Everyday Reading

Everyday Reading

Hindi Middlebrow and the North Indian Middle Class

AAKRITI MANDHWANI

SPEAKING
TIGER

SPEAKING TIGER BOOKS LLP
125A, Ground Floor, Shahpur Jat,
Near Asiad Village, New Delhi—110 049

First published by University of Massachusetts Press, 2024
This edition first published in India by Speaking Tiger Books, 2024

Published by arrangement with University of Massachusetts Press

ISBN: 978-93-5447-951-9

10 9 8 7 6 5 4 3 2 1

Typeset in Adobe Jenson Pro by Jojy Philip, New Delhi
Printed at Chaman Enterprises

For Madhu, Satya, and Pammi

Contents

List of Figures

Acknowledgments

Meharbani

This book first took shape as a curiosity. I had just finished writing an MPhil dissertation at the University of Delhi that examined the uncharacteristically good production quality of postmillennial novels of Hindi master crime writer Surendra Mohan Pathak. A series of accidents had led me to this deeply rewarding print historical project. My protagonist Pathak was everywhere, had sold millions of copies, was much beloved by everyday readers, and yet remained critically understudied and persistently misunderstood. After I submitted, I asked the obvious question: What would a study of magazines and books that inhabit every drawing room, and the ones rather pejoratively labeled "lowbrow" and often hidden away, reveal for reading, writing and publishing histories?

This question became a PhD project that found a warm home at SOAS, University of London. I am enormously grateful to Francesca Orsini for her attention to every step of the research process and for her infinite patience with which she helped shape these curiosities into coherent and thoughtful questions.

At SOAS, Eleanor Newbigin sent painstaking comments and always lent me a kind ear, and Rachel Dwyer provided cheerful conversations on film and life. My SOAS cohort, specially Chinmay Sharma, Daniel Luther, David Landau, Guanchen Lai, Maddalena Italia, Paula Manstetten, Poonkulaly Gunaseelan, Radha Kapuria, Sara Marzagora, Simon Leese, Yan Jia, and the South Asia Writing Group at large provided an intellectually stimulating and stable environment in which I could work, breathe, and inhabit these questions. I also had the best time teaching at the Summer School, London School of Rare Books, Senate House. It gave me gumption: I was a *proper* print historian now, I had arrived.

I am grateful to Vasudha Dalmia, who not only generously gave this PhD project time but also (literally!) helped pen my (then thesis) structure one evening in Delhi. She succinctly summed up my research findings in one line: "It made commercial sense to publish in the national language." That is what the book chases and hopes to deliver. Abhijit Gupta, Akshaya Mukul, Alok Rai, A. R. Venkatachalapathy, Baidik Bhattacharya, C. M. Naim, Douglas Haynes, Graham Shaw, Javed Majeed, Leigh Denault, Murali Ranganathan, Nandini Chandra, Padmini Ray Murray, Rashmi Varma, Ravikant Sharma, Rina Ramdev, Subarno Chattarji, Suman Gupta, Tapan Basu and Udaya Kumar, thank you for your warm conversations and interest in my current, past, and future work. Swapan Chakravorty was so attentive to the work and is dearly missed.

This book would not exist without its exciting archives spread across Delhi, London, and Allahabad. I thank Paresh and Anant Nath at Delhi Press, as well as Chandrama Prasad Khare, for their archives and time. The Malhotra family, particularly Priyanka and the late Shekhar Malhotra, so generously opened the archives at Hind Pocket Books to me. Many thanks also to the infinitely patient librarians and karamcharis at the Marwari Library, Delhi, and Hindi Sahitya Sammelan, Allahabad, who fished out bound copy after copy of the (very) copious archives. These two meticulously preserved archives still stand due to their very diligent efforts (at times despite all odds). Thanks are due also to librarians and staff at Bharati Bhawan, British Library, SOAS Library, and the Nehru Memorial Library.

My colleagues at the School of Humanities and Social Sciences, Shiv Nadar University, especially at the Department of English, have been generous to a fault and have provided me with the stillness and conviviality necessary to complete this book. Dadri life has been infinitely more colorful because of clubhouse dinners, campus walks, and Korean food jaunts to Greater Noida with Atul Mishra, Chinmay Sharma, Diviani Chaudhuri, Gautama Polanki, Hemanth Kadambi, Iman Mitra, Jabin Jacob, Ratheesh Radhakrishnan, Tuhina Ganguly, Subhashim Goswami, Sreejata Paul, Urmila Bhirdikar, Vasundhara Bhojvaid, and Vinayak Dasgupta.

Parts of this book have been both presented at and bettered because of talks and conferences at the Postcolonial Print Cultures Network workshop at Newcastle, Center for South Asia at University of Wisconsin–Madison, Centre for the Study of Developing Societies in Delhi, European Conference on South Asian Studies, Vienna, and IIT Bhilai. Parts of the introduction and first chapter of this book have been published as Aakriti Mandhwani, "*Sarita* and the 1950s Hindi Middlebrow Reader," *Modern Asian Studies* 53, no. 6 (2019): 1797–1815, and Aakriti Mandhwani, "Modernisms in the Magazine: A Case for Recovery in Hindi," in *Indian Modernities: Literary Cultures from the 18th to the 20th Century*, ed. Nishat Zaidi (Delhi: Routledge, 2023).

At University of Massachusetts Press, I thank the series editors and Brian Halley for giving me full reign to write the book I wanted to. I have benefited enormously from the meticulous notes given me by the two peer reviewers for this book. I have been absolutely blown away by Nancy Raynor's editorial attention and care. Speaking Tiger has made this book reach its Indian readers. I thank them, particularly Nazeef Mollah, for making this happen.

For this book to come into being, I needed to make journeys far and near: the PhD project was generously supported by the Felix Trust and the Doctoral Fieldwork Award, SOAS. While at Shiv Nadar University, the faculty development fund provided for subsequent travels to Allahabad that helped me substantially prepare the book as it is today.

Aditya Balasubramanian, Andrew Amstutz, David Landau, Manav Kapur, Paula Manstetten, Priyasha Mukhopadhyay, Radhika Iyengar, and Simon Leese: thank you for reading and writing with me between 2020 and 2022 over stimulating Zoom, Teams, Google Meet, and impromptu WhatsApp sessions. Vaid Rox with David Landau and

Rosina Vuille and Hindi Adab Mandal with Fazal Rashid, Zaen Alkazi, Somil Daga, and Melina Gravier: our weekly reading groups these two years sustained and colored my inner life. We were all locked in, but together with such reading magicians as Vaid, Husain, Bhandari, Bhuwaneshwar, and others, we could fly.

This book has received sustenance across many cities and time zones from many friends. London, where it all started: Anjumon Sahin, Anaïs da Fonseca, Jay Sharma, Priyasha Mukhopadhyay (pseudo-London resident), you made the city breathe and come alive. Special thanks to David Landau, Paula Manstetten, and Simon Leese, aka, the NW Hood, for the many impromptu coffees, cakes, neighborhood dinners, and park jaunts. Daniel Luther and Shantanu Singh, thank you for making the gray city come closest to feeling like home.

Each time Allahabad has been a wonder and a delight: Alok and Rajul Rai, your bel sharbats, espressos, and jalebis have sustained me during my Allahabad archival trips more than you know. Coming to the city and its archives for the first time with Francesca Orsini was a revelation. Trisha Das, from El Chico to Netram, thank you so much for always coming through with Allahabad tips and tricks.

In Delhi, I thank Alka Gupta, Aradhana Gupta, Harbans Jolly, Pramode Mishra, Sumit Mandhwani, Vandana Mishra, and Vatsala Sivasubramanian for your constant nourishment. Anaïs Da Fonseca, pseudo-Delhi resident: With each of your visits, I have loved Delhi more. Here's to eating many more dosas together. Ashutosh Bhardwaj, Aradhna Sharma, Bodhisattva Chattopadhyay, Chitranshu Tewari, Radhika Iyengar, Susan Christi, and Taiyaba Ali: some of you still stay here, some have since moved away. Dilli is always you.

I get my love of literature and history from my father, Suresh Mandhwani. From his father and my *dada*, C. S. Mandhwani, the family's most multilingual speaker who quietly practiced his politics of language, I witnessed firsthand that Indian independence also meant loss. A million thanks to my brother, Aashish Mandhwani (my Ocean of Notions, Shah of Blah), for being generous and kind to a fault (though he may vehemently deny it!) and Suhasini Mehta, who has taken more panicked calls and messages and made more on-demand chocolate wah-ve cakes than she should. Also, my little loves Jugmohan and Cattoo, Cheeku and Brownie, Auntie and Uncle, Julie and Jugnu: What would I do without your love.

Dhananjaya Mishra, fellow traveler, mirth-maker, it is a joy to live my everyday with you.

This book is dedicated to three very special readers in my life. To my mother, Madhu Mandhwani, enthusiastic magazine reader turned voracious OTT consumer, who has been the book's (and my) biggest support; to Satya Jain, her mother and my *nani*, elegant sari wearer, feisty straight shooter, insatiable reader, from whom I get my love of all things Hindi; and finally, to my father's mother, my *dadi* Pammi Mandhwani, who could not read or write a word until she turned sixty and then decided enough was enough and she wanted to learn, who would *probably* not approve of me reading these magazines and paperbacks, who most definitely did not know what an "academic" book was, but who would have been proudest of this work.

Note on Translation and Transliteration

All translations from the Hindi are my own unless otherwise indicated in the text.

In this South Asian edition of the book, I have adopted a commonsensical approach to transliterating Hindi terms. The transliteration aims to be intuitive and practical, focusing on clarity and accessibility.

INTRODUCTION
Middlebrow
Not Only in the Middle

READING IN THE 1950S, READING THE 1950S

In 1962, prominent Hindi writer Amarkant published the short story "Hatyare" ("Murderers"). It focuses on two (extremely) cynical students meandering through the marketplace at evening time. Occasionally, the students stop to smoke a cigarette. Sometimes, using heavy left-liberal rhetoric, they burst into pseudo-political speeches about the state of the nation. After this, they visit a drinking den and then a prostitute. Here, the story takes a dramatic turn: while fleeing the prostitute's lodgings to avoid paying for her services, the students unwittingly end up killing a man.

"Hatyare" evokes the disillusionment of an age, of promises not fulfilled. It provides a scathing critique, both of the contemporary ruling party Congress and the unhappy alternative of an empty Left opposition, whose language the students mockingly deploy. This heavy disillusionment is distributed across several spaces: the drinking hole, the prostitute's home, and the marketplace. Another such space is the market's magazine stall, where a young female student goes through the pages of the English-language magazine *Eve's Weekly*, "her face reflecting the hope that people would consider her extremely modern and intelligent." Flipping through a variety of magazines in both Hindi and English, the students nonchalantly harass her: "Coming and standing closer to her, they also began whistling softly, rifling through several magazines at the same time. One by one, they went through *Rekha, Gori, Reader's Digest, Illustrated Weekly, Life, Manohar Kahaniyaan* [Pleasing Stories], *Filmfare, Jasoos Mahal* [Detective Palace]."[1] These magazines and the story's many uncomfortable questions animated the world of the 1950s and 1960s, the two decades immediately following the Independence of India and Pakistan in 1947. These questions, negotiated through a wide range of these ubiquitous archives, are the concerns of this book. *Everyday Reading: Hindi Middlebrow and the North Indian Middle Class* takes as its focus the world of "middlebrow" publishing and attendant practices of reading of the North Indian middle classes in the 1950s and 1960s. In it I argue that this largely unexamined archive of Hindi magazines and paperbacks, commercially successful as well as desirable literary objects, is vital to understand the emergence, nature, and concerns of the North Indian, Hindi-reading middle classes in the post-independence period.

In and of themselves, the decades following 1947 deserve more scrutiny. After a comprehensive postcolonial scholarly deep dive into nineteenth- and early twentieth-century South Asia, historical, political, social, and anthropological studies have more recently begun to approach the 1950s with a degree of care. Here, too, the immediate post-independence period has predominantly been studied from the perspective of development: of economic planning under the aegis of the Congress government and, in the past two decades, of the failure of that planning.[2] Additionally, scholars have thoroughly studied the framing of, and debates around, the Indian Constitution, ranging from its first amendment over the right to free speech in 1951 to the formulation of the Hindu Code Bill and, most recently, through tracing the afterlife of colonial legal practices in the postcolonial period.[3] Jawaharlal Nehru, the first prime minister of India, often presides as a towering figure at the center of these investigations. Nehruvian India is understood through his policymaking processes, both in terms of his internal economic as well as his international diplomatic policies, particularly with respect to India's relationship with China and its subsequent collapse, which resulted in the 1962 Sino-Indian War.[4]

The period has also been studied from another, equally poignant perspective of the long partition and its consequences for the two new states and its citizens.[5] The violence of the partition was overwhelmingly gendered.[6] A vast body of work focuses on the literature representing and analyzing the silence around it.[7] Finally, scholarship on these years, understood as the golden age of Indian cinema, also attends toward 1950s Hindi films as well as their significance within public discourse.[8]

Among these alternative historiographies of the post-independence Indian state, culture, and society, print culture—specifically commercially successful print culture—has remained a largely uncharted terrain. A study of print culture does not only decode narratives of publishing, reading, and editing. For instance, colonial print culture has many poignant stories to tell us about the formation of public opinion as well as the "recasting" of gender, religious, even linguistic identities.[9] Popular and nationalist journals show us that the pre-independence rhetoric, of nationalism, collective service, and duty to an ideal beyond the family, continued to hold sway until the 1940s.[10]

In *Everyday Reading*, I suggest that enormously successful Hindi magazines and paperbacks offer an unexpectedly rich entry point to understand and reimagine the middle classes of the 1950s. In many senses, these social constituencies were considered fundamental to the wider dispersion of the Nehruvian vision that insisted on the deferral of pleasure in the service of the nation.[11] This archive, comprising best-selling middlebrow magazines like Delhi Press's *Sarita* (subject of the first chapter) and Bennett, Coleman and Company's *Dharmyug* (examined in the third chapter), as well as Hind Pocket Books, the first paperbacks in Hindi (the focus of chapter two), demonstrates that the pre-independence rhetoric as well as the post-independence Nehruvian tour de force was not able to rationalize, control, or regulate gender roles, relationships, and consumer behavior during the

1950s. The Hindi reading middle classes who eagerly lapped up these exciting materials were everyday active consumers who defied the state's prescription and imagined themselves outside the ambit of the institutional logic of the austere nation. In other words, the deferral of pleasure that was supposedly a key constituent of the middle classes in Nehruvian India needs to be reexamined and nuanced: through these publications and everyday reading practices, I seek to present an alternative narrative and shed light on the history of consuming classes during this period.

In this book I not only engage with narratives of nation and nationalism but also those of language and its strong links with nation and nationalism. I examine the history of Hindi and its post-independence trajectory in the commercial publishing sphere. Unfortunately, Hindi has long suffered from the sheer burden of its history: it did much more than simply serve the purposes of nationalist representation, much more than its well-established history as the "national" and simultaneously "nationalist" language of India from the nineteenth century onward.[12] Indeed, this story is predominant for a reason: many literary histories have charted the trajectory of Hindi and its claims and how a variety of Hindi periodicals in the pre-independence period configured Hindi in high literary, prescriptive, and nationalist terms.[13] The magazines and paperbacks that appear in *Everyday Reading* tell us another, equally significant story of how a variety of middlebrow Hindi periodicals of the 1950s also vocally defied such responsibility. I link this defiance to the concerns of not only the publishers but also, more importantly, the readers.

Given this, I privilege "everyday" over "literary" reading habits for the purposes of my investigation. Everyday reading habits offer clues into both active and *non*active resistance processes of the reading public. Some questions that the book proposes to unravel directly relate to one's relationship to the magazine. What does it mean to read separately rather than reading the book or magazine object together as a group? What does it mean to insist on possessing one's own copy of the magazine rather than sharing it with the family? I articulate this shift in post-independence reading through the emergence of what I call the "middlebrow" magazine and paperback, defined in this book as a "wholesome" readable object in the logic of the market that gave rise to individualized acts of and demands for reading. This, I show, took place within the family that had begun to covet the magazine as a material object and, most important, to reference itself in the light of its consumption. A primary attribute of the middlebrow was that such reading refused to fixate only on concerns of the pre-independence period—nationalism, austerity, poverty, and religious belonging.

Women readers are central to the main concerns of this book. *Everyday Reading* joins scholarship on women as agentive co-constitutors of their literary universe.[14] The book contextualizes these debates in popular print sphere, where female readers confidently assert themselves. It stresses the importance of female readers as creative actors within the magazine space. Indeed, women were strong, unabashed readers and consumers of material objects such as soaps, creams, shampoos, radios, and film music records, all of which were advertised, coveted, and discussed in the magazines.

Working with materials in a language separate from the language one writes and publishes in presents its own existential questions. The act of history writing then becomes tantamount to thinking about it as an act of translation. Am I just trying to "translate" from Hindi to English a sense, an experience? *Everyday Reading* examines extremely popular archives that, paradoxically, have not been seriously examined in scholarly debates, in either English or Hindi. For instance, this book is the first academic study of Hind Pocket Books, which regularly published half a million first-print runs of its titles.[15] Also, while *Dharmyug*, the weekly with more than 110,000 subscribers in the mid-1960s, has been referenced in countless memoirs of writers and readers, in this book I consider its significance beyond just introducing literariness.[16] Even though these publications were read locally, they offer themselves up for inspection to more wide-ranging imaginations: of the world, of the "other," and, concomitantly, of oneself. For instance, the model of Hind Pocket Books was inspired by the successful Penguin and Book of the Month Club experiments in the United Kingdom and United States, respectively. *Dharmyug* published calendar images of Hindu deities along with existential treatises of Kierkegaard. The lowbrow genre magazines of the period regularly published world literature in its pages. The writers, editors, and publishers of the paperbacks and magazines traveled the world, and as a result, readers, not as well traveled, imagined the world and their place within it. The confident Hindi middlebrow of the 1950s and 1960s, internally diversified, could be intellectual and cosmopolitan as in Dharmvir Bharti's *Dharmyug*, democratic and modern as in *Sarita*, and eclectic and more Urdu-friendly as in Hind Pocket Books. This book, therefore, actively expands the boundaries of what "literariness," "modernism," and "cosmopolitanism" meant in the 1950s and 1960s and shows that middlebrow publishing partly participated in all of them.

BOOK HISTORY BEYOND THE BOOK

Methodologically, I situate my project within disciplines of print history and history of the book, which is interested in questions of materiality of books, including texts of any kind that are written or digitized in any form, and the circulation and distribution processes by which books reach their intended—and unintended—audiences. Robert Darnton's seminal work in this field is enlightening and provides us with three prominent questions when confronted by the book object: "How do books come into being? How do they reach readers? What do readers make of them?"[17] Important volumes on Indian print culture have already widely investigated print cultures across several languages and time periods.[18]

Three out of the four chapters of this book focus on magazines, both middlebrow and lowbrow, as material to conceptualize a history of a middlebrow reading public. This focus on magazines was labored: I studied monthly issues of *Sarita*, *Maya*, *Rasili Kahaniyaan*, and

Manohar Kahaniyaan and weekly issues of *Dharmyug* spread over more than ten years. Also, by no means is this focus accidental. In the South Asian (and, in our case, a more specific Hindi-Urdu) context, the magazine has been as significant (if not more) as the book, in terms of its impact and thus as an object of study. Magazines were formative to the development of not only a literary consciousness in Hindi but also, in many senses, a consciousness *of* Hindi. Scholars have attributed the first journal in Hindi to Bharatendu Harishchandra, commonly referred to as the "Father of Modern Hindi." The journal *Balabodhini* (1874–77) declared itself to be "Stri jano ki pyari hindi bhasha se sudhari masik patrika" (beloved by women, monthly magazine improved by the Hindi language).[19] However, founded a couple of decades later in 1900, Indian Press's *Saraswati* towers over all other journals in the early twentieth century, literally dictating the terms for the language widely recognized and institutionalized as Hindi, one monthly at a time.[20]

Indeed, Hindi journals of the time articulated reading and writing in terms of *seva* (service) to Hindi and to the nation. Francesca Orsini identifies these journals as "animated by the new figure of literary activist" and that *sahitya seva* (service to literature) was the conceptual category created for this purpose.[21] First published in 1922, a hugely successful women's journal titled *Chand* (Moon) also epitomized another framework, that of *stri-upyogi* (useful for women) literature, which, as the name suggests, was highly prescriptive, linking women's work largely within the home to a broader duty to anti-colonial nationalism.[22] However, journals like *Chand* also experimented with these frameworks, significantly widening their scope: for one, *Chand* helped provide legitimacy to women's activities outside the home.[23] Moreover, the journal invested in legitimizing women's feelings at large. Orsini shows how "hybrid genres (confessionals, epistolary novels, social novels) mixing reality with fiction, instruction with entertainment" published in *Chand* ultimately made space for "taboo issues concerning women to be raised, directly and with the heightened impact of a melodramatic narrative."[24]

Although women's journals propagated fully formed ideas like sahitya seva, *stridharma* (women's duty), and *rashtraseva* (service to nation), popular post-1940 magazine archives tell other stories. This book demonstrates that, within post-independence magazines and reading practices, the hugely significant rhetoric of nationalism could no longer serve as a focal point holding everything together or provide the justification for gender roles, relationships, and behavior. Post-independence middlebrow magazines exhibit a notable shift of *seva* to new rhetoric such as *grahak seva* (service to the consumer). Additionally, these publications consciously configured themselves as magazines for *everyone* in the family and for women as an inherent part of it, fashioned as matter-of-fact readers and producers within the magazine. If the pre-independence period had its own discourse of women as mothers, women as mothers of the nation, and, finally, women as subjects of feeling, post-independence female readers can perhaps be understood more in terms of consumers, arbiters of taste and knowledge, and less in terms of either kinship or those seeking to expose oppressions.

In an entirely different context, that of Victorian women's magazines, Margaret Beetham writes, "Magazines are . . . deeply involved in capitalist production and consumption as well as circulating in the cultural economy of collective meanings and constructing an identity for the individual reader as a gendered and a sexual being."[25] Following from this, I critically deploy the term "magazine" to demonstrate the genre's direct relationship with the questions of consumption of not only the magazine as object but also the commodities advertised within the magazine. Forging close links between "the culture of commerce and advertising," periodicals are uniquely placed to trace consumption habits of its readers, largely the Indian middle classes.[26] Periodicals held power because of their placement in the public sphere—and also precisely because they were *periodical* in nature: in other words, serialization and sequentiality in 1950s magazines and paperbacks in themselves play an important role in the creation of the middlebrow reading habit. Serialization creates what I discuss in chapter two as a "repeatable" book-reading habit. This "repeatable" habit results in what Rob Allen and Thija van den Berg term "commodification of leisure."[27] The "everydayness" of the middlebrow reading habit was born from the pleasure derived from repeatedly owning, reading, and consuming one's *own* magazine and paperback.

Therefore, I study the middlebrow magazine also in terms of the reception history of the material object itself. How did Hindi magazines circulate as objects in the life of the family home? Who read these magazines first, and how did they read them? The price of the magazine, too, defines the threshold of access that it can provide and how it mirrors the aspirations of the reading audience. *Everyday Reading* considers magazines and paperbacks that were cheap at best or affordable at worst, with price points varying between forty paise and one rupee made easily accessible direct to home through postal delivery systems.[28] Technologies of production and government subsidies that aided low pricing are extremely relevant, specifically to a newly minted nation beset by shortages, but have not been considered in much depth within Indian book scholarship.[29] For instance, Hind Pocket Books discussed in chapter two was aided in its home delivery scheme pricing through a government subsidy as well as the establishment of post offices within the publisher's compounds, thereby facilitating easy and cheap circulation of the paperbacks.[30]

Apart from mapping readers and reading practices, in this book I engage in a close study of publishers and publishing history. What were the great publishing centers of the 1950s and 1960s? In the second half of the nineteenth century and early twentieth century, Calcutta, Lucknow, and Allahabad predominantly come to mind.[31] In the immediately post-independence period, the cities of Delhi and Bombay emerged in their own right as strong commercial publishing centers. The locations of the publishing houses under discussion confirms this. Although *Sarita* was published from Delhi by Delhi Press, the Bennett, Coleman and Company group published its major newspapers and periodicals, including *Dharmyug,* from Bombay.

Hind Pocket Books was also published from Delhi. On the other hand, Mitra Prakashan from Allahabad published the lowbrow genre magazines considered in chapter four. This (partial yet significant) geographic shift and the reasons for it have been noted in passing—and often anecdotally—by writers and historians alike. For instance, Neelabh Ashk's pioneering oral history of Hindi literature and literary milieu records accounts of a large number of writers who reiterate that, in the 1950s, prominent authors were shifting publishers from those in Allahabad to either Delhi or Bombay.[32] In a collection of writings on Allahabad, the author Gyanranjan writes movingly: "I ran away from Allahabad. I travelled to Delhi, Bombay and Calcutta. Walter Benjamin said that there is no face more real than the face of a city. I am hopeful about cities, but not about Allahabad."[33] Although writers did not provide precise reasons for why this was happening, throughout the recollections two things remain consistent: this change occurred rapidly, and Allahabad was growing empty. Ravikant Sharma discusses this shift from not just Allahabad but a larger-scale migration from other towns to Delhi and imagines that it occurred because of state requirements for Hindi and bilingual translators: "Poets such as [Harivansh Rai] Bachchan (Uttar Pradesh) and [Ramdhari Singh] Dinkar (Bihar) and [Maithili Sharan] Gupt (Madhya Pradesh) were some of the more illustrious names in a long line of migrant litterateurs who made Delhi their new destination and finally, as the mid-century moved towards the last quarter, a foremost center for Hindi language, journalism, and literature."[34]

While writers were flocking to Delhi for jobs in Hindi, publishers in the city were also choosing to publish in the language. The caste identities of the publishers under consideration and their decision to publish in Hindi are equally significant. Delhi Press and Hind Pocket Books, published from Delhi, are products of the Delhi Baniya family and the Arya Samaji Malhotra family, respectively. Although Dayanand Saraswati, founder of the Hindu nationalist reform organization Arya Samaj, was Gujarati, the state of Punjab was its major area of operation. Arya Samaj's hold over the region meant also linguistic control: Alok Rai writes, "Dayanand Saraswati was persuaded to adopt Hindi instead of Sanskrit, and the Hindi that developed under this complex of influences grew progressively distant from Urdu, and became more and more sanskritized 'Hindi.'"[35] Bennett, Coleman and Company Limited was purchased by the prominent Marwari businessman Ram Krishan Dalmia in 1946. Hindi was not the first language for these community groups but historically became the identifying language for them on the national stage.[36] *Everyday Reading* shows how Hindi was not only a national language but also a commercially viable one, not only for publishing textbooks and other instruments of governance but also for producing books and magazines for leisure and pleasure.

All the publishing houses discussed in this book were family-run businesses. Delhi Press and Hind Pocket Books were family owned, with the former still run and owned by the Nath family today. Hind Pocket Books was family-owned and -run as recently as 2018, when it was sold to Penguin Random House.[37] On the other hand, Sahu Shanti Prasad Jain, Dalmia's son-in-law, took over Bennett, Coleman and Company in 1948, and the publishing house has remained in the Sahu Jain family since then. Finally, Mitra Prakashan in Allahabad was headed by the Mitra family until its dissolution and is the only non-Punjabi, non-Marwari publishing house under study in this book.

Not only are these publishing houses family-run businesses, but publications of two of the four were also *edited* by the publisher-proprietors themselves. Delhi Press and Hind Pocket Books were published and edited by Vishwa Nath and D. N. Malhotra respectively. Of the editors on which I focus, only *Dharmyug*'s editor, Dharmvir Bharti, was well-known before he started editing the magazine. *Everyday Reading* places Bharti on a uniform stage with Nath and Malhotra. I show that these often cast aside editors-publishers of the commercially successful middlebrow magazines and books were, in fact, towering personalities and entrepreneurs who dramatically widened the scope of the Hindi reading public.

REFRAMING THE MIDDLEBROW—"NOT ONLY IN THE MIDDLE"

> The BBC claim to have discovered a new type, the "middlebrow." It consists of people who are hoping that someday they will get used to the stuff they ought to like.

This epigraph, which appeared in the December 1925 issue of the English satirical magazine *Punch*, is considered one of the first recorded usages of the term "middlebrow."[38] Clearly, in Eurocentric criticism, it started out as a pejorative category: discursive essays by Virginia Woolf and Q. D. Leavis have viewed the middlebrow as a pretentious, imitative, mediocre category, of both readers as well as literature. Woolf's 1932 essay "Middlebrow," penned as an (unsent) letter to the *New Statesman*, is particularly entertaining: in it, she derided the "middle-brow" as a people "betwixt and between," labeling this class "the bloodless and pernicious pest who comes between" the highbrow and the lowbrow.[39] Her terms of reference are unforgiving: to Woolf, the readers she called the "middle-brow" have nothing original to provide or learn from, since they passively position themselves in the middle of creators of culture, that is, the highbrow, and the lowbrow consumers who, according to her, were necessarily beholden to the highbrow. The highbrows were benevolent benefactors who derived their energies from the lowbrows' respect for their productions. Woolf wrote, "Lowbrows need highbrows and honour them as much as highbrows need lowbrows and honour them."[40]

The French theorist Pierre Bourdieu has a more nuanced theoretical formulation of the "middlebrow" than did Woolf. For one, Bourdieu is very conscious of the fact that distinctions take place according to the process of relationality. He notes: "Distinction and pretension, high culture and middle-brow culture, like, elsewhere, high fashion and fashion, haute coiffure and coiffure, and so only exist through each other, and it is the relation, or rather, the objective collaboration of their respective production apparatuses and clients which produces the value of culture and the need to possess it."[41]

However, Bourdieu uses the French term moyen, which the translated edition renders "middle-brow." "Moyen," in its other renditions, reads as "medium, average, common."[42] Theorist Caroline Pollentier critically reflects on the English translation of this key word in the same way Bourdieu asks us to reflect on the terms in translation: thinking of them as "equivalents." Pollentier highlights that, in the first preface to the English translation of his book *Distinction: A Social Critique of the Judgement of Taste*, Bourdieu warns his English-language readers against "the dangers of a facile search for partial equivalences which cannot stand for a methodological comparison between systems." That being the case, Pollentier returns to the French word "moyen" itself: "'Moyen[,]' meaning average, does not function on its own as a cultural keyword in French, and rather points to the average standard . . . The concept of culture moyenne therefore retains a semantic fuzziness, all the more so because Bourdieu never reflects on its problematic pejorative connotations."[43]

In his turn, Bourdieu argues that "the very meaning and value of a cultural object varies according to the system of objects in which it is placed," so that genres like detective novels or cartoons will be perceived as daring and imaginative within an avant-garde system. However, while he subtly layers the modern processes of cultural production, he writes that if these genres "combine to form a constellation typical of middle-brow taste," they "appear as what they are, simple substitutes for legitimate assets."[44] Here, middlebrow or "moyen" is doubly criticized, for working with "substitutes" and for aspiring to the "legitimate" art or culture.[45] Again, here, Bourdieu conceptualizes the "l'Art Moyen" as a position that, according to him, is not "legitimate." Pollentier writes, "The intermediary position of the *art moyen* is indeed that of a 'not-yet-legitimate' art, an art 'in process of legitimization'—that is, an art falling short of cultural legitimacy, or, at best, constituting a transition towards it."[46]

Much beyond Woolf and Bourdieu, enjoying well-deserved status of its own, "middlebrow" has lived a long, fruitful, and well-understood life. Two American feminist cultural theorists—Janice

Radway and Joan Shelley Rubin—are largely responsible for this reclamation. They delineate the middlebrow as a category separate from either the lowbrow or highbrow, recognizing it as a *type* of consumption practice rather than a *degree* within a cultural or taste hierarchy. Rubin highlights the expression "the average intelligent reader" that the successful subscription club in the United States, the Book of the Month Club, called its readers. She argues that the "general reader" or a "generalist" needs to be critically understood in order to make connections to "the current interest in the phenomenon literary scholars call canon formation." Therefore, Rubin views "generalist" middlebrow readers within the larger history of reading and cultural production, attributing them as major tastemakers with a role in canon formation. She concedes that, although canon formation is a result of market forces, consumers of these canons play a large role and are discerning in their consumption practices. In other words, "average intelligent reader[s]" *produce* a literary culture as much as they are produced by it.[47] Janice Radway also discusses middlebrow publishing practices, again focusing on the popular Book of the Month Club as an example of how the middlebrow readers can (and do) read an eclectic variety of curated genres. She argues that this varied and eclectic habit of reading does not indicate "passive" consumption by a "mediocre" middle class but, in fact, is a highly regenerative practice that is emblematic of middle classes and their interest in carving a different form of reading practice.[48]

Radway and Rubin have arguably paved the way for a school of enquiry that we can safely call "middlebrow studies" with multiple studies of the middlebrow underway such that, as Cecilia Konchar Farr and Tom Perrin note, "we no longer feel, as we once did, that a gloss on the term middlebrow is a vital component of any piece of writing on it."[49] *Everyday Reading,* firmly set in India, situates this conversation in a specific regional context. It takes its cue from this burgeoning field, which not only focuses its attentions on "reclaiming" the "middle" (which holds true specifically for women readers) but also reframes arguments about legitimacy: I understand the middlebrow as an essential category to unsettle or dethrone the very idea of a singular legitimacy, arguing instead for multiple legitimacies in the realm of the modern cultural field. I also see middlebrow publications and middlebrow readers as mutually constitutive. That is, readers not only constitute but are also constituted by the middlebrow publications and also read other kinds of highbrow and lowbrow texts. I also discuss these categories in the plural: there are as many kinds of middlebrow publications as there are middlebrow readers.

Indeed, the magazines and paperbacks I consider were not exclusively women's magazines and paperbacks. I consciously choose to term these "middlebrow" publications as opposed to the "family" or "women's" publications to stress overlapping readerships. Although many columns, short stories, and advertisements in the magazines were directed toward women, these magazines and paperbacks were not purely "feminine" texts. In addition to studying the extremely important development of women as unabashed readers, my impulse has been to understand this reading in terms of the family and of the growth of the individual self within the family. For instance, the examples discussed in chapter one show that *Sarita* often operated as an inclusive space where both male and female readers produced their own discourse. The structure and selection process of the magazines also points to this. Inclusions in the magazine such as articles on cooking, knitting, and makeup can perhaps be interpreted as a feminine gesture. However, different sections in the magazine are addressed to men, with some others directed to women. The readership of the magazines is the entire family. In turn, the family in question that reads these magazines is the middle-class family.

Everyday Reading foregrounds the importance of theorizing the middlebrow in its own right and showing that it comes into being because of specific historical conditions, tastes, desires, and publishing decisions, which may or may not take their cue from the highbrow. It understands the middlebrow as a multifaceted category with demarcations arising not only through a flattened view of class and legitimacy derived from it but also through such other postulates as reader participation based on political, religious, gender, and caste belonging, in addition to middlebrow views on consumption. In the post-independence context, the middlebrow is a reading practice that accords equal space to male and female readers for creative expression, focuses on nonnationalist subject matter, instead generating interest in consumption, of the magazine as well as the objects and services discussed or advertised within the magazine. In this book, middlebrow reading foregrounds the importance of the individual within the family as well as on the new morality of the nuclear, companionate, and aspirational family. Finally, middlebrow reading also comes into reckoning because of the modern circulation practices that facilitated the penetration of seemingly disparate kinds of reading material straight to readers' drawing rooms at a reasonable price.

Celebratory as such aspects may be, the study of legitimacy and the middlebrow is a tricky thing. For one, it certainly opens up and builds multiple legitimacies, but crucially, this work is also built on a fundamental notion of exclusion. As generously as they included, middlebrow publications excluded discussions on caste, poverty, minority religious belongings, and especially Muslim belonging, which were markedly absent from their texts in a newly partitioned India. If these themes made an appearance, they presented themselves as redeeming qualities of a championing majority, in the language of social reform discourses, reflected most strongly in the self-construction of Vishwa Nath, *Sarita*'s publisher-editor.

Middlebrow readers and publications themselves may have enjoyed aspirations similar to Woolf's in thinking themselves "better" than "others": the word "conservative," even "majoritarian," frequently comes to mind. *Everyday Reading* is not trying to be a triumphant story about celebration. It seeks to introduce and complicate. Indeed, books and periodicals were attempting to carve their consumption publics through a politics of distinction and exclusion. At the same time, all sorts of book and magazine objects circulated everywhere. Here, book historian Roger Chartier's work on "social areas" proves instructive. He critiques what he calls a "cultural separation" of readers by hierarchies based on wealth, status, profession, and class, prioritizing the "social areas where each corpus of texts and each variety of printed materials circulates."[50] Chartier's "social area" becomes more useful from the standpoint of understanding circulation processes, as it allows for class intersections in reading and consumption practices and, therefore, a more complicated understanding of the circulation of texts. I argue that while all middlebrow reading can be understood as a middle-class reading practice, readership intersections and overlaps did occur often. For instance, the advertisements of middlebrow magazines like *Dharmyug* in lowbrow publications like *Maya* show that readers were overlapping, reading beyond the consecrated middlebrow.[51] The fourth chapter of this book delineates how lowbrow magazines, printed on paper of cheap quality, carrying genres such as thrillers, romance, horror, and detective fiction genres that were kept outside the middlebrow publications, instead presented subjects that middlebrow publications deemed taboo.

How can we constitute this broader category of the middle class? Some answers are offered below.

THE MIDDLEBROW AND ITS MIDDLE-CLASS READERS

The archive of the 1950s and 1960s Hindi magazines offers us abundant clues to access identity construction of the middle classes. The term "middle class" as a category itself is a fairly contested one in Indian historiography. Leela Fernandes traces the history of the middle classes from the colonial to the post-independence period, arguing that "culture" was "defined in relation to socioeconomic location" and was "not simply a homogenized product of middle-class self-identification." For instance, English language and skills, along with what she calls a "'respectable' socioeconomic and family history," were some of the primary requirements to enter middle-class positions in the colonial period, where "socioeconomic criteria such as occupation and property ownership were critical in demarcating this upper tier of the colonial middle class."[52]

Eleanor Newbigin focuses on the Hindu family unit at the cusp of entry into a "legal modernity," for instance, through the identification of the Hindu coparcener/joint ownership unit as taxable under the 1886 Income Tax Act along with incumbent questions of how to tax professional salaries received by a member of the Hindu Undivided Family.[53] Such negotiations, she argues, are fundamental to understanding changes in the Hindu Undivided Family system not only as ones brought by the post-independence state but also as those affected during colonial rule. The focus on the Hindu family is deliberate: Fernandes, like Newbigin, also demarcates the formation of middle classes along the lines of religion, writing that "the formation of the upper tiers of this class was often marked by the exclusion of Muslims." Finally, the middle class was also framed through the discourses of female chastity and morality.[54]

This complex history of stratification and regulation in the middle classes continued in the post-independence period. These classes in this period have predominantly been framed in two ways: as the bureaucratic class that cohered to the Nehruvian vision and, later, as the class that thrived on business entrepreneurship during the strict control of the Indian economy pejoratively termed the "License Raj." Pavan K. Varma writes: "The important thing is that there was an ideology, a vision, a calling which the middle class could owe loyalty to. It was this loyalty to something other than merely its own gratifications that gave it a larger cause and purpose. This is not to state that the middle class had completely transcended its self-interests—in any society, to expect this to happen with respect to any class is utopian—but its natural proclivity, in the absence of a larger ideal, to a cyclical, spiralling materialism was kept in check."[55] All the same, middle classes also need to be examined through their own cultural imaginary. For instance, Sanjay Joshi and Haynes et al. argue that consumption in the late colonial period was intrinsically tied up with a deliberate construction of a class identity and that, in many senses, the new middle classes came into being not so much through new income levels but in how they chose to spend their disposable income and, in doing so, differentiate themselves from "aristocratic" groups.[56]

Returning to the larger socioeconomic history of the middle classes from the colonial to the post-independence period, the book shows that the Hindu salaried professional family with some disposable income is the predominant consumer of middlebrow magazines and paperbacks. However, this family needs to be seen simultaneously through all the lens of "'respectable' socioeconomic and family history," property ownership, and political representation. More specifically, I imagine these middle classes as consuming classes, as groups that identify themselves in terms of how they either spend or, indeed, *imagine* spending their disposable income. For this, the Hindi middlebrow magazines and paperbacks offer a valuable entry point. Here, I consider how the middle-class family spends its disposable income on consuming the magazine and book objects, which, in turn, manufacture tastes, ideals, class, gender, and caste differentiations and relationships. I focus on the magazine structures and the different objects of consumption scattered within, such as the stories, narratives within the stories, readers' letters, editorial comments, and their inclusions and exclusions to unearth how the middle classes read and construct themselves. One thing remains certain: the middle classes that emerge from this study are middlebrow consumers who do not wish to contain themselves within the definition of either service or austerity.

While I discuss the middle classes in the context of a cultural imaginary deeply invested in consumption, I do not suggest that they are merely passive consumers. I deploy the term "everyday" particularly from Michel de Certeau's classic paradigm, which stands out in understanding the value of reading practices: "everyday" reading is not routinized or static but an "'art' which is anything but passive." In de Certeau's formulation, the reader "insinuates into another person the ruses of pleasure and appropriation: he poaches on it, is transported into it, pluralizes himself in it like the internal ramblings of one's body."[57] The middle classes as middlebrow consumers and readers emerge in my analysis as nonpassive consumers and creators of literature and discourse. The middle classes reading these magazines and paperbacks may or may not have incomes commensurate to the objects advertised or lifestyles depicted within the pages. Nevertheless, in addition to holding opinions on what kind of literature they wished to read and how they sought themselves to be represented, they actively participated and imagined themselves as consumers of these objects and lifestyles.

Here, the middlebrow as a phenomenon connects practices of reading within the middle classes within a specific kind of literature that is central to the fashioning of class identity. Therefore, while I do not conflate all middle-class reading as middlebrow, I investigate Hindi middlebrow reading practices in the 1950s as one of the definitive ways that middle classes visualize as well as articulate themselves. While all middlebrow readers were middle class, all middle-class readers were not necessarily middlebrow and could be reading a variety of other lowbrow and highbrow publications.

STRUCTURE OF THE BOOK

The book begins with what I identify as the first Hindi middlebrow magazine, *Sarita* (River), which first appeared in 1945, published by Delhi Press, a Delhi-based publishing house. Chapter one argues that, through its structure, stories, readers' letters, advertisements, fiction, and nonfiction, *Sarita* promoted consumption as its primary impulse. *Sarita* packaged what it deemed as wholesome and educational for the family as a unit and promoted segmented consumption, focusing on each member's reading desires, with something on offer for everyone according to age, gender, and marital status. This magazine increased women's access to reading: women began to demand the magazine and construct their own creative space within it. The chapter shows women as confident rather than surreptitious consumers of reading material.

Chapter two investigates Hind Pocket Books, the first Hindi paperback established in 1957. Here I argue that we need to read the commercial book market in India as part of the global commercial publishing landscape, demonstrated through Hind Pocket Books's relationships with foreign publishers. Hind Pocket Books was influenced by, and partially implemented, the business models of Penguin and the Book of the Month Club from the United Kingdom and the United States, respectively. Inspired by the Book of the Month Club's success in America, the Hind Pocket Book paperback was available at a low price not only at such commercially viable points of distribution as railway stations and roadside pavement stores but also adopted a third distribution model, that of the Home Library Scheme, where books in a range of fiction and nonfiction genres were directly—and periodically—delivered to readers' homes, creating a "repeatable" book-reading habit that included a variety of genres. This book is the first academic study of the organization that regularly published half a million first-print runs of its titles.[58] At the peak of the Home Library Scheme, Hind Pocket Books counted around 600,000 subscribers, and forty thousand packets were delivered monthly out of the publisher's own premises through a post office set up in the compound because of the sheer bulk of the orders.[59] The books themselves were printed by different companies spread across Old Delhi as the print runs were much larger than what Hind Pocket Books's own printing machines could produce.[60] Because the books that were delivered home in sets of six were nonnegotiable in terms of titles—according to the company's policy, readers could only refuse or return titles but not choose or recommend them—readers at home expected books to be chosen for them. This created reader dependability on the "list," which was not only aspirational but also standardized diverse reading as an everyday practice. This chapter specifically foregrounds D. N. Malhotra, Hind Pocket Books's enterprising editor-publisher, and his self-fashioning efforts as traveler, publishing entrepreneur, and tastemaker.

Chapter three focuses on *Dharmyug* (The Age of Dharma), a weekly magazine published from Bombay by the Bennett, Coleman and Company group, which also published the hugely successful

Illustrated Weekly of India in English. Published in broad A3 format on glossy photogravia paper, *Dharmyug* started as a weekly magazine that provided readers with full-page illustrations of Hindu gods as well as religious and moral stories. The chapter demonstrates the changes that the magazine went through after an editorial change in 1959, when the company invited the prominent modernist Hindi poet Dharmvir Bharti to take over as editor of the magazine, leading to a steep rise in subscribers from around 60,000 in 1958 to more than 110,000 subscribers in the mid-1960s.[61] With Dharmvir Bharti, the magazine changed visibly, and *Dharmyug* came to include more "high" literary content, with articles as varied as reportage on beatniks in America and a literary analysis of Albert Camus's fiction, albeit in an engaging and accessible style. *Dharmyug* provided wide-ranging and boundary-challenging literary content and articles that were mediated by two middlebrow attributes: ease of accessibility as well as emphasis on emotion. The shift in *Dharmyug*'s content also allows me to trace the trajectory of the "middlebrow" from *Sarita* onward. Middlebrow magazines need to be studied not only in terms of shifting ideologies but also through the lens of the commercialist logic of profit making. The success and centrality of Hindi middlebrow publishing is supported by the fact that it made commercial sense for the Times of India group to alter the magazine. I trace how the largest selling Hindi magazine of the period incorporated "high literary" articles on Kierkegaard, Camus, and the Beat Generation, situating its readers within the global cultural discourse of cosmopolitanism, opening up questions about perceived distinctions between the "popular" and the "literary."

The contours of Hindi middlebrow publishing are sharpened through a comparison with lowbrow magazines of the time, which are the focus of the book's final chapter. I examine three successful magazines from Allahabad: *Maya* ("Magic"), *Rasili Kahaniyaan* ("Delicious Stories"), and *Manohar Kahaniyaan* ("Beautiful Stories"), published by Mitra Prakashan.[62] While I elaborate on the term "lowbrow" in greater detail, I use the word primarily to denote publishing practices—low-quality paper, lower price—rather than a particular type of textual production or a segment of readership in a qualitative or derogatory manner. In addition, I discuss the differences in articulation between middlebrow and lowbrow magazines, particularly with respect to the differences in the genres and content of the magazines. Significantly, these lowbrow magazines raised questions of livelihood, living spaces, troublesome neighbors and the lack of privacy, as well as post-partition Hindu-Muslim mistrust, that were kept out of the purview of the middlebrow magazines. Using fear and uncertainty on which to base their stories, I argue that the lowbrow magazines unsettled readers' expectations and, wittingly or unwittingly, unraveled the aspirational narratives of the middlebrow magazines. In a way, the lowbrow magazines carried short stories that provided alternative moral universes to the reader, challenging the middlebrow aesthetic that focused on consumption.

CHAPTER ONE

Sarita and the Birth of Middlebrow Publishing

"Every day my sister-in-law and I quarrel. She says she'll read it and I say I will. Mother gets very angry at these quarrels. She says, don't bring books that cause quarrels in the house. You say, one shouldn't give one's book to anyone. Should we buy two copies then?"[1] This letter appears prominently in *Sarita*'s January 1950 issue. In asking this amusing question, Babulal Ahir, the clearly distressed reader from Bombay, echoed the concerns of other households across North India witnessing a similar tussle for the Hindi monthly. Recording family arguments over a Hindi magazine, Ahir's question is crucial to unpacking the history of reading in Hindi in the post-independence period. This chapter focuses on *Sarita* (River), one of the best-selling Hindi magazines of the 1950s.[2] *Sarita* performed the function of a digest, providing something for everyone in the family. In doing so, it promoted segmented consumption that focused on each member's reading desires, with reading material for each individual according to age, gender, or marital status. Through *Sarita*, I delve into the emergence of what I call "middlebrow magazine culture" in Hindi which promoted consumption as its primary impulse. Marketing itself as a viable alternative to literary and highbrow magazines on the one hand and the existing range of lowbrow genre magazines on the other, *Sarita* was one of the pioneering magazines that created a middle ground in Hindi publishing.

Significantly, this middle ground nurtured a range of female readerships. *Sarita* shows us confident women: women as subjects of writing, women as writers, and, most poignant, women as readers. The chapter unfolds the story of how these readers not only entered this world but actively interacted with it. Babulal Ahir's distress makes this evident: crucially, his battle was with his sister-in-law, who posed as an openly confident reader of the magazine as opposed to reading these magazines surreptitiously.[3] Ahir's sister-in-law did not write this letter herself, but she could have. Crucially, rather than experiencing this reading through another reader, Ahir's sister-in-law fights for the right to read the magazine for herself. This argument is not being made for the growing literacy rates of women or about a smooth transition from communal reading to individual, silent reading. At the same time, *Sarita*'s world is that of poised women who wrote letters, responded to other readers' questions in agony aunt columns, debated the quality and veracity of short stories and nonfiction the magazine published, and also authored short stories themselves for submission. While these women were well versed with nationalism—both as recent colonial subjects and as citizens of a newly independent nation—they did not necessarily subscribe to its beliefs and incumbent responsibilities. *Sarita* poignantly opened up a rich world of women confidently asserting themselves, initiating a space for debate both within and outside the framework of the nation and the family.

The chapter also examines *Sarita*'s relationship to Hindi and, consequently, its place within Hindi literary history. In the context of post-1947 India and the Constituent Assembly debates, Hindi was viewed as overbearingly nationalist and Sanskritized, claiming its status as the national language at the expense of the other Indian languages and its own regional varieties.[4] *Sarita*, however, illuminates an alternate and vibrant trajectory: how Hindi in middlebrow magazines functions as a nonnormative and democratizing medium, providing a space for ordinary readers to express the right to a language that they would understand and enjoy. *Sarita*'s challenge to an institutional Hindi was embodied not only in its choice of fiction and nonfiction articles but also in its editorials.

Sarita's editor-publisher Vishwa Nath prominently features in these choices and decisions. I specifically examine his active stand against religious nationalism in the magazine, which often got embroiled in lawsuits because of it. In the only focused essay available on him in English, the writer V. S. Naipaul records Vishwa Nath's views on religion: "I think religion is the greatest curse of mankind. It has killed more people, destroyed more property, than any other thing." Vishwa Nath fashioned himself as a veritable magazine activist: "I didn't put on those saffron robes and start going about to those conferences, or preaching in public. I published my magazines."[5] Vishwa Nath wore many hats at Delhi Press: he was a smart entrepreneur, successful publisher, multilingual editor of flourishing magazines in English (most notably *Caravan* and *Women's Era*), Hindi (*Mukta* and *Champak* apart from *Sarita*), and Urdu (such as the Urdu *Sarita*). This chapter tells the story of the first of his efforts.

SARITA AND THE NEW *SEVA*

Launched in 1945 by the Delhi-based printing-turned-publishing house Delhi Press, *Sarita* was among the widely read Hindi monthlies of the 1950s. Munshi Thakur Das established Delhi Press in 1911 exclusively as a printing press, and Vishwa Nath, his great-grandson, was the first in the family to begin publishing with the launch of the English-language magazine *Caravan* in 1940, which, along with *Sarita*, he edited through the 1950s. *Sarita* was priced at one rupee (roughly thirty pence),[6] and an average issue ran into 120 pages, with some issues running up to even 200 pages. *Sarita* catered to a variety of readers, made evident from its structure (see figure 1).

Sarita comprised separate sections not only for different fictional genres such as short stories and one-act plays (*ekanki*), but also for the more "serious" nonfiction articles (*lekh*), averaging four to six pieces of each genre. A self-help or assorted section usually followed,

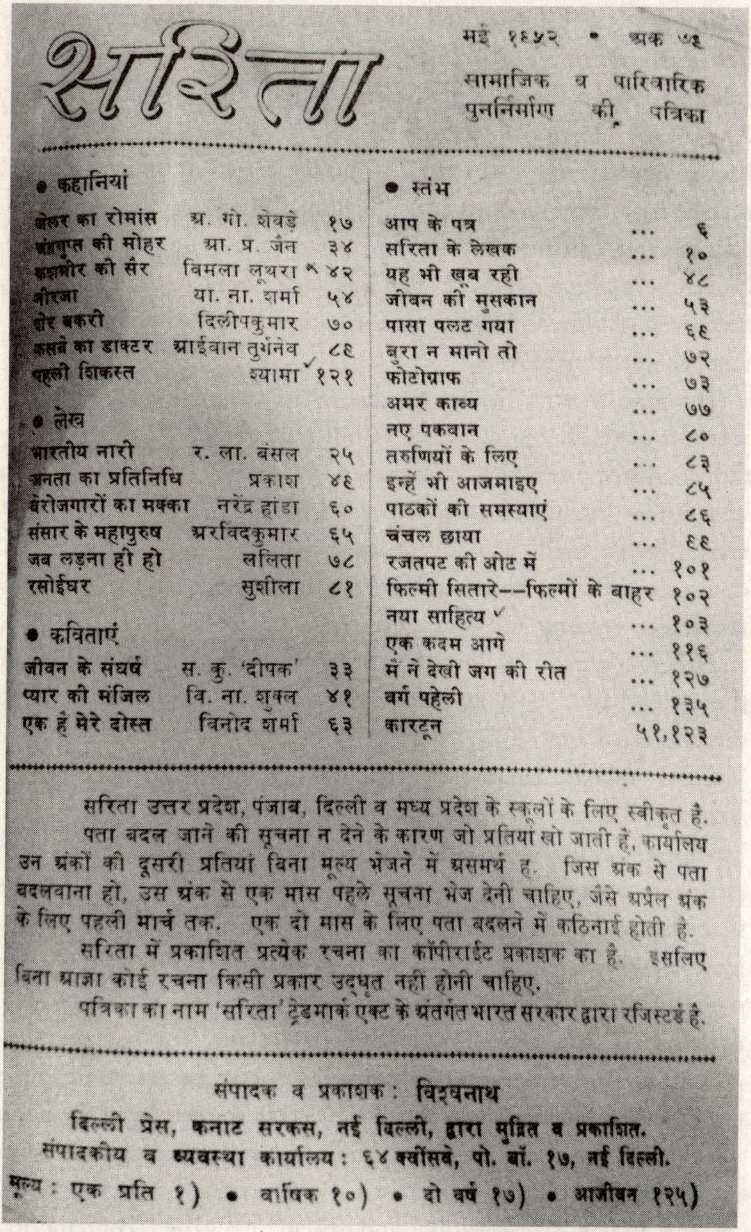

सरिता

मई १९५२ • अंक ७१

सामाजिक व पारिवारिक पुनर्निर्माण की पत्रिका

सरिता उत्तर प्रदेश, पंजाब, दिल्ली व मध्य प्रदेश के स्कूलों के लिए स्वीकृत है.

पता बदल जाने की सूचना न देने के कारण जो प्रतियां खो जाती हैं, कार्यालय उन अंकों की दूसरी प्रतियां बिना मूल्य भेजने में असमर्थ है. जिस अंक से पता बदलवाना हो, उस अंक से एक मास पहले सूचना भेज देनी चाहिए, जैसे अप्रैल अंक के लिए पहली मार्च तक. एक दो मास के लिए पता बदलने में कठिनाई होती है.

संपादक व प्रकाशक : विश्वनाथ

दिल्ली प्रेस, कनाट सरकस, नई दिल्ली, द्वारा मुद्रित व प्रकाशित.

संपादकीय व व्यवस्था कार्यालय : ६४ क्वींसवे, पो. बॉ. १७, नई दिल्ली.

मूल्य : एक प्रति १) • वार्षिक १०) • दो वर्ष १७) • आजीवन १२५)

FIGURE 1. Table of Contents, *Sarita*, May 1952, Delhi Press Magazines.

including advice columns on how to solve small household problems. The serialized novel (*dharavahi*) was next; then came all the regular columns, placed together at the end of the table of contents: Apke Patr (readers' letters), Chanchal Chhaya (film reviews), Naya Sahitya (book reviews), and Varg Paheli, a Hindi crossword competition with cash prizes. Later, sections added included Photograph and those on cooking and knitting; Pathako ki Samasyae (Agony Aunt, added in November 1951); Priya Mitr (Pen Pal, added in December 1949); and Bal Sarita (children's literature). *Sarita* thus provided everyone in the family something to read.

The magazine as an artifact that offered something to everyone was not novel to the world of Hindi publishing. Widely read pre-independence journals like *Saraswati, Madhuri,* and *Chand* (Moon) had similar intentions and formats.[7] However, as Francesca Orsini argues in her study of early twentieth-century Hindi journals and their role in the formation of the Hindi public sphere, these journals articulated reading and writing in terms of "service" (*seva*) to Hindi and to the nation (*rashtraseva,* or "service of nation").[8] *Sarita,* on the other hand, used familiar formats and structure to highlight very different questions from the ones that the pre-independence journals asked. Therefore, although pre-independence journals articulated a seamless, unhesitating agreement between "service of literature" (*sahitya seva*) and the nationalist framing of "women's duty" (*stridharma*) and "service of nation," the pages of *Sarita* told a different story, ignoring or reconfiguring the concerns that had animated journal cultures and, by extension, the public sphere.[9] In fact, it was by distancing itself from classic questions of nationalism that *Sarita* came to define what I term the "middlebrow magazine." For instance, *Sarita* did not carry any sections on nationalist poetry. Essays on imagining either an ideal nation or idealized subjects in the service of the nation were notably sparse: the monthly did not, however, completely isolate itself from the realities of the new nation, carrying a recurring section on the Indian Constitution and discussing varied contemporary concerns like language policy and the Nehruvian government's stand on communism.[10] At the same time, the exclusion of the discourse of nationalism, so soon after independence, is remarkable precisely because of its emphasis in the pre-independence journals.

This change can also be seen at the level of language politics: again, Hindi was one of the primary concerns of pre-independence magazines, but *Sarita* did not champion or defend any particular form of institutionalized or literary Hindi. By contrast, in an editorial in the March 1958 issue, Vishwa Nath began, "Hindi—or should we call it Hindustani—because it includes both Hindi and Urdu . . ."[11] This editorial declaration is significant, especially given the wide promotion of Hindi as national language in pre-independence Hindi periodicals in general.[12] This choice, preferring "Hindustani" to Hindi or Urdu, also comes from a long drawn-out public debate. For instance, in the latter part of his life, M. K. Gandhi was an advocate of Hindustani. In a presidential speech delivered at the influential Hindi Sahitya Sammelan (Society for Hindi Literature) in 1935, Gandhi used Hindi, Urdu, and Hindustani interchangeably, saying, "Hindi, Hindustani and Urdu are different names for the same speech," categorically stating, "Hindustani is the language which is spoken and understood and used by Hindus and Muslims both in cities and villages in North India and which is written and read both in the Nagari and Persian scripts and whose literary forms are today known as Hindi and Urdu."[13]

Sarita, therefore, did not prioritize service to an institutionalized, nationalized Hindi. Vishwa Nath categorically argued against a homogenized nationalist imagination, advocating language syncretism instead. *Sarita*'s writing style on the whole followed this avowal, deploying words from the shared language bank. This sentiment was also visible in the magazine's script itself, which employed the diacritic marks, termed nuqta, to denote Urdu phonemes. In acknowledging the nuqta, rather than erasing or avoiding it, *Sarita* linked the script with Hindustani rather than Hindi, registering a protest against the deterritorialization of language.

Sarita addressed not only the Hindi-Urdu debate but also the prominent one between Hindi and English, subject of heated arguments in the parliament regarding India's official and national language. When an irate reader complained to *Sarita* about its use of what he called an "English" full stop, recommending that *Sarita* "return" to the "Hindi" punctuation style of the *purna viram* to mark the end of each sentence, Vishwa Nath responded, "If other punctuations such as , ; - can be used in Hindi, then why take issue with the 'full stop'? Also, the English 'full stop' takes up less space compared to the Hindi 'purna viram.'"[14] *Sarita* argued for practicality, functionality, ease, and syncretism, both at the level of words themselves and of the script.

Vishwa Nath also addressed the debate around the possibility of Sanskrit becoming mandatory in schools. He argued that Sanskrit was no longer in common currency and, historically, could never be given its Hindu upper-caste connections. Instead, he advocated English as the lingua franca: "If it is a question of the country's equality and literature, then no other language can lead it apart from English . . . because the unity that exists because of English today cannot be obtained through any other language."[15] In proposing English as a unifying national language, Vishwa Nath showed that *Sarita* did not partake in the Hindi nationalist anxieties vis-à-vis English. This stance, in turn, built its reputation as a middlebrow magazine that fed its readers' imaginations as being an all-knowing, unbiased, and confident space that was also, at the same time, easy to understand, approach, and, if needed, call out. Another constituent of the middlebrow emerges from this discourse: just as it did not center its concerns around the rhetoric of nationalism, the magazine followed a similar practice when dealing with the subject of Hindi as national language. It addressed the question for its readers but, at the same time, refused to defend it. Curiously, therefore, in its multipronged approach to contemporary language debates, *Sarita* established itself as a "serious" magazine that thought beyond its own language of operation.

The editor also questioned social conservativism that emphasized clinging to silence around sexual and reproductive health. For instance, an embarrassed reader, Vijay Singh Nirmal from Calcutta, complained about an article that *Sarita* had published on birth control, saying, "It is inappropriate to publish things related to birth control, because we are Indian. Our Indianness (*bharatiyata*) has not been so distanced from us." In response, the editor sardonically replied, "Yes indeed, if our population is increasing uncontrollably at a time when sex is so distant from Indianness, then only God can save us when these two actually come together!"[16] The editor's satirical response here is noteworthy: he reproached the reader for taking a regressive view of the article tackling a social taboo.

In addition to his opposition to the nexus between Hindi and the Hindu nationalist idea of India, Vishwa Nath took a consciously anti-religious stand, and for this reason, *Sarita* often became embroiled in lawsuits. For instance, Arvind Kumar, one of *Sarita*'s editors, authored a poem called "Ram ka Antardvand" ("Ram's dilemma"). Kumar wrote the poem from the point of view of the Hindu mythological King Ram and his doubts about his morality. Ram asks himself: To test her faithfulness, should he have subjected his wife Sita to a terrible trial by fire (*agnipariksha*)? This provocative question ultimately resulted in a court case and ban on *Sarita*'s July 1957 issue.[17] *Sarita* also periodically produced several polemical essays criticizing the ritualistic practices of Hinduism.[18] For example, the May 1949 edition of the magazine carried an article titled "In the Name of Religion!" (Dharm ke naam par!).[19] The author of the piece, Indu Shekhar, wrote in the style of a social reformist text, arguing that although he did not consider religion itself a problem, what needed examination was how it was being misused to cause oppression. Shekhar considered the caste atrocities inherent in Hinduism: "A prominent part of society was boycotted in the name of being untouchable [*achhyut*] and sudra and the foundation of discriminatory caste system was established. A woman was forcefully enslaved under male authority for all time; even after the death of the husband, the woman was forced to commit sati in order to fly the flag of dharma."[20] Here, the writer spoke forcefully against inequitable religious practices, naming both the perpetrators of violence as well as the groups of people suffering from discrimination in the name of caste and gender. This reference to religious discrimination is the most direct I could trace in the magazine archive available for the time period. The article's tone borrows from the language that was deployed to speak about caste and gender reforms by social reformers in the nineteenth and early twentieth centuries.[21] This article can also be read in terms of Nehruvian secular ideology and can, therefore, be understood as a continuation of the social debates of the nineteenth and twentieth centuries reflected in the body of the magazine.

Critiques of religious practices, however, were not always so weighty. The article "The Importance of Makeup in a Woman's Life" ("nari jivan mein sringara ka mahatva") is one such example. Written by Parvati Mishra, the article holds forth on why women should wear makeup: "It isn't only lecherous men, old people, or young men who look at her [the woman], but other women also see her. There are immediate comparisons when one woman passes by in front of another. A woman feels content when you feel discontent."[22] Written in a humorous vein, the article makes its intentions clear: women dress not only for men but, in most cases, also for other women. However, the article also has some things to say about Hindu marriage conventions. It casually declares that the *sindoor*, the Hindu vermillion mark that married women are obligated to put in their hair, is rather unnecessary: "The sindoor is deemed necessary for married women, but there is no point to doing this. How correct is it that women carry around a signboard to declare that they are married? There is no grace in wearing red sindoor in black hair. It is another thing that it is a conventional practice [*rurhi*]."[23] The article enforces a logic of beauty, attacking social and religious practices that dictate that women wear the signifying mark. The English word "signboard" is used to protest this patriarchal marking of territory. The article reinforces the notion that if a woman wishes to commoditize herself through the act of makeup, she needs to step outside the bounds of how beauty has been defined for her by convention.

Although *Sarita*'s and Vishwa Nath's views on religion can perhaps be read as conforming to Nehruvian secular vision, this becomes complicated by *Sarita*'s blatantly open antiestablishment, anti-Nehruvian, and, in many instances, anti-Congress stance—visible, for instance, in cartoons lampooning Nehruvian tactics to rally public opinion and obtain votes.[24] For instance, a cartoon advised Nehru to establish more new cabinet ministries in the government so as to employ (even) more Congress ministers, as well as "a hundred, two hundred representatives, superintendents, section officers and clerks removing India's unemployment utterly so that they [Congress] can secure some more votes in the next election."[25] Here, Vishwa Nath openly satirized Nehru's overstaffed cabinet and bureaucrats.

This critique did not only emerge from Vishwa Nath's pen. In the article "Income from Above" ("Upar ki Amdani"), the writer Santosh Narayan Nautiyal adopted a moral tone in discussing Congress's state of corruption. Nautiyal criticized the figure of the freedom fighter who, when found guilty of corruption, used his past sacrifices to deflect attention: "Nowadays another kind of corruption is rampant. A Gandhi cap (*topi*) and the sentence 'we had gone to jail . . .' ('*aji ham to jail gaye the* . . .'). Going to prison should be indicative of your patriotism, sacrifice, etc., and not the ability or qualification for a particular position."[26] Through the above illustrations, we can see that the Congress Party was portrayed as manipulative and duplicitous rather than idealistic and egalitarian, and Nehru himself is caricatured as power hungry rather than as the revered leader of the nation. Thus Vishwa Nath's pronouncements on religion should not be read as merely Nehruvian or secular but, I argue, further in another, well-established Hindi literary tradition of the 1950s: the discourse of *moh bhang*. Loosely translated as "disenchantment," moh bhang questioned if, even after formal independence from British rule, India had achieved any real freedom at all. This "official" freedom, it was argued, was merely nominal. This sentiment was particularly strongly expressed among the Progressive leftist writers affiliated with the Progressive Writers' Association. Literary historian Gopal Rai writes, "At that time, critiquing the Congress, the Communist party declared 1947's freedom as an 'untrue freedom.'"[27] This, however, was not the only disillusioned faction. While the Progressive-Communist literary faction focused on literary representations of the lower classes and championing collective struggle, another literary formation, labeled the Nayi Kahani or the New Story literary movement, focused instead on the individual, subjective disenchantment.[28] Given this, the Nayi Kahani movement coined the slogan "felt experience" (*bhoga hua anubhav*), which meant that the writers' and their characters' personal, individual, independent experience was necessary if one were to articulate and write of experience in fiction.[29] That experience was one of loss, alienation, and disenchantment. Against this backdrop, I argue that *Sarita* articulated its own sense of disenchantment. The magazine regularly published Nayi Kahani as well as such Progressive writers as Mohan Rakesh, Rajendra Yadav, and Yashpal. Readers and editors were familiar with these movements and their ideas.[30] But while publishing their stories, *Sarita* found ways to express disenchantment without privileging the progressive emphasis on poverty and collective struggle. Similarly, *Sarita* also expressed disillusionment with the Nehruvian ideal nation without favoring individual alienation of the Nayi Kahani.

In fact, *Sarita*'s moh bhang uniquely blended practical and consumer concerns within its fabric. This combination can be best demonstrated through Vishwa Nath's interpretation of the term "service to literature," which he connected to the need for readers to support magazines by buying individual copies for each family member: "How long will writers be able to do service to literature if they remain starving? If they do not ask for anything, is it right for us to escape from their service (*seva*) and try to rob them? The development of literature can only be undertaken if literature lovers buy more and more magazines and books. If these do not sell, then publishers will suffer and creations will remain limited to the writers."[31] Again, the "service to literature," plucked from the well-established vocabulary of the pre-independence period, is creatively adapted and deployed in the context of middlebrow publishing, with the ostensible aim to support writers by encouraging readers to buy more magazines. Moh bhang, here, acquires another strain and trajectory. Disenchantment is expressed not only through a rejection of nationalism and language politics but also, rather ingeniously, by molding ideas such as "service to literature" to sell more magazines.

Sarita further played with the nationalist notion of service by introducing another rhetoric into the picture: that of *grahak seva*, or "service to the consumer." An advertisement published in *Sarita*'s May 1949 edition proudly declared, "*Sarita* has only one aim—to serve readers." Another advertisement stated that *Sarita* did not accept film advertisements because that would create bias, whereas the magazine's film reviews were unbiased.[32] *Sarita* projected an active sense of obligation toward its readers and their creative, intellectual, and ethical interests. Indeed, if we map the structure of the magazine onto the family, in a marked departure from the pre-independence discourse, *Sarita* asked not what the family could do for the sake of the country but instead informed the family about what it *must* and could do to nourish itself. Again, this possibly emerges from the disenchantment that was contemporary to literary movements, feeding into the readers' particular concerns about language, literature, and religion, also dramatically altering it, however, by ingeniously adding ideas of consumption and consumer service.

Even though Vishwa Nath's editorial voice and subject position appears throughout the magazine, what emerges from reading *Sarita* is a sense of readers not as passive objects editorialized into submission but rather as autonomous minds who speak back to the magazine. The following three sections focus on the value of the readers as producers and primary creative entities in *Sarita*.

ON LANGUAGE AND "LITERARINESS"

One of the ways in which readers of *Sarita* fashioned themselves as creative minds with an active stake in the magazine was by writing to the magazine, in the form of letters to the editor (at least six to seven letters were published each month), advice columns, and contributions to its content, to name just a few. These were often deeply critical, and readers were not afraid to take the magazine to task, contributing to the production of the middlebrow, for which the reader as creative entity and producer of ideas is paramount. An illuminating example are the debates over language. Readers actively expressed what kind of language they did or did not want to read. Many wanted to read simpler, more accessible registers of Hindi. Some readers expressed the older ideas of literacy and dharma, whereas others increasingly emphasized the idea of choice and vociferously asked for a simpler language for a variety of other reasons. "Simpler" Hindi could be read both as complaint over the "sanskritization" of language as well as a defense of reading for pleasure.

Although *Sarita* prided itself on simplicity of language and style, readers were quick to catch any slips and express their displeasure. In the June 1949 issue, Bamchand Surana from Sadulpur, Rajasthan, wrote about a column that meant to cater to the magazine's female readers: "It is beyond doubt that the 'something of the home, something of the world' column is very beautiful, current and entertaining, however, alas, only if the language were a little simpler! You know how many people are [actually] literate in our India and how many of them are women. We would despair if we were to count the number of well-read sisters. Moreover, you will have to concede that this column has especially been introduced for women, however, simple and common literate sisters are not able to derive full benefit from it."[33] Surana's comment cloaks the demand for coherent and simple writing in the rhetoric of nationalist "useful for women" (*stri upyogi*) literature: the purpose of *Sarita*, in his mind, was to be useful for women and to help them carry out their women's duty (*stri dharma*). Thus the discourses of the pre-independence period are not completely absent from the magazine, and the list of duties was still prevalent and part of the magazine. Alongside such comments, *Sarita* also published others, such as a terse note from Balswarup "Rahi" from Timarpur, Delhi, expressing his dissatisfaction about the magazine's use of language: "*Sarita* often satirizes radio's sanskritized Hindi, but what was the kind of language employed in the first two [to] three contexts of 'Crime,' the short story published in the December issue?"[34] The story, according to "Rahi," deliberately employed a more "unnatural" language register, a kind of Hindi that did not serve any purpose for the magazine's readers. When the reader rejects "radio's sanskritized Hindi" in the story, the assertion of choice derives from an expression of the right to read freely without the weight of institutionalized Hindi that *Sarita*'s readers have no interest in engaging with.

The readers of the magazine also sought to comment on the idea of "literariness" of the material within the magazine, as well as the "literariness" of the magazine itself. This point is illustrated by a letter from Ambalal Manilal Patel from Naya Deesa which compared reading the stories in the magazine to reading the Hindi/Urdu canonical writer Premchand: "Just as a memorable image gets etched on your mind when reading Premchand, the same thing occurs for many of the stories in *Sarita*." However, although this reader praised the magazine in its selection of short stories, he was quick to criticize the fact that the same standards are not maintained when it comes to geography, science, and poetry. The letter continues, "They should take care of these subjects the same way that they do for literature."[35] Another reader, Mahabirprasad Agrawal from Nohar, Rajasthan, also craved more poetry, "This [*Sarita*] has all sorts of things for everyone. It would be very good if you could publish at least one poem each month."[36]

Often, the magazine played out the question of literariness by publishing conversations between readers, best illustrated in readers' comparisons of the magazine with other contemporary highbrow literary journals like *Pratik* and *Himalaya*.[37] The magazine often recorded readers' discontent with it. Vallabhdas Gupta, a reader from Amravati, Maharashtra, compared *Sarita* unfavorably with literary magazines: "*Sarita* will take ten years to match them. These are magazines as well as literary books."[38] Other readers differed from Gupta's analysis and wrote replies to the editor, hailing *Sarita* as the magazine of genuine ease. One such female response, by Rajkumari from Ahmedabad, Gujarat, directly addressed Gupta: "Even I have read *Himalaya* and *Pratik*, but they don't possess the pleasure I get from reading *Sarita*." Another female reader, Kaminilata, from Allahabad, Uttar Pradesh, was even more profuse in her praise, providing a rather sardonic response to Vallabhdas Gupta: "But Editorji, you didn't provide this Progressive sir with a correct answer. I would say that he isn't evolved in his knowledge of magazines. He does not know that magazines cannot progress one step without advertisements. For example, the magazines he has named—*Himalaya* and *Pratik*—perhaps he does not know that no new issue of theirs has appeared in public for many months now. Regarding *Sarita*—this sir can himself keep his hand on his heart and ask, is there any other magazine currently that can take the place of *Sarita* as Hindi literature's primary magazine?"[39] *Pratik* was definitely one of the most respected literary magazines of the time,[40] and for Kamanilata to take on its cult status and link it to its lack of advertisement revenue is remarkable. The informed and articulate female reader not only counters the literary magazine's specific claims to literariness but is also aware of the link between the publication of a magazine and advertisement revenue, deriding the "Progressive" reader about his lack of awareness on the matter. To her, a magazine with a large circulation base cannot survive without advertisements, and it was obvious that a smaller and more exclusive magazine such as *Pratik* should actually fail in its *literary* endeavors given a lack of knowledge on publishing successfully over a sustained period of time.

The question of literariness was tied not only to circulation but also to accessibility. Yet another reader wrote that his "ahindi" friends—those who did not count Hindi as their primary language—were able to read stories in *Sarita* because of their simplicity. This fact actually worked in Hindi's favor, as compared to writings in *Himalaya*: "If you place *Himalaya* in front of them, will they show that much love towards Hindi?"[41] This battle over literariness continued many months later into February 1950, when another reader, Shyam Hari Tiwari from Lucknow, Uttar Pradesh, wrote: "We should not overlook the second aspect. The other two magazines are not as close to life as is *Sarita*."[42] Tiwari's argument about the magazine's ability to be "close to life" is an intellectual assertion to take this desire to be represented seriously and to unapologetically read the accessible magazine.

I dwell on the readers' comparisons between the literary and middlebrow journals here to establish three points. First, the consumer of *Sarita* was indeed familiar with the Hindi literary sphere and the publications circulating therein. Second, that the reader was making an intervention of choice, declaring not only the use value derived from *Sarita* but also in terms of the pleasure gained from reading it. Finally, subscribers expressed an intellectual assertion, arguing for the right to read a middlebrow magazine such as *Sarita*. The emphasis on how the middlebrow magazine is ordinary, accessible, close to life, and therefore *more* valuable to the reader than literary magazines is expressed as a well-argued, well-articulated choice.

That said, studying letters to the editor is only one way of understanding readers' engagement with the magazine. Consumers also made themselves visible in the text through other contributions, most notably via the stories they themselves wrote and submitted. *Sarita* launched a section called Naye Ankur (New saplings) in January 1952. Vishwa Nath explained the rationale underlying this section: "*Sarita* has, from its birth, stopped itself from being influenced by big names. It has always given more importance to the work—who wrote it has been uninfluential."[43] *Sarita* thus invited stories from its readers. This was a novel way of participating in the economy of the middlebrow magazine that also significantly published prestigious Nayi Kahani and Progressive fiction alongside it in the same space.[44]

Readers also communicated extensively with the editor and, indeed, one another, through advice columns. Although many readers wrote in with questions about physical appearance such as how to solve their hair and skin problems, other questions were more fraught with social and familial conflicts. For instance, one reader asked if it was socially acceptable for his friend to marry a girl who had, at a point in time, tied a *rakhi* on his wrist.[45] The question essentially was this: Was it possible to overcome the ritual implications of tying the ceremonial thread that converted the relationship between any man and woman into a bond between a brother and sister, or can one establish a marital or conjugal relationship? In the same column, another reader wondered if it was possible for her to marry her sister-in-law's brother's son.[46] The editor answered these questions of marriage within the family, providing technical loopholes to confused readers. In these two cases, it was acceptable for both readers to establish relationships and marry the people they wanted to because there were no direct blood ties between them. Social ties because of marriage in a family as well as symbolic ties because of a band on the wrist should not deter people in love from getting married to each other, the editor reasoned.[47]

Often, the editor would offer a reader's question for other readers to answer. This is where things get even more interesting. In the December 1951 issue, a reader wrote in about his wife who had confided in him about a premarital sexual relationship with someone else. He wondered what to do in this situation. Reader responses in the January 1952 issue addressed this dilemma, insisting that the husband should not dwell on this because this relationship had occurred before their marriage. The advice extended beyond the husband's personal relationship with the wife: it also addressed the possible social humiliation if the community at large came to know about this relationship. In that case, readers suggested, the husband should definitely support the wife. If the social pressure proved unbearable, the couple should move away from their current neighborhood. Often, these columns concluded with other questions inviting reader responses, to be published in the coming issues.

By creating a pool of replies in the article with direct quotes from readers' suggestions, the editor made space for readers as integral to the magazine. The next section discusses the space that female readers inhabited in *Sarita* in which they were an active part of the readership of the magazine and routinely wrote in with their observations and concerns.

THE ASSERTIVE FEMALE READER

"One thing irks me. Why would a (District) collector's son buy earthen utensils from a potter? Everyone knows that no one cooks in earthen pots in officers' houses. Then he takes a loan and refuses to give the money back in the end. All these things sound made up. A clerk and a potter can become friends, but a collector's son buying earthen pots on loan sounds impossible."[48] In this letter, Pratibha Singh from Ranchi fact-checks a few details in a story by Neelkan Perumal titled "The Story of a Hut" ("Jhopri ki Kahani"). This reader contests a fictional detail based on her position as a housewife well acquainted with the price of pots and pans. On the basis of this detail, she concludes, "All these things sound made up," calling the veracity of the story itself into question. The reader here confidently situates herself as a woman possessing a wealth of practical knowledge, writing a letter to the editor to so demonstrate it in order to educate the ignorant storyteller in the magazine.

Another reader, named Neeraja, from Meerut, Uttar Pradesh, writes in not about a story but about applying makeup: "The pieces that you publish for women, the ones that talk about makeup, are they for married women or for everyone? If it is for everyone, can you please tell me why an unmarried girl is called 'fashionable' if she dresses according to the suggestions of *Sarita*, and is therefore disliked by the people of the family, because of which she can then later not dress herself up. What should she do in such a situation?"[49] Neeraja is direct in her question to the magazine and wants to know why unmarried women like herself are censured if they wear makeup based on the magazine's suggestions, a magazine she clearly trusts. According to Neeraja, if *Sarita* recommends it, then the family should accept it too.

The two letters above, written by two women, one within the home and the other not, show fearless and assertive readers, self-confidently spelling out clear likes and dislikes, reporting concerns directly and confidently to the magazine. Both examples illustrate how women in *Sarita* define themselves both in relation to the parameters of the home and the world outside, stitching the two entities together within the fabric of the magazine. For both kinds of women, *Sarita* offered space to express themselves as thinking subjects quite apart from the nationalist or even the domestic sphere. That is, the magazine flattens the differences between what it means to be inside or outside the home, not privileging one for the other.[50]

A cover image of the magazine, depicting a modern Indian woman dressed in a fashionable sari, serves as an example (see figure 2). This image of women as confident and assertive needs to be understood with respect to the pre-independence debates of women as subjects of feeling. In the context of women's journals and their usual conflation of womanhood with motherhood and, in the nationalist framework, with woman as mother of the nation, Francesca Orsini argues that the journal *Chand* also invested in feeling, "recognizing women as emotional beings, questioning their home-bound existence, and envisaging new public roles." She shows how "hybrid genres (confessionals, epistolary novels, social novels) mixing reality with fiction, instruction with entertainment" published in *Chand* ultimately made space for "taboo issues concerning women to be raised, directly and with the heightened impact of a melodramatic narrative."[51] In her book on nationalism and women's periodicals, Shobna Nijhawan argues that "the periodical was a site to expose patriarchal, social, and political ideologies that negatively impacted the lives of women."[52] Mapping the readerships of women's periodicals as "by default upper class and Hindu," she notes that the periodicals addressed the readers "as an entity, indicated by the terms *stri jaati* (womenkind), *stri samaj* (women's society), *sri gan* (women's group), and even Hindi *bhasini narisamaj* (the Hindi-speaking women's community), or through the more intimate kinship terms mother and sister."[53] Nijhawan's study of periodicals invokes a sense of women's place at the center of public discourse, which they otherwise could not attain because of their inability to physically be present in it. Significantly, she imbues the magazines as a space for expansion of the roles of women's subjectivities during the nationalist struggle.[54]

FIGURE 2. Cover, *Sarita*, June 1953, Delhi Press Magazines.

However, as the examples so far show, *Sarita* did not particularly address women exclusively in kinship terms or as a separate audience, nor did it directly seek to address social ills that oppressed women. In fact, Nijhawan's argument about the collapsing of divisions along the lines of gender finds continuation in middlebrow magazines such as *Sarita*. This publication acts not as a prescriptive manual reproducing a normative formula for what a woman ought or ought not to be but consciously configured itself as a magazine for everyone in the family and for women as an inherent part of it, fashioned as matter-of-fact readers and producers within the magazine. If the pre-independence period had its own discourse of women as mothers, women as mothers of the nation, and, finally, women as subjects of feeling, *Sarita*'s female readers perhaps can be understood more in terms of arbiters of taste and knowledge and less in terms of either kinship or seeking to expose oppressions. Notably, women's voices are not cloaked in apology. Instead, the magazine serves to make available a multiplicity of subjectivities to the different women who engage with, and are integral to constituting, it.

Female readers' direct, assertive relationship to the magazine is reflected in Kumari Vimla's letter from Shahdara, Delhi, complaining about the magazine's cost: "The price is definitely expensive, but it can be tolerated because of *Sarita*'s beauty. However, please don't step even further, otherwise *Sarita* will escape middle-class and reach upper-class status."[55] Vimla asserts her opinion over price, linking it directly to a question of class status and the limited disposable income of the middle classes. She expresses an entitlement over the right to read, which is tied not to her gender but, rather, to her class identity. This assertion, of value for money, stands in stark contrast to the discourse around other such book publications for women, namely, religious chapbooks and almanacs.[56] *Sarita* notably marketed itself as a family magazine, not as a women's magazine. The reader in question is accessing the magazine in terms of the same rhetoric. Kumari Vimla's concerns about price then reflect her role as consumer of "*Sarita*'s beauty"; she does not feel the need to cloak the pleasure she derives from reading the magazine and expresses direct economic stake in the material object, fully aware of her choices as well as how much money she should pay for the magazine. This idea of beauty linked to price, which, in turn, is linked to class identity and readily disposable income, is another important middlebrow attribute, and Vimla squarely presents her concerns as separate from that of a highbrow or upper-class reader.

How do these readers' positions correlate with the cultural imaginary expressed in the short stories published in *Sarita*? In the next section I move away from both the reader and the editor-publisher figure and concentrate on the short stories within the magazine. As the examples show, the short stories situate their concerns around consumption, class, and marriage and thereby reflect the concerns of the readers as well as the editor of the magazine.

SARITA AND THE SHORT STORY

The women written about in *Sarita*'s stories are surprisingly varied: we find young women working within the household as well as women stepping out of the home; women who stay within the marriage as well as women who choose to leave. The stories—or, indeed, any story at all—are representations and cannot directly be taken as obvious "mirrors" of authenticity to understand the women or households who were reading the magazine. However, certain commonalities running through the texts reflect the readers' anxieties and desires about their subject position within marriage and can help reach certain conclusions about *Sarita* and the stories that consumers wanted to read. The stories transported readers not only into the modern world of alternative family bonds and commodity consumption but, crucially, also reflected women's fears and desires of achieving and retaining subjectivity within the sphere of marriage. The recurrence of themes in the stories specially tell us this: the female protagonists in the stories provided certainty of conflict resolution within the framework of marriage without surrendering their sense of self.

Some other commonalities persist. The first compelling one is the general absence of the larger joint family in the stories, albeit with a focus on love within the marital sphere. In other words, the energies of the short stories are concentrated on the young, recently married couple. Nonmarital love is almost absent from the pages of *Sarita*, except in some instances where the love conflict is played out between the rebellious female protagonist and her parents' rejection of the man she has chosen to marry. The other, more prevalent theme of love of the young married couple is almost always under threat. Significantly, the two are neither directly confronted by the undivided family nor even by its specter, in the form of the absent but looming voice of the parents or parents-in-law. The conflict lies squarely between the two primary characters. By the end of the story, however, the couple return to each other, marking a space that they have negotiated as the "familial ideal," one that necessarily begins with the restoration of the marriage and marital relations.

Additionally, the short stories in *Sarita* embody the generally understood definition of melodrama as an expansion of the ordinary into a question of resolving ethical binaries, between good and bad, right and wrong, truth and untruth. Peter Brooks's definition of melodrama serves as a major formative argument to explain the melodramatic turn in writing: "The promethean [sic] search to illuminate man's quotidian existence by the reflected flame of the higher cosmic drama constitutes one of the principal quests of the modern imagination."[57] I suggest that the route of resolving these binaries is displaced. For instance, the return to the "familial ideal" is indeed reached through a series of ethical turns, but it is the couple who actively make these interventions. The stories emphasize that both parties possess equal agency. The melodramatic turn in the story is essential to reading clues into the inner lives of the protagonists. Significantly, although the closure itself is dramatic conforming to the familial ideal, first, it is an ideal entirely of the couple's own crafting and, second, it conforms to the conventions of the modern nuclear family model, a relatively new entity in the magazine.

The January 1953 short story "Pride and Obstinacy" ("Man aur Hath") by a writer called Usha may serve as an example.[58] A very beautiful girl, Amrita, is married to Mukul, who happens to be an ugly (*kuroop*) man. She decides to reject him and their marriage, even though, as is repeatedly pointed out to her, the man comes from a very rich family and works for himself, separately and unrelated to the family business, thus in accord with the idea of the new Hindu nuclear family.[59] An altercation occurs between the two where Mukul, after trying hard and failing to woo Amrita—not because she is stubborn but because he is unable to generate any desire in her with declarations of his monetary accomplishments—tells her that he can find many replacements for her. At this point, Amrita leaves and moves back to her parents' house. The story is narrated from Amrita's point of view, dramatizing her state of mind. The story's tension is built through Mukul's frequent letters that anxiously inquire about her return to her husband's home. In the meantime, Amrita returns home to study further and tells her family that she will find a job rather than go back to a man who believes that he can easily buy her love. She does find a job in the metropolitan city of Pune, but as the years go by, she develops regrets. In the meantime, Mukul marries someone else.[60]

One day, Mukul suddenly arrives at Amrita's house with a child. The second wife has died, and Mukul declares: "Her death did not change anything for me. I was as alone with her living as I was with you gone. I know that you will not accept me, but I don't know what drew me here. A slight hope . . ."[61] The story ends with Amrita picking up the child and walking into the house, with Mukul following them inside.

The story, then, ends with the restoration of marriage. At first glance, the "choice" of the protagonist may not seem to be a radical act at all, because she chooses to return to her husband and care for his second wife's child. However, this is not a simplistic return of the prodigal wife. The story is built not so much on familial interventions as on the protagonist's own understanding and expectations of marriage and her refusal to compromise or make peace with her circumstances: she chooses to walk away from the marriage rather than give way to her rich husband. This is not a stubborn young woman brought back to the fold but rather a young woman growing through her decisions while the young man she married grows through his own. She has time to reflect on her life when she moves away and works in another town, and she reaches the conclusion that she desires the familial ideal which is dramatized in the story in the form of a dialogue much before Mukul reenters the narrative. The author displaces the ethical binary of right and wrong, of the wronged husband and errant wife, because Mukul's provocation that he can easily replace Amrita if she is unwilling to accept him stands at the center of the narrative. The husband has erred too. Both wife and husband reach narrative growth, and by the time the husband comes to reconcile with his wife, they have both realized the fruitlessness of their excessive reactions.

Although the emphasis on building dramatic tension within the story is crucial, the ending points to the logic of resolution because, ultimately, the excess of feeling must be curbed. Yet this resolution is not born out of deference to the national ideal or to the feminine ideal within marriage, which were the logics typically employed in pre-independence women's journals. Instead—and this is again a prominent aspect of the middlebrow—it occurred owing to arriving at the ideal by one's own introspective process. This process is particularly valuable because, first, the woman is not given these templates in the beginning of the narrative and needs to reach them in the face of her own opposition, and, second, as suggested, the template of the "familial ideal" itself has shifted.

As I noted above, the undivided family is almost absent from the short story in *Sarita*. The space that the family inhabits also shrinks as a consequence. The couple's space becomes more intimate. The protagonists imagine the space of the home in terms of their relationship with each other. Published in June 1950, "Loose Bonds" ("Kachche Dhage") by Vimla Kapur stands as an example.[62] The newly married couple in the story are estranged and inhabit separate bedrooms, because the wife believes that the husband had a hand in her father's bankruptcy. She refuses to dine with her husband when the maidservant asks her but is eager to notice her husband's reaction to her rejection. The narrative reads: "Surprised by this utterance, the servant went away, and Sunita eagerly started waiting for the answer."[63] Soon, the servant returns and informs the wife that her husband insists on dining together. It seems that, in this power play, the wife has failed. The walk from the bedroom to the dining hall takes on epic proportions because of the estrangement between the two.

After the meal, they move from the dining hall to the drawing room, another long walk for the female protagonist of the story. Not only does time expand for her, but so does distance. There is empty space between her and her husband, only crossed by the servants of the house. Most striking, the female protagonist has easy access to both the inner and outer spheres of the house, that is, the bedroom and the sitting room. In fact, the entire space of the house has now become a private space, closed off from the public, serving as a modern marker of privacy. Such easy movement, as well as the ability to grieve in private (albeit under the watchful eyes of servants), is a mark of class position: in an essay, Nirmal Verma famously remarked, "There is no word for privacy in Hindi, because Indian families have never felt any necessity for it."[64] The configurations of space, family, and relationships within *Sarita* imagine the modern nuclear family model.

Indeed, the households in the stories in *Sarita* are closed spaces, that is, spaces that neighbors can no longer constantly visit or pry into. Sometimes, they are lived places where people come to visit, leaving after the meal that they have been invited to has ended. The woman of the house is hurrying the servant along. These, again, are visible class markers for not only the modern nuclear family but also the upper-class family. The popular writer Vimla Luthra's one-act play (*ekanki*) titled "Pretenders to Art" (Kala ke Davedar) is set in "a room of an important officer's house in Delhi."[65] A woman is seen urging another on the telephone to come home for tea to meet an artist. Clearly, these women belong to an upper-class set: "There's a party today in the Belgian Embassy, dinner tomorrow at the Afghan Embassy, and a cinema show at the American Embassy the day after."[66] The preparation of tea is always at hand in the household. Items like snacks and pastries are served. Tea was not a common object of consumption in the Indian subcontinent and was a "phenomenon largely confined to the latter two-thirds of the 20th century." Philip Lutgendorf argues that the Indian public started being understood as a lucrative untapped market in the 1920s and 1930s, and tea was subsequently marketed as a colonial object, as the national beverage, and as a "medium for women's 'awakening'—a progressive and empowering tool for smart, modern homemakers, who understood the importance of good nutrition and domestic hygiene."[67] Despite great efforts at marketing, at the time of India's independence, tea was a commodity that privileged—often bureaucratic—upper-class elite drank. The spatial configuration of the drawing rooms of *Sarita* provides a contrast to middle-class lived experience. These are, in short, aspirational spaces.

These spaces are open to one more interpretation: that they may not even be aspirational, that they are spaces that the reader of *Sarita* wishes to *know* about. Middlebrow readers of *Sarita* who wrote to the magazine confidently specifying the prices of pots and pans or inquiring about makeup tips for unmarried women may not have been interested in confidently holding a tea party but could wish to know about the objects and ceremonies in an intimate manner. Such impulses resonate in Vinod Kumar Shukla's 1979 novel *The Servant's Shirt* (Naukar ki Kameez), where the male protagonist residing in a small town justifies buying women's magazines for his wife to read at home: "I had understood much by looking through these mirrors, my general knowledge had increased. I had never sat on a horse but books and the cinema had made sitting in an airplane so common that I knew how to sit on an airplane . . . I knew the services available at Bombay's Oberoi Continental . . . It is important to do it in order to be modern. I wanted this for my wife. Meaning, one should be in the know about modern comforts. She could learn how to put makeup on through advertisements, even though she, as well as I, didn't like powder on her face, because it's wasteful expenditure."[68] *Sarita*'s world is indeed an intimate world, in terms of relationships, the imagination of the home, and its imagination of heartbreak within domesticity, in its generation and facilitation of desires.

In this plethora of exploration of desires, what of sexual desires? A story of longing that deserves mention is called "Boundaries" ("Seemayein"). Written by the prominent Nayi Kahani writer Mohan Rakesh, it narrates the story of a girl named Uma, who, he tells us in the very beginning, is not beautiful. The narrative voice informs us that it has been four years since Uma has passed her examinations, and since then, she has only been waiting to get married: "From then until now, it has been a waiting time [*sandhikal*]—waiting to get married [*vivah pratikshakal*]. Parents will make a decision about her marriage. She will leave as a wife. Perhaps, this month. Perhaps, two years later." The narrative is ridden with pathos—clearly, Uma is very unhappy. She is excited about going to a friend's wedding for a while, yet even that becomes a moment of unhappiness because she does not feel beautiful. She compares herself with her friend Raksha, who has come to pick her up for the wedding: she looks beautiful and desirable even in coarse *khadi* cloth. Uma tries hard to dress herself and applies makeup but feels immediately ashamed: "She went down the stairs. She started walking with Raksha. She thought that she was crossing her boundaries. Boundaries, that are her own and natural to her—her mother, the house, the temple, the festival, and the suffocating desire inside her heart."[69] Rakesh poignantly etches a narrative that communicates what it means to lose self-respect and how marriage—and in this case, the lack of it—can erode a person's selfhood. At this point, before Uma leaves, her doting mother gives her a gold necklace to wear to the wedding, which she does absentmindedly. Uma's mother also reminds her that before she returns home, she needs to go to the neighboring mandir. This moment—the interest of Uma's mother in adorning her daughter with the gold necklace kept aside for Uma's future wedding, as well as telling her to go to the temple—are significant not only to the story's conclusion but also in terms of establishing that Uma's sense of emptiness and despair does not necessarily emerge from lack of affection or familial pressure to get married. Uma's subjectivity is not directly tied but rather more ambiguously: she is able to move in and out of these given narratives and constraints, still despairing of their existence.

Uma does reluctantly go to the wedding and finds herself in a group of girls excitedly discussing the groom. One of the girls at the wedding has managed to obtain the groom's photograph and passes it around for everyone to see. Uma remains silent throughout the scene, and the circulation of the photograph and the following conversation leaves her completely untouched:

> "This is a nice lottery," Kanta said after seeing the photograph.
>
> "Why lottery?" Kanchan asked.
>
> "It is a lottery only. Parents decided on the match, the girl acquiesced, she got to see the man when the curtain was lifted, she folded her hands, did a *namaskar*—Hail the husband! [*Jai patidev*!]"[70]

At home, while Uma was despondent about her "waiting time [*sandhikal*]—waiting to get married [*vivah pratikshakal*]," this moment, Kanta's joke about how a wedding is nothing more than commodification of the female self, only reestablishes what Uma already believes. She laughs mirthlessly at Kanta's joke.

Unable to participate in the joy of the wedding celebrations, she is left alone while the others mill about. However, at this point, Rakesh introduces a moment of realization for Uma. Even in this loneliness, Uma keenly notices one such interaction that is playing out in front of her—a conversation between her attractive friend Raksha and a man unknown to Uma. Uma wistfully keeps looking in their direction, suggesting that while the wedding celebrations or the constant bustle around her do not interest her, a developing intimacy between these two characters does. The story foregrounds intimacy as the missing link in Uma's life. While the readers are still guessing what exactly Uma is attracted to—a flirtation between Raksha and the man, a longing for a deeper intimacy, or something else entirely—Rakesh introduces the appearance of a second unknown man, who is looking directly at Uma. She feels her entire body heating (*Sharir mein lahu adhik bharne laga*), as if someone had stabbed her with a dagger. The man's unwavering stare in her direction makes Uma completely and literally lose her footing, and she decides to flee the celebrations. While Uma's state of mind is described actively throughout, the readers are left hanging at the last sentence of this moment of fleeing: "She felt as if she has heard the first sentence of a story and left the rest of the story in the middle. There's eagerness building, however."[71] This passage indicates that Uma is unclear about what has transpired, but while she is shocked by this encounter, she is not averse to it.

After this, Uma returns home and leaves quickly to visit the temple on her mother's chiding. At the mandir, Uma encounters the same man, again looking at her directly. Suddenly, in the crowd, she feels that the man has touched her, and it is in that moment that Uma "realizes" herself: "She only had knowledge of one thing, that one hand is touching her—here, near the arms, here, near the shoulders, here . . ." While the wedding encounter is striking in terms of Uma's possible desire for this man, the introduction of sexual desire at the very end of the story is telling. Uma realizes that she not only seeks a man to marry her but also desires someone's desire of her. More important, Uma discovers that she is also seeking a story: "Now her soul (atma) is full. Today, even she has a story."[72] The visit to the temple follows from the visit to the friend's wedding celebrations, with the narrator suggesting that Uma needed to go through the process of being a participant at the wedding, where she was first looked at and desired, to understand her own desire for this at the temple. The friend's wedding celebrations then become a rite of passage.

The narrative voice that enumerated Uma's created boundaries above, that is, "boundaries, that are her own and natural to her—her mother, the house, the temple, the festival, and the suffocating desire inside her heart"—resonates with the readers in how the story ends. Yet the last part of the story where Uma imagines the unknown man's hands all over her is meant to be read as emancipatory. Uma escapes her boundaries in, of all places, a religious place of worship, which shows those boundaries that were "natural to her" have suddenly opened up within her. The story, then, hints at a predominant aspect of female desire, that is, sexual desire. This desire is, however, questioned, or even curtailed, by how the story ends: when Uma leaves the temple for home, she realizes that her gold necklace is missing. Readers are left guessing: What will actually become of this new knowledge, undercut by the loss of precious jewelry at the end? The story written for an audience of the middlebrow magazine explores desire, but also undercuts it.

Although *Sarita* addressed significant ideas, it also actively kept out certain narratives from its pages, again reinforcing its status as a middlebrow magazine. For one, *Sarita*'s world was an insular one: it limited fiction that transcended class concerns. The publication included some upper-class narratives, but the characters are mostly middle class. Only a few stories about lower-middle-class poverty are included. For instance, "Red Sari" ("Lal Chunar"), by writer Usha Saksena in the December 1951 issue, voices this third anguish, that of the "housewife" protesting a lifestyle of imposed austerity. The story opens with Sunaina cleaning utensils and missing everyday comforts, screaming at her husband for not being able to provide adequately. After the husband goes to work, her neighbor visits her wearing new jewellery, reminding her of the time when she had to give away her own jewellery for her sister-in-law's wedding: "Sunaina thought to herself: my jewellery got sold because of my sister-in-law's wedding, and my lord husband's tongue has worn out from talking but . . ."[73] The incomplete sentence poignantly points to Sunaina's loss. It creates an implicit identification with the universally pervasive idea of *stridhan*, which, translated literally, means "woman's wealth": Sunaina has had to sacrifice her own property for another woman's stridhan.[74]

By the way of exclusions: the short stories in *Sarita* are remarkably secular, with religion absent from the pages. If there is a reference to a deity, it exists as a cursory entity, in the form of impromptu exclamations from characters in times of distress. This idea of secularism does come at the cost of the near absence of Muslim plots and characters. Apart from token representations in one story per annum at times—1950 and 1951 had one story each focusing on Muslim protagonists—no reference to Muslim characters exists in the genre.[75]

Consumers read these stories, constituted their worlds through these stories, and also interrogated these stories. But *Sarita* also took cognizance of other books and publications. The final section provides an in-depth analysis of how the magazine presented and reviewed these other works.

BOOK REVIEWS

Sarita strove to create and promote a middlebrow reading habit not only through its own consumption. It found many direct and indirect ways to urge its readers to buy and read contemporary books as well as classics. There were advertisements: one set of books published by Delhi Press, *Sarita*'s parent organization, while the other set of books from other, smaller publishing companies. Apart from these ads, the magazine approached books in three other ways. First was the New Literature (Naya Sahitya) section, a monthly review of books; the second type was a special yearly review of books usually published during January or February of each year. While the first column is unsigned and seems to have been written by the editor, the prolific writer Manmath Nath Gupta was invited to pen the yearly special review of books. Finally, *Sarita* also carried a regular one-page column titled Literary Diary (Sahityik Diary).

The category of advertisements decidedly differed from the monthly review of books, which, in turn, differed from the yearly review of books. The advertisements, for instance, contained popular books that had already been crystallized in people's memories as classics. "Books Selected from Hindi" ("Hindi ki chuni hui pustaken"), an advertisement by the Delhi Book Company, urged readers to buy from a variety of novels authored by canonical Hindi-Urdu writer Premchand.[76] This focus on classics from a publishing house that ordinarily thrived on contemporary publications, most importantly through its periodical magazines in Hindi and English, is notable. The press also advertised other, more contemporary authors such as Santosh Narayan Nautiyal and Manmath Nath Gupta who both regularly wrote for *Sarita*. In this way, Delhi Press benefited from *Sarita* in terms of business for its other books and publications, additionally publishing its prolific writers so that they, too, could benefit from the exposure and sale of their books.

The advertisements by other publishing houses are telling signs of what the readers of *Sarita* were likely reading outside the magazine.

Rangbhoomi Book Depot, for instance, advertised in the January 1952 issue of *Sarita* with the title "Useful Books and Magazines in Hindi" ("Hindi ki Upyogi Pustaken aur Patrikayein."). Some of the advertised titles included *Saral Radio Guide* (*The Easy Guide to Radio*) that, as the name suggests, tells one about parts of a radio: "You can, through this book's help, open up your radio, fix its problems and fix it back, all by yourself." The publishing house offered manuals for other parts too, namely, *Electricity* and *Motor Guide*. Other kinds of titles were also up for consumption, for example, *Married Entertainment* (*Vivahit Manoranjan*), strictly advertised for "married women who want to further enrich their married life."[77]

Therefore, the advertisements, both from Delhi Press itself and other publishers, seem to suggest a consensus regarding the taste of its reading public, providing it with a reading list that has already existed, such as in Premchand's case, or presenting it with an array of literature guaranteed to mark an improvement in its readers' lives, as in learning to fix a radio. In other words, the advertisements follow a usefulness (*upyogi*) pattern in their selection of books on display. Here, the notion of middlebrow lists comes into play: the readers are urged to possess "must have" books. Janice Radway, in writing about the Book of the Month Club launched in 1926 by Harry Scherman, compares it to Ford's production line, saying, "He assured his subscribers that they could keep up with the tempo of modern cultural production without sacrificing their appreciation for distinction."[78] Radway extrapolates this on the book list and shows how distinction is possible through duplication. The advertisements in *Sarita* urging readers to possess certain kinds of books function in a similar vein.

Through the book review sections, the magazine provided readers an even wider scope of engagement. The Naya Sahitya section, published monthly, reviewed an eclectic variety of books, including a wide spectrum of genres such as poetry, short stories, and even plays. Predictably, the review sections were also a vehicle for self-promotion. Delhi Press's own books were constantly reviewed in it. For example, *Mrignayani* (Doe eyes) by Vrindavanlal Verma was advertised by Delhi Book Company in the February 1951 issue and glowingly reviewed.[79] As mentioned, books by many of *Sarita*'s regular contributors were reviewed as well.

The widest scope for engagement can be found in Manmath Nath Gupta's yearly reviews of books. His evaluations created a critical space for readers to think about literature because of wider contextualization: pedagogic in nature, clearly stating which books should be read and which safely discarded, Gupta's reviews did not stop there but often provided deeper engagement with writers, literary movements, and the publishing industry at large. For instance, the January and February 1960 issues of the magazine see a long, well-formed discussion of the Nayi Kahani (New Story) and Nayi Kavita (New Poetry) movements. Indeed, some Nayi Kahani writers such as Mohan Rakesh and Rajendra Yadav had already been stable presences in the magazine, writing short stories and nonfiction pieces for *Sarita* from as early as 1949. However, what was the context of the movement? Gupta's reviews created that ground for engagement.

We find another example of this larger contextualization where Gupta talks about the publishing landscape of Hindi at large in the introduction for the books published in 1959: "With much unhappiness, we declare that Hindi publishers are barely ready to publish any serious work (*gambhir granth*). The reason given for this is the absence of market. Yes, a lot of books of oral criticism are published. Over 95 percent of these are published with the view of becoming textbooks, or it will have useless pedantism, because of which useless investigations become weightier instead of improving the level of thought. Criticism also becomes decorative."[80] Gupta goes on to name and shame commercial booksellers like Hind Pocket Books (the subject of chapter two and, paradoxically, the press that went on to publish his works),[81] Satsahitya Alpmoli Sanskaran, and Ashok Pocket Books, urging them to "concentrate on the publication of serious literature as well, thanks to which the intellectual level of the community is improved."[82]

Some books that Gupta criticizes in his reviews are ones the magazine features in advertisements and other reviews. Returning to Vrindavanlal Verma's *Mrignayani* is useful because, as mentioned above, Delhi Book Company advertised in the February 1951 issue and *Sarita* glowingly reviewed it in the Naya Sahitya section on the very next page. In the yearly review, however, the book is cited as an example of one such failed venture. When Gupta reviewed it in the January 1952 issue, he criticized historical fiction as a genre, sensing it to be blind to the ethical responsibility of also commenting on the present: "It would not be inappropriate to hope that, in addition to narrating history and using the past, it also says something about the present. Although Vermaji's novel is successful, it seems that he completely forgets the present when he is looking through the binoculars of history."[83] Notably, the same book had been reviewed glowingly, praised specifically for its grasp of the historical narrative. This incongruity, I suggest, lies at the heart of *Sarita* as a magazine. While the advertisements pitch the books as objects of use (radio repair, sex manuals), the book reviews, especially the yearly reviews, create a different, more critical narrative. *Sarita* here performs its function as a vehicle that brings together the many contradictions of Hindi literature, not only creating what I call "middlebrow literature" but also demonstrating how this readership is also in the making, actively in flux, in a way that other sections in the magazine cannot register. This array of different kinds of literature and book reviews cannot be simply dismissed as unregistered incoherence. It actually speaks for the contradiction that lies at the heart of *Sarita*: of how literature is being produced for sale and yet at the same time being molded into a new consumable category, all the while negotiating with more settled expectations of what literature is supposed to be.

Finally, Literature [Sahityik] Diary, written by Chandrama Prasad Khare, is another manner in which literature is introduced in *Sarita* in late 1959, upending the conversation around what and how to read.[84] For instance, one column of the diary warns against "serious" and therefore potentially destructive criticism that takes away from the everyday reading process: "The development of literature was stalled by those teachers (*acharyas*) who had the power to lay the foundations of rules of literature but instead wasted their time in limitations and rote learning, themselves becoming the root of feudal environment. The need of the hour today is to stop earlier ways of critiquing literature and understand particularly how much and how successfully literature has become part of everyday life (*janjivan*)."[85] The ethics of literature here are rooted literally in the practical and the everyday. The acharyas are stripped of their power to dictate what literature means, and everyday criticism is preferred over serious criticism. A different diary column targets another institutional practice: regulating bookselling. The column's anonymous author criticizes the All-India Publishers Association, specifically its commission process of unlicensed publishing houses, arguing that licensing increases the price of the book, which, the writer argues, hinders the reading habit: "The problem is that the All-India Publishers Association does not provide books to those booksellers who have not been registered by them. The state of Hindi has not so improved that the reader and the library can buy expensive books. If we really want to promote literature, it is necessary that booksellers should get full benefits."[86] Thus *Sarita* provided the reader with not only different kinds of reading material within the magazine itself but also various avenues of exploration for the reader to buy and read books beyond the magazine. Additionally, the magazine features diverse perspectives on books through its reviews, as well as creating a space for the reader to be part of the larger debates within publishing, criticism, and reading itself.

CONCLUSION

"I am a soldier and I live in Tamil Nadu. We have been getting *Sarita* in our information room for three months now. Essays written on ordinary topics, as well as an essay called 'Rifle,' have increased the enthusiasm of all the soldiers here. If you publish more samples of [how to knit] sweaters, then soldiers as well as their wives will be very grateful to you."[87] Abhayram Sharma's letter to the editor from Jalahalli, Tamil Nadu, is a great example of *Sarita*'s place within the family. The soldier congratulates *Sarita* for its essay on rifles that has inspired all soldiers. At the same time, he requests that the magazine publish more pieces on sweater patterns for which both the soldiers and their wives would be grateful. The soldier feels no incongruity mentioning both these rather varied topics and interests in the same discussion. This mix, of enjoying an essay on rifles and looking forward to a new knitting pattern, is what forms the basis of the middlebrow. In this chapter, I have foregrounded the middlebrow reading habit as a valuable part of the discourse in the 1950s, drawing attention to Hindi middlebrow readers promoting service to the self, of the individual within the family, through various forms of consumption and creative self-representation.

Sarita is important to this story of expansion: significant because of its pioneering nature, it soon became one among several best-selling magazines that ushered in new forms of reading. Reconfiguring biases toward gendered reading and consumption processes, *Sarita* of the late 1940s and early 1950s opened the doors for other possibilities in middlebrow publishing, the most successful example of which is *Dharmyug*, discussed in chapter three. The next chapter, however, considers Hind Pocket Books, another publishing house in Delhi. The focus of Hind Pocket Books was not magazines but paperbacks.

CHAPTER TWO

Hind Pocket Books

The House of Exploding Hindi Paperbacks

"When we would go abroad, people would talk in terms of a million copies. We said, we did not print a million at a time, but we did manage half a million." In the 2012 interview, Dina Nath Malhotra, the founder, publisher, and editor of Hind Pocket Books, looks visibly frail with age.[1] In a barely audible yet measured voice, Malhotra recalls his company's unprecedented massive print runs and successes, also recounting the time when he first commissioned such a print run. In the early 1970s, Malhotra's friends and other publishers would often talk about an extremely prolific and wildly popular romance fiction writer named Gulshan Nanda. During a road trip, giving into curiosity, Malhotra decided to read one of Nanda's novels put out by another publishing house.[2] By the end of the trip (and of the novel), Malhotra had decided to publish Nanda. *Jhil ke us Par* (Across the lake), published in 1972, is the novel that holds the distinction of having been published with a first print run of half a million copies, a figure unprecedented in the history of Hindi publishing. The novel ultimately sold twice that number.[3]

This chapter focuses on the beginnings of the Hind Pocket Books success story: it returns to 1957, the year it all began. I examine the first paperbacks produced in Hindi, which, at their initial cost of one rupee each, were priced the same as *Sarita*. The story of Hind Pocket Books is significant for several reasons. First, it was extraordinarily successful. Second, the genres it published further contextualize the preoccupations of the post-independence Hindi-speaking middlebrow readership. The genres on offer were many. Printed at the back page of one of the paperbacks, an advertisement enumerates some of them:

> Books from writers famous both at home and abroad—Hind Pocket Books publishes novel[s] [*upanyas*], short stor[ies] [*kahani*], poetry [*kavita*], plays [*natak*], Urdu poetry [*urdu shayari*], scientific knowledge [*gyan-vigyan*], comedy and satire [hasya-vyangya], health [*svasthya*], "useful for women" [*stri-upyogi*], and "useful for life" [*jivan upyogi*]. Hind Pocket Books is famous throughout India for its writers of the highest standards [*uchcha koti ke lekhakon*], attractive getup [*akarshak getup*], beautiful printing [*sundar chhapai*], and cheap rates. Every book is just priced at one rupee.[4]

Hind Pocket Books published even more genres than those given above. Fiction included melodramatic social novels, Progressive social satires, literary classics written in both Indian and foreign languages; poetry comprised both Urdu and Hindi high literary poetry and film songs; nonfiction ranged from household management literature and self-help to political treatises; and, finally, manuals and guides included topics like health and first aid. However, the books were also curated through notable exclusions. Genres such as detective fiction, horror, thriller, and pornography were not included. Also not included were other popular genres such as patriotic novels and poetry, popular wedding songs, folk songs, and seasonal songs. This middle ground, where the publisher provided a variety of genres with clear exclusions of some prominent lowbrow categories, as well as some acceptable but deemed unnecessary-for-consumption genres such as nationalist writing and folk songs, again created a middlebrow space. This choice of genres, along with several standardization decisions in terms of pricing, branding, and circulation of the books, comprises the first half of this chapter, where I examine what Dina Nath Malhotra termed a "paperback revolution" ushered in by Hind Pocket Books, where the large print runs, cheap print technology, and paper quality contributed to the burgeoning middlebrow consumer of the years following India's independence.

What Malhotra rightly called a "paperback revolution" also owed its success to one of its highly successful circulation schemes called the Gharelu Library Yojana, or the Home Library Scheme. Hind Pocket Book paperbacks were available at cheap prices at time-tested and commercially viable points of distribution such as railway stations and roadside pavements, yet the publisher also adopted a third distribution model, that of the Gharelu Library Yojana, where books in a range of fiction and nonfiction genres were delivered directly to readers' homes every month, a proposition made sweeter by offering six books for the price of five. This scheme led to three pivotal results: First, given its inexpensive pricing, targeted branding, and, most importantly, easy reach for consumers, the scheme firmly enshrined Hind Pocket Books into the everyday, domestic middlebrow economy. In other words, the scheme was substantively responsible for enforcing and ensuring what I call an everyday "repeatable" reading habit: a variety of books were delivered home every month, a variety of books were read. Second, again uniquely, the scheme famously mixed into one bundle its numerous genres and authors established elsewhere as "high" literary and ones that were "not." In this way, the everyday repeatable reading habit developed a robust palate: books cut across genres, concerns, and demarcations of "good" and "not *quite* so good" literature. Lastly, and closely linked to the second feature, was the scheme's other unique attribute: readers did not choose books but instead read titles that Hind Pocket Books had curated and made available for that month. The everyday "repeatable" reading habit solidified here on a consensus about taste: because these books were approved by Hind Pocket Books, they must surely be worth reading. Through this method, Hind Pocket Books made its range of curated genres not only aspirational or desirable but also habitual for its sizable readership.

Indeed, through this system, Hind Pocket Books not only expanded or defined a variety of new reading genres but also actively suggested, even encouraged this eclectic reading. Through its Home Library Scheme, a canonical novel by Rabindranath Tagore came home in the same reading bundle alongside a biting social satire by Krishan Chander. A songbook based on the theme of romance accompanied an autobiography of Nehru. These selections created a wide-ranging and eclectic library at home. And repeated subscriptions to the Home Library Scheme were an important component that kept Hind Pocket Books' printing and publishing expenses low, which then enabled it to procure a variety of genres and, in turn, ensured continuation of this varied reading list. Also important was the very successful efforts of Hind Pocket Books at book branding. Given the uniformity in size and design of the book cover, the Hind Pocket Books brand came to be identified as much as and, in many cases, even *more* than the title or the author's name on the cover.

The emphasis on branding the series emerges largely from Dina Nath Malhotra's own focus on his role as a conscious publisher-editor. Therefore, a substantive part of the chapter investigates Malhotra's "self" and how he projected himself as a pathbreaking visionary responsible for creating a middlebrow publishing space for a burgeoning reading market. At the same time, self-fashioning efforts can often be deceptive, and I do not aim to read them at face value. In fact, members of the Malhotra family tell different stories about this publishing legacy.[5] However, his self-canonization makes Malhotra's presence felt throughout our discussions of Hind Pocket Books. Although Hindi literary histories of the twentieth century provide us with examples of visionary writers, critics, and editors who understood their role emphatically in relation to the literariness of the language and literature and its often nationalist goals and connections,[6] Malhotra's project and projection interrogated none of these questions. Reminiscent of the service of his contemporary Vishwa Nath to readers (*pathako ki seva*), discussed in chapter one, Malhotra's first goal focused on how to make the book reach its reader. In this, the role of the publisher-editor was paramount. At the peak of the Home Library Scheme, Hind Pocket Books counted around six hundred thousand subscribers, and forty thousand packets were delivered monthly out of the publisher's own premises through a post office setup in the compound.[7]

Significantly, Malhotra's publishing influences were outside India: he vocally owed a debt of inspiration to Penguin's Sir Allen Lane and the Book of the Month Club in America, from which he chiseled the ideas of the paperback and the Home Library Scheme, respectively. Thus Hindi publishing was a story of being at home in the world, confidently engaging and importing ideas and refashioning them for a vast readership.

The final section of this chapter returns to the genres themselves. It provides a close reading of some of the genres in the series, such as the Progressive satire of Urdu writer Krishan Chander and the social romances of the prolific and popular writer Guru Dutt, the high seriousness of Urdu poetry that frequently appeared on the list, as well as the self-help publications imported from America and Britain. Here, genre-naming is also an important part of the story. Genres were often not defined in terms of how the authors themselves intended them or how they were formulated in the realm of literary criticism but with respect to what the publisher-editor deemed either as marketable, acceptable, or both. For instance, Hind Pocket Books did not market Progressive novels under the well-established nomenclature of "Pragativad" or "Pragatisheel" (literally translating as "progressive") and instead used a more neutral term of "world-famous."[8] What does it mean for Hind Pocket Books to position itself as a publisher that encouraged Progressive ideas without adhering to specific ideological frames?

DEFINING THE "FIRST" HINDI PAPERBACK AND UNCOVERING THE MALHOTRA PUBLISHING SELF

In recollections from interviews, written memoirs, and editorials ranging over his long publishing career, Dina Nath Malhotra continually maintained one thing: that, right from the beginning, he had a clear vision in mind for Hind Pocket Books. From its inception in 1957, Malhotra sought to distinguish the Hind Pocket Book paperbacks from a sea of other already existing non-hardback books in the Hindi publishing market. In his memoir titled *Dare to Publish*, Malhotra continually stressed the uniqueness of his project: Hind Pocket Books did not model itself on an existing Indian publishing house because it did not have any clearly well-formed predecessors. The first aspect of Malhotra's model was to include a range of genres in the same paperback series, by linking and bringing together those that were categorized elsewhere as "highbrow" and "low," easy to consume, literature. Malhotra's memoir further explicates this: Hind Pocket Books deliberately distanced itself from the implicitly self-selecting Penguin/Picador "quality" and "egghead" paperbacks that claimed respectability on the basis of the titles that they chose. He objected to the term "quality paperbacks" as it "seems to imply that the other paperbacks lack quality in production," and as "egghead" paperbacks "include only books of high-intellectual input, it is always understood that the editions of these books will be small and only highly intelligent readers or intellectuals will buy them."[9] It's telling that Malhotra rejected the "highly intelligent readers or intellectuals" as well as the lowbrow equally as categories of engagement, amalgamating genres from both categories for this "middle" consumption.

Malhotra not only sought to distinguish Hind Pocket Books against Penguin's paperbacks but also acknowledged a debt of inspiration. He had actually met Sir Allen Lane, the founder of Penguin, at a publishing conference in the United Kingdom. In his memoir, Malhotra claimed a friendship with him.[10] Like the Penguin publications, the first Hind Pocket Books paperbacks were pocket sized and limited in length to between 100 and 150 pages. All the paperbacks were, without distinction, priced at one rupee each, thereby setting a tone of similarity between the different titles and genres from the first collections. In doing this, Hind Pocket Books sought to break the distinction-by-genre paradigm by simultaneously providing a diversity of reading matter while standardizing it in terms of length, packaging, print quality, and, more important, pricing. In this way, like Penguin, Hind Pocket Books sought to build itself as a brand. Following Penguin's lead in emphasis on the stylization of the book using simple fonts, Hind Pocket Books became an instantly recognizable book commodity. The back covers of each book were especially uniform, with the spine of the book prominently carrying its serial number along with the company logo. The effort at standardization was unmistakable: before the writer and title of the book itself could be identified, Hind Pocket Books was recognized.

Hind Pocket Books' paper quality had to contend with Indian paper availability and paper prices. The different qualities of paper available in 1950s included cream wove, airmail, maptho, check or security paper, poster paper, Xerox paper, bond paper, and—relevant to commercial newspaper, magazine, and paper production—newsprint and lightweight coated newsprint.[11] Malhotra used "bulky book printing paper" or "double weight newsprint" (*lugdi*) as the paper to carry out the paperback project. By contemporary standards, the production quality was inferior. For instance, *Sarita* was printed on better quality paper, whereas the weekly *Dharmyug* was printed on vastly better "photogravia" paper.[12] However, according to Malhotra's vision for the titles on offer, design and pricing would supersede these differences in paper quality.

Malhotra's vision of Hind Pocket Books was influenced by and tied to outside influences, with Penguin being only one of them. Malhotra forged alliances with publishers in both Britain and America so as to arrive at novel circulation and distribution systems for Hindi publishing. At the same time, Malhotra was at home in India as he was in the world. He participated in key national publishing conferences and worked as part of publishing federations issuing several informational and commemorative volumes on the profession. We know these travels through his memoir of his time as publisher, which speaks to many significant decisions: not only in the conscious self-construction of a cosmopolitan, well-traveled editor-publisher but also of an editor-publisher who very consciously etched himself in history as a legitimate player in Hindi literary publishing. Indeed, Malhotra saw himself as the driving force behind commercial publishing in Hindi in general. He fashioned himself as an innovator and a visionary who had transformed consumption patterns by carving a new readership category. Therefore, while his success at directing consumer tastes is a significant strand of the narrative, Malhotra built legitimacy even among other Hindi publishers and editors. Put differently, Malhotra's deep sense of his publishing self is key to rethinking the very formula of a Hindi literary success story. For and through Malhotra, volume and reach became crucial. Literariness rested on the back of, and was determined as a result of, this volume and reach.

To understand this formula better, we need to return to the Malhotra family. Malhotra began his career as a university teacher.[13] His family migrated to Delhi from Lahore in the wake of the Partition. In Delhi, Malhotra found employment as a printer, but his new role as printer-publisher was not entirely unfamiliar to him. Malhotra's father owned and ran a publishing firm in early twentieth-century Lahore. The firm did well, "publishing books on religious, political and social subjects in four languages—English, Hindi, Urdu and Punjabi."[14] Malhotra's brother, Vishwanath—not to be confused with *Sarita*'s proprietor and editor Vishwa Nath—was also a publisher and ran Rajpal & Sons in post-partition India.

Malhotra subsequently collaborated with Vishwanath in 1949 as a contractor and publisher of much needed, frequently commissioned, and vastly profitable school textbooks.[15] When the nationalization of textbooks came into effect, rendering commissioning and publishing of private school textbooks unprofitable, Malhotra decided to foray into the paperback business.[16] Hind Pocket Books issued the first paperbacks in 1959; its business model from the very beginning emphasized large print runs and sales to offset lower profit margins per book.[17]

The two brothers often worked together to produce the same books, albeit in different formats: while Hind Pocket Books published only paperbacks, Rajpal & Sons published the hardback version simultaneously.[18] Although Hind Pocket Books defined itself as a paperback company, the brothers understood the Hindi market at large, with the firm business sense that there was an institutional market for hardbacks and that, even among individual readers, not everyone could be seduced by the paperback and its poor-quality paper.[19]

In addition to setting their roles as businessmen and tastemakers, the Malhotra brothers were simultaneously interested in the process of institutionalizing the Indian publishing industry. This process by itself was not new, and there seem to have been a small number of publishing federations in place earlier in the period. But the brothers were deeply involved with running the Federation of Indian Publishers (FIPA), which was founded in 1955; they became president and office-bearers of the organization at different points in time.[20] A later FIPA document, *50 Years of Book Publishing in India since Independence*, published in 1998 when Vishwanath was its president, shows the Malhotras' vision of their own standing in publishing. The book breaks up the publishing landscape into eighteen different chapters, with contributions on markets for different languages. The commemorative issue also features articles on different areas of publishing such as school-level textbooks, college-level publishing, and so on. The chapter titled "Publishing of Paperbacks" considers the impact of Hind Pocket Books and the Home Library Scheme that inspired the same scheme in other languages. In his entry on Hindi publishing, Vishwanath mentions "the few that have made their mark" in Delhi and includes Hind Pocket Books and Rajpal & Sons alongside names such as Bhartiya Gyanpith, Rajkamal Prakashan, National Publishing House, Radhakrishna Prakashan, Saraswati Vihar, Kitab Mahal, and Kitab Ghar, the most prominent Hindi literary publishing houses of the post-independence period.[21] To include a paperback publishing house of the diversity and range of Hind Pocket Books contributed to its legitimization, elevating the paperback to the same level as literary books, and shows the middlebrow company carving an identity for itself alongside the already established identity of literary highbrow publishers.

This self-canonization continues in Malhotra's recollection of trips abroad. His first such trip in 1956 to London was "to be in time to participate in a Book Publishing Workshop of ten days organized by the British Council."[22] This trip also included other destinations in Europe, where Malhotra excitedly participated in even more publishing conferences and workshops. During this visit, Malhotra met Penguin's founder Allen Lane. This relationship forged in England provided Malhotra with the validation he needed to begin publishing paperbacks in India. In an interview with Rajya Sabha TV, Malhotra adds to this story: although the paperbacks were inspired by Penguin, their success apparently exceeded Lane's own expectations in the Indian context, which he thought of as having a limited readership market.[23] Malhotra's implicit boast is clear: despite being one of the paperback pioneers of the world, Lane's understanding of the Indian market was limited. That Malhotra was able to not only identify but actively cultivate a very large pool of readers is evident throughout his recollections.

America followed Europe. Its Book of the Month Club provided another publishing milestone. In June 1961, Malhotra received a UNESCO fellowship enabling him to spend three months exploring the publishing markets of the United States and Japan. In the United States, he visited the offices of the Book of the Month Club, where he borrowed the idea of the postal service.[24] The cosmopolitan nature of a seemingly local commercial publishing enterprise is pointedly visible through Malhotra's inspirations for Hind Pocket Books. Malhotra studied not only the publishing models but also the publishing selves of two major middlebrow publishing processes in the world at that time and made those contexts local and relevant to the Hindi reading market. The Penguin and Book of the Month Club experiments, with their long legacies of being associated with middlebrow consumption, were successfully fused in the form of the Home Library Scheme, discussed in the next section of this chapter.

Malhotra, well-traveled, well-connected, and at the helm of the Hindi publishing universe, also championed himself as the center of editorial and commissioning decisions. Although Hind Pocket Books had a well-established team of curators, editors, and translators, in his recollections Malhotra insisted that he remained personally in charge of the library scheme and personally commissioned books for it. Malhotra remained in control of both intellectual and business decisions until he passed the company to his son, Shekhar Malhotra.[25]

How did this self-image translate into the process of genre selection? As we have seen, Malhotra chose the booklist on the basis of commercially viable inclusions of Bengali classics even while excluding such equally commercially viable categories as detective fiction because he thought them unfit for consumption. He provided the readers with a plethora of genres, giving into the middlebrow need for accumulation of knowledge, discussed in this book's introduction as the "need to know." Most significant, he created an aura of seriousness around reading for pleasure: although pleasurable genres such as romance and satire were the mainstays of the booklist, humor in the form of joke books and songbooks was completely excluded. This publishing strategy—of simultaneously providing the reader with multiple genres, cultivating generalist reading, and maintaining decorum and seriousness around pleasurable reading—is discussed at length in the following sections as the basis for the middlebrow readership.

DISTRIBUTING THE PAPERBACK: THE HOME LIBRARY SCHEME

"I remember being shocked by my sister-in-law's repeated usage of the proverb '*bhoga hua yatharth*' (one's lived reality) in a village in Mithila because till then I had imagined that this is a "New Story" (Nayi Kahani) slogan and therefore only used by literary critics. I believe that no one ever succeeded in tying Hindi readers together quite like Hind Pocket Books."[26] In his pioneering and possibly the only dedicated study published on Hind Pocket Books, Hindi writer and academic Prabhat Ranjan registers his amazement about his sister-in-law's familiarity with the phrase "bhoga hua yatharth," or "one's lived reality," a slogan identifiable with modernist New Story sentiment in writing.[27] To Ranjan's mind, only Hind Pocket Books and its wide circulation could explain such an eclectic reading habit. This section focuses on how Dina Nath Malhotra established a distribution system that made such a readership possible and how the intrinsic value of the paperbacks was enhanced from this distribution strategy. Through the Home Library Scheme, rather than abandoned after reading, cheap book objects became coveted and preserved at home.[28]

How did Malhotra reach this circulation model in the first place? Again, his travels helped. As we have seen, Malhotra borrowed what were successful concepts of distribution and circulation elsewhere and adapted them to the Indian book market. First, the much-acknowledged inspiration from Penguin, which rested on making its books available at other traditionally nonbook or nonliterary bookselling platforms,[29] such as Woolworth's, the department store "whose motto was 'nothing over sixpence.'"[30] Hind Pocket Books did not necessarily have to borrow this idea; the paperbacks became available at the A. H. Wheeler stalls at railway stations. Since the late nineteenth century, Wheeler stalls had been dependable and well-established distribution channels in North and North West India.[31] In the 1950s, Wheeler paid publishers only for the books that the stalls actually sold, returning those that did not sell. Malhotra negotiated with Wheeler to pay upfront for at least 50 percent of the books taken.[32]

However, these distribution points could not reach all its target consumers. As other consumption histories in India from the period show, despite being urban, mobile, and in large numbers female, consumers were either not able or ready to physically reach the marketplace to make purchases.[33] This made Malhotra turn to America and think about the success of the Book of the Month Club. He wrote, "Having studied the working of the Book of the Month Club in the United States, I had come to the conclusion

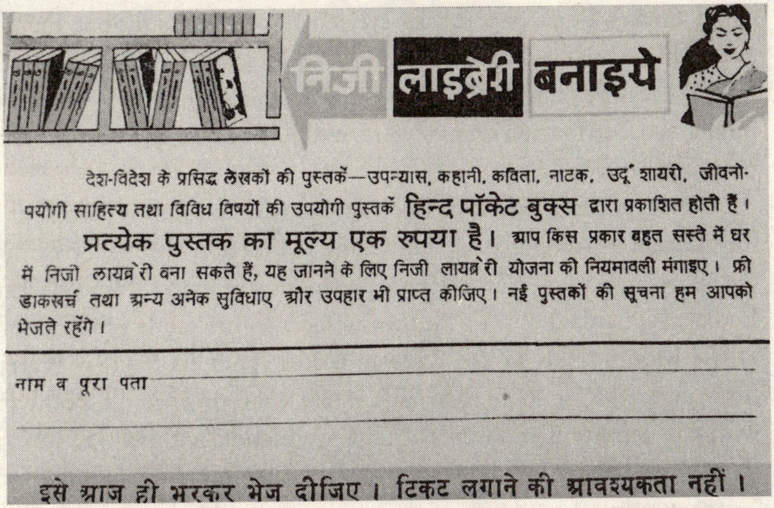

FIGURE 3. Postcard from Gharelu Library Yojana, Home Library Scheme, Hind Pocket Books.

that the residual hidden market that we were not able to tap could be reached only through book clubs."[34] Therefore, Malhotra set up a third distribution model, that of the postal method, of delivering books home.

Malhotra was not satisfied with delivering only one book every month. From the mid-1960s onward, Hind Pocket Books, at its expense, began delivering six books for the price of five straight to consumers at home,[35] which became known as the Home Library Scheme (Gharelu Library Yojana).[36]

Much like the success of the paperbacks themselves, the Home Library Scheme was hugely successful and, at its peak, had around six hundred thousand subscribers.[37] Forty thousand packets were regularly delivered out of the publisher's own premises: a post office had been set up in the compound because of the sheer bulk of the orders.[38] Although variants of cheap or nonhardback books such as several *pustak mala* (book series) that serialized novels and other genres had flourished from the early twentieth century, the

Hind Pocket Book paperbacks created favorable conditions for an affordable, socially acceptable, eclectic, and what I call "repeatable" middle-class reading habit.[39] Like the magazine or the newspaper model, the distribution scheme rendered the book a taken-for-granted household commodity.

A study of the American Book of the Month Club is instructive for another reason, that is, cultivating distinction through creating the allure of modern cultural mass production practices. Hind Pocket Books also banked on this idea to succeed. In her study of the Book of the Month Club, Janice Radway writes about its founder Harry Scherman, "He assured his subscribers that they could keep up with the tempo of modern cultural production without sacrificing their appreciation for distinction."[40] For Scherman, distinction and "modern cultural production," therefore, ran hand in hand. He built a book distribution system that streamlined the consumption practices of his subscribers, purporting that this system "offered the generalized and highly abstract promise that his open-ended collection of new books, because they were the best, were sure to become classics."[41] This emphasis on what books "were sure to become classics" is significant. In the past, Scherman had run a phenomenally successful venture called the Little Leather Library, which published only acknowledged classics. For the Book of the Month Club, he published just new books, ones "sure to become classics." In other words, classics would become so not only through the club's recommendation but, significantly, through the mass—and simultaneous—readership of the books that the club recommended.

The Hind Pocket Books Home Library Scheme mixed both ideas. It already included canonical books along with contemporary works. Classics mingled with new books, and then there were the other, newer genres and writers. The circulation of these different genres by themselves is not remarkable and not new to Hindi. However, the genres being bundled together certainly gives one a moment for pause. Through the library scheme, Hind Pocket Books facilitated two simultaneous processes. First, as already discussed, because of its emphasis on the seamless merging of the literary highbrow and the self-help lowbrow, it arguably created a symbiotic culture of reading in Hindi. Second, this distribution method created reader dependability on the "list" to define the Hindi middlebrow. The books delivered in fixed sets were nonnegotiable in terms of the titles—according to publisher policy, only at certain times could the reader refuse or return titles; consumers could not, however, choose or recommend books.[42] The readers at home grew to expect books to be chosen for them. In my archival visits to the publisher's office, an undated postcard advertising the Gharelu Library Yojana popped out (see figure 3). It exhorted its readers to build a personal library (*niji library banaiye*). Yet this "personal library" featured books already decided for it by the publisher.

The list was also important for other reasons. In the context of Anglocentric middle-class reading history, starting from the Victorian or Arnoldian moment, much critical and scholarly work has focused on the idea of the literary canon resulting from middle-class aspirational reading practices, with the reading list functioning as an expression of literary ability and the ultimate marker of respectability.[43] While the list emerging from the library scheme did contribute to the creation of a canon, the listmaker and, by extension, the tastemaker here were not academics, editors, or writers. The list in this particular case emerged out of the publisher-editor's decisions.

Related to these decisions, the list also carried ramifications for author selection. Indeed, as discussed earlier, authors published regularly in the series were chosen because of their sheer popularity or legitimacy. They were also published because Malhotra at the helm chose them. However, perhaps we also need to account for the selection that transpired because of royalty and copyright negotiations, which is important because of the sheer bulk of books: the company register records 5,072 published titles over its lifetime. Because of Hind Pocket Books' balance between supposed classics and nonclassic new authors, it is possible to see the law of "supplementation" that tentatively took off with other commodities in 1950s India followed by the liberalization in the 1990s: buying one commodity gave another one free, making one unsure of what commodity was being bought in the first place.[44]

As a detailed analysis of these writers and the overlaps forms the last section of this chapter, I return here to Prabhat Ranjan's shock at his sister-in-law's knowledge of the New Story saying "one's lived reality" in the small village tucked away in North India. As discussed above, we can speculate that this scheme reached the large potential audience of largely homebound female readers. Statistics are unfortunately not available for the scheme distribution, by region, gender, or even age group. The company records that, I was assured, did exist at one point containing complete information about print runs and such details are now lost.[45] It is difficult to find out about the identity of the readers through markers such as advertisements, editorials acknowledging the readers, or even readers' letters, since Hind Pocket Books kept these markers absent from its paperbacks, either because of space constraints or general design decisions. However, given the nature of the delivery process, women are likely to have constituted a large reader base with the entry of the paperbacks into the home. Malhotra does record that, at the height of the scheme, the company conducted an informal survey of the readership and found that "there were professors, teachers, traders, students and in the higher echelons, High Court judges, doctors, actors and engineers."[46] While we can read this as yet another self-legitimizing gesture, a detailed study of the genres can help us to better identify the reading habits between the different professionals and, also, the missing link until now, that is, the family. Indeed, the broad variety of genres does provide a peek into how the Hind Pocket paperback was possibly consumed by the entire family. Alternatively, the range can perhaps be read in terms of how it might represent the interests of the whole family.

The final sections of this chapter closely examine the dominant genres of fiction, poetry, self-help, and knowledge textbooks.

THE BOOKS

I have argued for the significance of Hind Pocket Books—through its sheer print volumes and circulation strategies, Dina Nath Malhotra created an everyday, repeatable, and middlebrow habit of reading a wide range of genres. Although I have discussed these books in terms of their inclusions and exclusions, in terms of their exciting genre-mixing strategies, what exactly did the books contain?

The first ten books offered by the company included poetry and fiction classics like Rabindranath Tagore's *Gitanjali* translated from Bengali, Mirza Ghalib's *Deewan-e-Ghalib* translated from Urdu, R. L. Stevenson's *Dr. Jekyll and Mr. Hyde* translated from English, alongside novels by contemporary popular Hindi writers like Acharya Chatursen. Later in the series, Malhotra published such major Nayi Kahani figures as Mohan Rakesh, Rajendra Yadav, and Mannu Bhandari, who, as chapters one and three show, were also being published by *Sarita* and *Dharmyug*.[47] Progressive writers such as Krishan Chander and Rajinder Singh Bedi, too, were published. Along with Tagore and Chander, fiction by the extremely popular Guru Dutt appeared, as did fiction by now-forgotten writers such as Hansraj and Yagyadutt Sharma. For instance, Hansraj's novel *Sankalp* (Resolve) was the second title ever published.[48] The back cover tells us that the author belonged to a "poor family" (*nirdhan parivar*) and had attained a master's-level education completely on his own merit. The author's blurb reads: "He's always been interested in writing, and whatever he's written, he has written really well. *Sankalp* is his latest novel whose special characteristic is its newness and freshness."[49] Yagyadutt Sharma is described on the back cover of his book as an author who "is a representative writer of the new age." Again, "he stays away from different debates and writes realistic stories centered around Indian life, putting forward national, societal, and human consciousness."[50] Apart from this variety, manuals on letter writing, self-help, and high serious poetry also circulated.

This brings us to a related question: although the first paperbacks adhered to this mixing that distinguished Hind Pocket Books from other publishing series, in the larger scheme of things, how many of these genres were published more than the others? To understand this, I undertook an intensive close study of the different genres of the first two hundred paperbacks that Hind Pocket Books issued between the years of 1959 and 1963. Because the paperbacks themselves are no longer in circulation and are found only as stray titles in libraries and private collections, I quickly realized that my only chance at obtaining a comprehensive list rested in finding a very avid and willing collector of all titles or accessing Hind Pocket Books' archives, if there were any. In the summer of 2015, I met Shikhar and Priyanka Malhotra, Dina Nath Malhotra's son and granddaughter, and asked them to let me have a look. They kindly agreed. What followed was a dream-come-true moment for any print historian who works on the popular: the Malhotras had a meticulously kept register that recorded all company titles ever published. Therefore, I make my observations from the list of titles in the archival register of Hind Pocket Books' Noida (Uttar Pradesh) office. This location also holds a large number of the books themselves, perfectly preserved, from the 1950s and 1960s. I had struck gold.

Despite this relative ease of access, the genre survey became a difficult task from the point of view of methodology. The records have methodically been manually penned up to the last Hind Pocket Books paperback series, running into the 5,072nd title. However, the company list itself, that the publishers reconstructed in 2015 on the basis of the physical books in their possession, is incomplete because many of the first books themselves were missing. This leads to several gaps in this analysis. For instance, of the first 200 titles analyzed, 28 titles were missing in the main records, being left as blanks. Therefore, I have taken 172 books into consideration for the present study. Of these titles, 45 books have disappeared from the company archives. I have been unable to trace these books through other library and market sources, thereby lowering the number of titles under study to 127. Some of the other titles are, in many cases, widely available, but many times through other publishers and editions. Although I have drawn some approximations from these other editions, the first Hind Pocket Books editions may or may not have adhered to the same content. For instance, in the archives I found the early editions of Acharya Chatursen's *Abha*, which was first commissioned by Hind Pocket Books and was republished later by other publishing houses. However, I could not find many Hind Pocket Books titles, such as Rabindranath Tagore's novels, that it republished after changes in translation, commissioning, abridging, and editing. Moreover, as there is no history of other pulp paperback enterprises in the Indian and, more important, Hindi publishing context, it becomes rather difficult to measure the Hind Pocket paperback against any comparable enterprise. Finally, the list of titles that I discuss in this section should not be confused with the Home Library Scheme, which was issued from mid-1960s onward. Despite these gaps in analysis, I have nonetheless attempted a genre breakdown so as to arrive at a more precise range available from Hind Pocket Books.

Now, to the findings themselves. In terms of the first paperbacks that Hind Pocket Books published, I found that fiction was the dominant genre on offer: at least 65 novels and nine collections of short stories, constituting 58 percent of the known 127 titles. Other genres of fiction, such as satire and drama, stand at six and five titles, respectively. From the figures, it is safe to say that the paperback enterprise leaned heavily on fiction. Among the other genres, self-help, health, and household nonfiction comprised 22 titles, forming at least 17 percent of the total. In the first 127 examined titles, we find a limited number of nonfiction titles, mostly limited to science and general knowledge.

A larger genre breakdown of this nature reveals that Hind Pocket Books relied largely on creating repeat consumers for commodities that they were already used to, such as novels, poetry, self-help, and the like. A closer analysis of these genres reveals a more complex story. Although the Hind Pocket Books series conformed to genre conventions for each genre, presenting them together breaks genre expectations in terms of readership. Let us take the case of novels, for example. I begin with a close analysis of fiction, as the genre had the largest presence in the booklist, which as middlebrow emerges most clearly in this selection. While classics are celebrated within the list with a broad selection made available in translation from English and Urdu, contemporary Progressive satire, too, finds a place on the list. Social romances also dominate, concerned mostly with questions of negotiating selfhood within the family space.

Among the first 127 considered titles, the popularity of modern classic Bengali writers like Rabindranath Tagore (nine titles), Bankim Chandra Chatterjee (five novels), and Sharat Chandra Chattopadhyay (twelve titles) is conspicuous. However, the other popular genre that had featured substantially from the nineteenth century onward, that of Bengali detective writing, is strikingly absent from consideration.[51]

In fact, the three Bengali writers mentioned above largely filled the space for modern fiction classics on the Hind Pocket Books list. In terms of Hindi writers who wrote roughly around the same time period were Pandey Bechain Sharma, with the pen name "Ugra" (with two titles), and Jainendra Kumar (one). Both these writers were not quite as canonical as the three Bengali writers were in the Bengali (as well as the Hindi) canon. The choice of "Ugra" is striking, as he was often the center of controversies around obscenity. However, Hind Pocket Books did not publish *Chocolate,* which created a furor in the Hindi literary sphere with its focus on male same-sex relations when it was first published in 1927.[52] Instead, it republished *Chand Haseeno ke Khutoot* (Some letters of beauties), also first published in 1927.

The genre of romance gained easy admittance into the booklist. In fact, some of the Bengali titles in the list, *Devdas* and *Srikanta,* for instance, were extremely well recognized as romances, as Sharat Chandra had already been marked as a writer of social romances.[53] In the list, the Hindi romance was represented by the genre of the Hindi social romance, particularly in the writing of the famous contemporary writer Guru Dutt, not to be confused with the famous filmmaker who, in fact, did not write these novels but directed some of the most iconic films during the same period, such as *Mr and Mrs 55* (1955) and *Pyasa* (Thirsty, 1957).

In addition, as mentioned before, Hind Pocket Books also published several Progressive writers. Krishan Chander's widely popular *Ek Gadhe ki Atma Katha* (The autobiography of a donkey), the first of the political satirical trilogy series about the life of a donkey in the post-independence nation, was the twenty-second book in the series. Chander, a very active member of the Indian Progressive Writers' Association, was clearly well regarded by the publishers and wrote eight other books in the series during the time period under consideration, including one collection of short stories. Other contemporaries, either among the Progressive or the Nayi Kahani group, like Kamleshwar, Rajendra Yadav, Mannu Bhandari, Upendranath "Ashk," and Rajinder Singh Bedi, also feature in the list, though with only one title each. Bhairav Prasad Gupta, the editor of the magazine *Kahani* (*Story*), who later shifted to *Nayi Kahaniyaan* (New Stories) in 1960, is included with two titles. Through this strand of patronage, one sees Hind Pocket Books tapping into another literary strand that worked well with mass publication, that is, Progressive fiction. However, there lies another contradiction. As stated before, Hind Pocket Books did not market Progressive novels under the widely understood nomenclature of "Pragativad" or "Pragatisheel," and instead used a more neutral term of "world-famous."[54] Hind Pocket Books clearly did not seek to position itself as a publisher that encouraged Progressive ideas without adhering to leftist/Marxist ideology itself.

Poetry is another genre that gives one moment for pause. Hind Pocket Books published a variety of poetry collections, all of which emphasized the "seriousness" of poetry. None of the poetry collections in the series dealt with humorous poetry as its subject matter. Also, all poetry collections under study carried an introduction to the poet or the collection as the case may be. This "need to know," coupled with the weighty introductions in the case of poetry, adds to the impulse of "seriousness," another middlebrow attribute, which again corresponds to the novels where "world-famous" social satire is the only humorous genre, if any.

In fact, the books' emphasis on "serious" genres contributes to a more comprehensive understanding of the paperbacks as middlebrow. In the case of Hind Pocket Books, seriousness was imported in the form of self-help from America, romance/melodrama from Bengali novels, satire from largely Progressive sources, literary poetry from Urdu, and contemporary emphasis on individualism and Nayi Kahani. Subsequent sections dive into a close reading of the genres that comprised the Hind Pocket Books paperback.

Hindi Social Romance versus Satire: Guru Dutt and Krishan Chander

In its formative years, Guru Dutt was one of Hind Pocket Books' prolific contemporary Hindi novelists and one of its most popular as well. Born in 1894 into a family of a devout Arya Samaji father and a Vaishnavi mother, Guru Dutt went on to become an extremely prolific and popular writer, producing eight to ten novels per year on average.[55] Even though his primary profession was that of Vaidya or Ayurvedic doctor, Dutt strove to make his living primarily through writing and, therefore, kept a keen eye on the paperback publishing industry.[56] Ashok K. Shah "Pratik" notes that even though the canonical Hindi-Urdu writer Premchand appreciated and published Dutt's first stories, he was strictly excluded from the Hindi literary domain from very early in his writing career. He was often published through numerous popular pocket book series and even came to prefer this mode of publication. Since Dutt never exclusively contracted with one series, Hind Pocket Books was only one of the publishers to acquire rights to his novels.[57] However, even though Dutt was not writing exclusively for Hind Pocket Books, he was very important to the publishing house, and not just because of the enormity of his sales figures.[58] He was, like Acharya Chatursen, one of the few best-selling Hindi authors of social romance that Hind Pocket Books regularly published, being indispensable in terms of their contemporary Hindi fiction.

Dutt's oeuvre consisted of a mixture of social fiction, historical fiction, political drama, and mythological fiction. However, the two novels published by Hind Pocket Books that I analyze below—*Mamta* and *Lalsa*—fall under the "social novel" category. Guru Dutt's novels of this type find parallels in a well-theorized field of the "social film." The Hindi social film has been theorized multidirectionally in the context of family, romance, and melodrama, with particular recourse to nationalist and Nehruvian ethics, and where, as Ravi Vasudevan points out, it "is singularly indifferent to mechanisms of suspense and surprise; the moral universe of the fiction, the figuration of guilt and innocence, is always already known."[59] Rachel Dwyer similarly notes, "The Bombay films of this period blend melodrama with realism, foregrounding the emotions, while dealing with the regulation of social relationships to create a framework of desire, self, family and romance."[60] Narratively, the above themes are central concerns of Guru Dutt's novels: the sustained action is used to mold scenes of continuous interactions between its primary protagonists. The narrative concern lies in developing a romantic or familial union—or both—based on the tenets of renunciation, restraint, and the code of morality.

While the relationship between Bengali and Marathi literature has been charted with reference to the post-independence Hindi film, little has been written with respect to the relationship between Hindi literature and the post-independence Hindi film.[61] Apart from sharing thematic resemblances, Guru Dutt's social novels also share similarities with the Hindi social film's visual narrative. Although these similarities in visual narrative could, arguably, be the result of the comparable use of melodrama in both film and novels, I trace the outline of Dutt's popular social novel as a separate subgenre of the many categories of social novels that had already been established in Hindi beginning with Premchand's writing, characterized by "social realism."[62] I seek to do so by foregrounding what I call the "cinematic imagination" of Guru Dutt's novels. His narrative techniques carry an acute understanding of an audience attuned to *watching* the social film and conform to this cinematic imagination. For instance, many of the primary protagonists in Dutt's novels look at the other characters in ways reminiscent of the point-of-view shot. As I discuss with regard to the two novels below, the psychological narrative of the story is well in place, yet much of the feeling in the story is directed outside the character onto an object. Even though this is a standard melodramatic device, it becomes significant to look at the narrative construction and thematic similarities in tandem with the Hindi social film. The two were produced at the same time and were intertwined and, arguably, referenced each other.

Mamta (Maternal love), published in 1962, is a social novel set in the late colonial period. It places its male protagonist, a doctor newly returned from England in stark opposition to the English (and presumably white and upper-class) wife, Lily, he married while studying medicine there. The wife stands for values constitutive of a good Indian *bahu* or daughter-in-law—she forges a relationship with the doctor's mother, whom he has rejected. She also attends *kirtans* (religious gatherings often centered around devotional music), symptomatic of the traditions that the doctor has rejected. Finally, she rejects the allure of the club and its glittering evening gowns. Her husband is a staunch representative of English habits: he loves the English style of dressing, the tradition of spending his evenings at the club, and, most important, his insistence in living separately from his mother, whom he finds too traditional, religious, and, therefore, backward looking.

In time, the husband's opposition to his mother is revealed as not merely an ideological one. He suspects that his mother was responsible for his father's will, in which he left a very small amount of money to his son and instead bound a sizable portion of the family property to a trust for Ayurvedic medicine with a provision for the study of Sanskrit. Therefore, Ayurveda and Sanskrit stand not only in direct opposition to modern medicine and English but also in the way of the son's inheritance, causing him acute pecuniary loss. Against this background, it is curious to note the son's sexualization of his mother: the doctor alleges that his mother's beauty drove his father to distraction and to change the will. The mother and her sexualized self stand in the way of the father's relationship with his son and ultimately his inheritance, which leads to the son's unequivocal rejection of his mother.

The first half of the novel engages in a complex set of discussions about desire, sexuality, even psychology, all within the ambit of the social space of a town and its clashes between different notions of modernity, but the novel's second half takes a sudden turn toward sensational action. Some years have elapsed. The doctor, it seems, has grown tired of his English—by now, Indian—wife and has an affair with a nurse, who, it turns out, has decided to poison Lily during her difficult third pregnancy. Enter the doctor's mother, whom, despite his protests, Lily has invited to stay in the house. Completely unaware of her son's affair and role in the poisoning, when the mother discovers the poisoning, she immediately alerts the police. In the meantime, the nurse has absconded. The police arrest the other prime suspect, the son. After a revelation of the events, unable to believe that she has unwittingly had her own son arrested, the mother, feigning hatred for Lily, comes forward to take the blame for the poisoning. *Mamta*, as the novel's title suggests, ultimately triumphs. The morality that lies at the center of the narrative is unmistakable: even a murderer son is, after all, a son. The mother in this social novel functions as an "iconic" image in the Hindi social film, "an image into which symbolic meanings converge and in which moreover they achieve stasis."[63] However, whereas the mother functions as an "iconic" image, change is imminent in the marital economy of the couple: after this event, Lily, the ideal wife, leaves her husband's house along with her children. She departs not for London but stays instead in her mother-in-law's home, awaiting her return from prison and immersing herself in the study of the Bible. The union here is an unlikely familial union between an English daughter-in-law and Indian mother-in-law. It is based on a renunciation of marital vows and an emphasis on gods and religion. The Hindu kirtan ceremony is invoked several times in *Mamta*. It is also elaborately described to Lily, as she is an outsider to the Hindu tradition of worship. The kirtan, like the extra-diegetic film song, "inhabit(s) a space outside the fiction and alert(s) us to a certain point of view or emotional disposition which we find highly intelligible."[64] In the case of Lily and her mother-in-law, it is the kirtan that symbolizes their union and Lily's marital break.

Lalsa (Desire), another novel by Dutt published later in 1968, approaches morality in similar ways. This novel is also set in the pre-independence period. A sexualized mother once again lies at the narrative's center. But this is a story of rape. Bhagwati, the protagonist, has just witnessed the zamindar's eldest son leaving his house. After this visit, he finds his mother hiding under the covers in her room: "Bhagwati kept standing near his mother's cot for a long time. Then, assessing his mother's shame, he went away to his room and sat down on his own cot, and started thinking, is this rape [*balatkar hai*] or his mother's lack of faithfulness to his father [*ma ki pitaji mein nishtha heenta*]." Rape is soon spelled out as rape—the humiliated mother admits to having been forced. Bhagwati thinks about his mother's state: "He believed that his mother would commit suicide if the night's events [*raat wali baat*] happened again."[65] What does rape mean in the context of a married and, here, the widowed woman? Again, we return to the site of film scholarship on rape in Hindi film. Jyotika Virdi links the suffering female subject of the Hindi film to state apotheosis: "The veneration reinforces suffering as a value in itself, monumentalising it, rather than resisting patriarchal norms. The suffering woman is held up as a model of womanhood, idealized, honoured and decorated. In a fantastic and wholly fabricated gesture, the films have the son/state recognise the mother's martyrdom, making her suffering 'worth it all.'"[66] The way the scene is set is worth noting. Bhagwati first encounters the zamindar's son stepping out of the house and pauses. He then steps into the house where he notices, from a considerable distance, his mother cowering in her bed. The physical distance between the two of them is palpable as Bhagwati steps out of the room to think if his mother had given consent or not. The readers, aware of such scene settings in films, are expected to linguistically translate the literary/textual experience into a cinematic one.

Again, the mother is beautiful and desirable, sexualized by the son but only in the context of her rape because, for him, and the readers, she is also equally virtuous. Bhagwati is the perfect sixteen-year-old son who bases his entire life on self-restraint and, on account of her abuse, uproots them from their village, moving to Lucknow to work and study English. Bhagwati practices strict vegetarianism as a Brahmin, preferring to read the *Gita* instead of playing chess with his companions at night. He also refuses an offer of marriage from a family friend's young daughter, Vimla. He refuses to marry her only because her Christian parents do not want their daughter to wed a Hindu. Impressed by his renunciation, Vimla offers herself to Bhagwati. To appeal to him, Vimla dedicatedly starts wearing plain saris, reading Sanskrit *shlokas* with Bhagwati's mother as well as giving up meat.

Both these novels are cloaked in Progressive social rhetoric but are also deeply moral in their depiction of Hinduism. In turn, Guru Dutt's novels sat beside often biting and popular satire written by Progressives-turned-film writers, such as Krishan Chander, K. A. Abbas, and Kanhaiya Lal Kapur, contributing to the range at offer from the publisher. Many Progressives had, by the 1950s, already embedded themselves in popular imagination through their collaborations and contribution to the Hindi film industry. Krishan Chander was a prolific screen writer. K. A. Abbas was both a screenwriter and director, the latter for *Dharti ke Lal* (Children of the earth) in 1946, which holds the distinction of being the only film produced by the Indian People's Theatre Association. Abbas also wrote prolifically for Raj Kapoor's popular and iconic films, such as *Avara* (Wanderer), *Shri 420*, *Mera Naam Joker* (My name is joker), *Bobby*, and *Henna*.[67]

However, these writers wrote and treated their fiction writing as projects completely separate from their film projects. An active member of the Indian Progressive Writers' Association (IPWA), Krishan Chander in particular was famous for his leftist, propaganda-laden short stories and satires. According to Rakshanda Jalil, Chander "remained associated with the IPWA till the end of his days, and, more importantly, the only one who was consistently praised by fellow progressives for being one." Chander was "a poster boy for the Progressives" because of his ability to write on topical events, or *waqti adab*.[68]

Under the Hind Pocket Books banner, the first books that Chander published were his famous satires *Ek Gadhe ki Atma Katha* (The autobiography of a donkey), *Ek Gadhe ki Vapsi* (A donkey's return), and *Ek Gadha Nefa mein* (A donkey in NEFA), a book trilogy featuring a donkey as its central character. The books show the donkey as more mindful and compassionate than all the intellectuals, politicians, and bureaucrats of the time. *Ek Gadhe ki Atma Katha* tracks the donkey's movements across the capital city of Delhi, where he meets the prime minister and experiences firsthand the futility of bureaucracy; *Ek Gadhe ki Vapsi* has the donkey produce a film in Bombay; and *Ek Gadha Nefa mein* sees the donkey caught in the middle of the Third Indochina War, even flying to Beijing. Throughout the books, the donkey acts as a social commentator on the acts of the new republic and is particularly acerbic in the first book. He has traveled from a small town in Uttar Pradesh to Delhi, a city that he had imagined from a distance to be a liberal socialist haven for such donkeys as him. In Delhi, he is immediately tethered by an overworked washerman who eventually dies at his ghat, swallowed whole by a crocodile. The donkey feels the misery of the washerman's family, which has lost its sole earning member. Thus begins the donkey's quest to get justice in the form of monetary compensation for this family. The donkey travels from one government department to another. He is rejected at every step of the way. He finally catches the prime minister taking a walk in his garden: this prime minister is named explicitly as Jawaharlal Nehru. Nehru confesses his inability to help the washerman's family; he offers private compensation but no governmental recourse. The highlight of the donkey's meeting with the prime minister is when Nehru asks if he can take a ride on him around his garden. The deeply satirical image carries an embedded political message. Nehru riding a donkey was a bold sketch on Chander's part, with a writer metaphorically taking the prime minister to task, demanding that the nation serve its people. What does it mean that Nehru can help personally but not institutionally and that he wants to ride the donkey publicly around the garden? Here, Chander separates the prime minister's persona from this bureaucratic political persona, where the man himself accepts that he can do no more for the Indian public beyond the personal acts of charity. Nehru's desire to ride the donkey, which he does around the garden, signals both his playfulness and his acceptance of being a fool. Perhaps it signals that the government is happy living off the "backs" of its citizens.

Ek Gadhe ki Atma Katha also shows the readers another vision of Delhi, that is, high-society Delhi. After his meeting with Nehru, the donkey becomes famous, and a businessman (*seth*) invites him home to stay with him. The infamous License Raj under Nehruvian Era is invoked in the latter half of the work, with the donkey invited to judge beauty pageants and dine at fashionable homes just on account of presumably having won a contract from the prime minister. The author's message is clear: a donkey is no longer a donkey if the prime minister has given him a contract. For the sake of securing a contract, the seth even tries to persuade his daughter to marry the donkey. Chander's satire is a scathing comment on how the two pillars of post-independence planning and prosperity—bureaucracy and business community—are hollow, are false, and reek of corruption.

The second book continues the donkey's journey in Bombay, the budding center of commercial Hindi film. There, the donkey has many strange experiences: for his new owners, he becomes a physical tanker transporting contraband alcohol in his belly and even turns into an unwilling sadhu forced to predict lucky numbers to Bombay seths addicted to playing the lottery. The donkey eventually also produces a Bombay Hindi film, an experience that not only completely drains him of all the wealth that he had accumulated from his lottery profits but also strips him of any self-respect. With the right amount of material possessions, even a donkey can be a star. The donkey is a donkey only when he has nothing to offer.

Krishan Chander's satires offer a tantalizing insight into the writer's disillusionment with the new nation and its unfulfilled promises. While Hindi literary criticism often discusses this moment as *moh bhang* (disillusionment), Chander's satires with the donkey as protagonist spell the extent of its brutality. Nehru sitting atop the donkey in the first book is the ultimate indictment of the state—the state is being taken for a ride, and one can do nothing but feebly laugh about it.

Self-Help

Apart from fiction, Hind Pocket Books also paid great attention to the inclusion and curation of self-help books. Of the 127 Hind Pocket Books titles surveyed, self-help, health, and household nonfiction books constitute a total of twenty-two titles on offer, a significant proportion.

One of the most prominent subgenres within pre-independence self-help was self-improvement through sayings and manuals on letter writing. Hind Pocket Books followed this style of self-help and included it in the first titles. An illustrative example of this is *Amar Vani* (Immortal voice), which, the title page declares, included fifteen hundred inspirational sayings from "saints, mahatmas and wise men" from "many countries." The point of such sayings was to be inspirational as well as to provide "healthy and knowledgeable entertainment . . . during holidays."[69] The seventh book published by the company, *Amar Vani* enabled the reader to use a table of contents to reach sections that listed problems alphabetically, such as *agyanta* (ignorance,) *asafalta* (failure), *alasya* (laziness), and so on. Readers could use the contents to reach the page number of the desired inspirational quotes. *Agyanta*, for instance, carried quotations from a wide range of philosophers, writers, and politicians such as Socrates, Confucious, Dickens, Plato, and Gandhi.

Indeed, from the 1920s onward, this was a genre that had come to dominate the *pustak mala*, or "book series." From some pre-independence publisher accounts, self-help books had proven to be a lucrative genre. One of the first self-help writers to break into the Hindi market was James Allen, an English motivational writer and philosopher who lived between 1864 and 1912. Allen was immensely successful in England. In an introduction to the second edition of Allen's book *Atma Rahasya*, the Hindi translation of *Out from the Heart* (the first Hindi edition of which was published on 15 December 1916), translator Dayachandra Goyalinka wrote, "In the West, one can estimate Mr. James Allen's books and their renown through the knowledge that every book of his has sold thousands of copies . . . If Hindi language speakers have benefited at all from this book, then we will soon present them with other books of the author."[70]

This subgenre is the more identifiable of self-help books published in the pre-independence period. The company also published other subgenres that broke away or were distinct from the self-help pustak mala books of the 1920s. In other words, although the pustak mala books of the 1920s transcreated the largely nineteenth-century Victorian self-help books to suit the nationalist, religious, and collective-oriented context of its consumption, I show that translations by Hind Pocket Books were far more direct and literal, favoring a more individual-oriented text.

What were these books like to begin with? The self-help, health, and household nonfiction book genre began flowering in the Hindi publishing market from early twentieth century, with books put out by several Hindi pustak malas covering an extensive range of topics, from thinking about practical and monetary questions, such as how to run one's household and be thrifty, to the more metaphysical questions involving self-improvement, such as how to better one's self and soul. Samuel Smiles (1812–1904), the famous Victorian English motivational writer, was one of the first people to use the phrase "self-help" and bring it into currency in his writing in 1859. He was first published in Hindi by Indian Press in Allahabad in 1914 and became so popular in

Hindi that his books went into multiple reprints. The introduction to the 1927 edition of Smiles's 1875 work *Thrift*, translated into Hindi as *Mitavyaya*, begins with a glowing biography of Smiles.[71] Although the book was lifted from the Victorian context of middle-class thrift, domesticity, and household management, the central concerns of Victorian middle-class England, the 1927 Hindi edition of the book modified the content of the book, adding local, specific historical references and examples.[72] The introduction hails Smiles's book *Self-Help* as one of his most popular. Written by translator Ram Chandra Varma, the introduction to *Mitavyaya* threaded the question of what it means to be a human (*manushya*) with being self-reliant (*atma nirbhar*) and possessing good behavior (*sadachar*). Only then does Varma turn to the question of money. Varma writes, "It cannot be said that a poor person cannot possess the strength of character, however, it cannot be denied that man needs money in order to further his progress in terms of good deeds."[73] Therefore, the question of *charitra*, or "character," is, albeit apologetically, linked to the question of money, and money is supposed to be saved only to further one's character. Self-development, then, takes on a particularly unique middle-class character.

Not only was the nineteenth-century Victorian ideal of household management transported into the Indian middle-class context of linking thrift with character development, but the 1920s pustak mala editions of self-help books also catered to the loftier ambitions of human self-development. For instance, the 1918 Lucknow edition of James Allen's 1904 book *Out from the Heart*, was meant to cater to the Indian theosophists, a group that practiced tenets of universal truth and brotherhood.[74] The book was published as part of the Hindi Sahitya Bhandar's *Sadvichar Pustak Mala* ("The good thoughts book series"), a telling signifier of how self-help as a print genre had, by this time, progressed to being promoted with its own series. The above examples help historically contextualize the birth of this genre, which at its inception catered to nationalist-minded middle-class readers who wanted to orient themselves differently with respect to the questions of nation, religion, and belonging.

Hind Pocket Books took on this legacy of self-help books, publishing authors such as James Allen and Swett Marden, who were already in Hindi circulation in the rubric of what the publisher labeled "useful for life literature" (*jivan upyogi sahitya*). However, the treatment and content of the books themselves had significantly changed, with these texts being more literal translations that addressed readers as individuals. James Allen's works published in Hindi in the 1920s featured Indian inspirational quotes by contemporary and historical heroes like Govind Ranade, Keshav Nath Choubey, Chanakya, and so on, thereby *customizing* his work to the Indian context, often with Sanskrit shlokas as epigraphs, the Hind Pocket Books narrative veers from this. In fact, the James Allen that one finds in the Hind Pocket Books series is bereft of such embellishments. Not only that, the question of individual progress is also directly addressed to the readers. This transforms the nationalist, religious, philosophical text into a secular and more individualist articulation of self-help. We can see this through a close reading of one of Allen's texts that Hind Pocket Books published. The blurb at the back of Hind Pocket Books' edition of Allen's 1911 work *Eight Pillars of Prosperity*, translated into Hindi as *Safalta ke aath sadhan*, reads, "Countless people have been inspired by Allen's powerful thoughts and found success in their lives . . . The lines of this book will inspire you to turn the pages of your lives."[75] The book itself begins with a compact introduction, written by Mahavir Adhikari, who declares, "Blaming conditions and difficulties is just another name for weakness." The idea, then, is to reach success despite obstacles and oppositions. To reach success, all one needs are eight steps: "This book lists these eight steps of success in a correct and scientific manner."[76] The emphasis is on "scientific" method. But though the introduction emphasizes a deeply "scientific" manner, the main text itself is a literal translation of Allen's work in which he speaks of the direct link between success and morality. For Allen, prosperity and ethics go hand in hand: "The boundary lines of a man's morality mark the limits of his success. So true is this that to know a man's moral status would be to know—to mathematically gauge—his ultimate success or failure. The temple of prosperity only stands in so far as it is supported by its moral pillars; when they are weakened, it becomes insecure; when they are withdrawn, it crumbles away and totters to ruin."[77] The conditions spelled out are translated into Hindi, with the eight pillars of success being *shakti* (energy), *mitvayayta* (economy), *satyanistha* (integrity), *shram vyavastha* (system), *sahanubhuti* (compassion), *sachchai* (sincerity), *nispaksta* (impartiality), and *atma viswas* (self-confidence).

The other major writer covered by the series was the American motivational writer Swett Marden (1848–1924), who was already a very successful and long-running author in Hindi translation. Of the titles included in the study, Swett Marden's books number five. The "useful for life literature" advertised by Hind Pocket Books also includes other genres that had become fairly customary in series, with titles such as *Patr likhne ki kala* (The art of letter writing) and the intriguing *Pati Patni* (Husband wife). Sex education for married couples, then, sits side by side with letter writing.

Poetry and the Paperback

At Hind Pocket Books, poetry was a comprehensive, well-curated, and well-edited genre. Hindi poetry sat alongside Urdu poetry, and single-author books featured as many words as did multiple-author poetry compilations. Miscellaneous *Prem geet*, or "love songs," a historically successful pocketbook genre, were also part of the list.[78]

While the genres themselves are multivaried, some commonalities persist. A long preface usually accompanied each title. I read this form of the long, weighty preface in two ways. First, quite simply, it set the ground for its readers: the well-appointed editors explained the rationale for the particular poetry collection at hand, its historical significance, its authorial and generic legacy. Second and closely related to the first reason, the long preface also added to Hind Pocket Books' larger emphasis on the volume's "seriousness." This impulse of "seriousness," where the book deserves readers' full and scholarly attention, ties to the other middlebrow attribute of the "need to know." In short, the long preface built the book's claims to literary legitimacy.

The anthology *Hindi ke Sarvasrestha Prem Geet* (The best love songs of Hindi) begins with a lengthy preface. Among many things, it first lists the importance of love poetry. The preface then insists that this compilation was produced after obtaining permission from the poets themselves. In the introduction, its compiler-editor, Kshemchandra "Suman," writes: "We have been aided in this sacred gathering by many respected poets of Hindi, who have fully supported us, with the result that we got such unparalleled material that we were unable to print it all in the small format of the 'pocket book,' so we could not use all the material here even if we wanted to."[79] We soon understand the preface's emphasis on "support" of "this sacred gathering": the poets who contributed to the book firsthand, and exclusively, for this Hind Pocket Books collection include celebrated contemporary Hindi poets such as Agyeya, Upendranath "Ashk," Kailash Vajpayi, Dharmvir Bharti, Harivansh Rai "Bachchan," as well as fiction writers like the Nayi Kahani writer Rajendra Yadav and the popular Rangeya Raghav. Clearly, Hind Pocket Books invested in providing high literary poetry to its readers at the usual price of one rupee per book.

The long preface continues across Urdu poetry collections as well. Of the eight poetry titles, four—*Deewan-e-Ghalib* (Complete works of Ghalib), *Jigar ki Shayari* (The Shayari of Jigar), *Urdu rubaiyat* (The Rubaiyat in Urdu), and *Aaj ki Urdu Shayari* (Contemporary Urdu Shayari)—are of Urdu poetry. This emphasis on Urdu poetry collections is evidenced not just by the number of titles on offer but also by the treatment given to each collection. In these volumes, the long preface emerges again, with each collection first presenting the poet's biographical details and, should readers want to explore the poet further, providing the poet's complete bibliographic information as well. For instance, in the case of *Deewan-e-Ghalib*, the first part of the book consists of a long *jivani*, or "biography," of the poet. Each preface spells out both the translational and the selection rationale of the poems.

Apart from the impulse of "seriousness," requiring the readers' full and scholarly attention, the long preface makes clear that the reader is a reader of Hindi and, as such, is provided with more context. This becomes more evident when we engage with the poetry itself, consciously introduced in the Nagari transliteration, with extensive footnotes on each page to explain the words the readers may not understand. Significantly, the Urdu words are kept "as is," supplemented by explanations. The *Deewan-e-Ghalib* from the series can again serve as an example here (see figure 4). The preface of the book praises him in lofty terms: "It is without doubt that Urdu has many good poets [*shayar*], however, Ghalib's style of expression [*andaaz-e-bayan*] is not only different but much better than them. He cannot be compared to any other poet."[80] Here, andaaz-e-bayan is transliterated into Hindi, while the image below from the first page of the *Deewan* shows how Ghalib's original verse is preserved "as is," with extensive footnotes for the Urdu words. The format of the book, as well as the care given to the visual presentation of the poem, ghazal, or song, is also striking, with the patterns of calligraphy replicated on the front page. This useful representation is not only limited to classics such as Ghalib but also extends to contemporary poets such as 'Jigar' Muradabadi, who is described as "the king of the modern Urdu ghazal." Moreover, he is described as "one of those fortunate poets, whose creations became 'classics' in his own lifetime."[81]

What consequences does this have for the relationship between Hindi and Urdu? In many senses, we can see an extension of the argument about Hindi in *Sarita*: *Sarita* functioned as a nonnormative and democratizing medium, providing a space for ordinary readers to express the right to a language that they could understand and enjoy. Here, Hind Pocket Books' construction of these poetry books says this: Urdu, Hindi's perceived "other," also deserves to be enjoyed in its splendor. Whereas in the context of post-1947 India and the Constituent Assembly debates Hindi has been constructed as overbearingly nationalist and Sanskritized, claiming status as the national language at the expense of the other Indian languages and

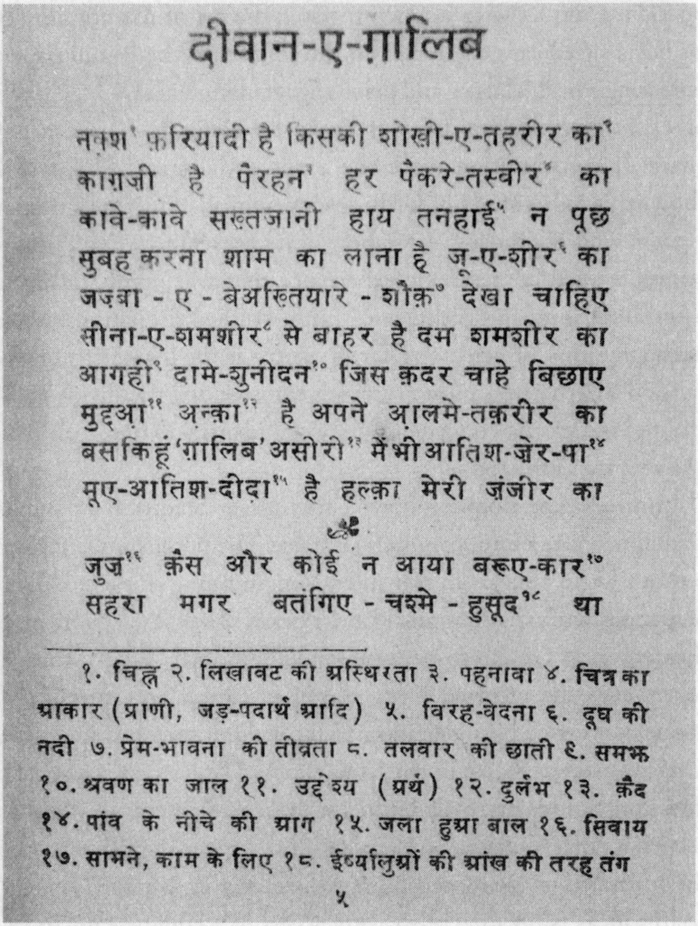

दीवान-ए-ग़ालिब

नक़्श[१] फ़रियादी है किसकी शोख़ी-ए-तहरीर का[२]
काग़ज़ी है पैरहन[३] हर पैकरे-तस्वीर[४] का

कावे-कावे सख़्तजानी हाय तनहाई[५] न पूछ
सुबह करना शाम का लाना है जू-ए-शीर[६] का

जज़्बा-ए-बेअख़्तियारे-शौक़[७] देखा चाहिए
सीना-ए-शमशीर[८] से बाहर है दम शमशीर का

आगही[९] दामे-शुनीदन[१०] जिस क़दर चाहे बिछाए
मुद्दआ[११] अन्क़ा[१२] है अपने आलमे-तक़रीर का

बस कि हूं 'ग़ालिब' असीरी[१३] में भी आतिश-ज़ेर-पा[१४]
मूए-आतिश-दीदा[१५] है हल्क़ा मेरी ज़ंजीर का

जुज़[१६] क़ैस और कोई न आया बरूए-कार[१७]
सहरा मगर बतंगिए-चश्मे-हुसूद[१८] था

१. चिह्न २. लिखावट की अस्थिरता ३. पहनावा ४. चित्र का आकार (प्राणी, जड़-पदार्थ आदि) ५. विरह-वेदना ६. दूध की नदी ७. प्रेम-भावना की तीव्रता ८. तलवार की छाती ९. समझ १०. श्रवण का जाल ११. उद्देश्य (अर्थ) १२. दुर्लभ १३. क़ैद १४. पांव के नीचे की आग १५. जला हुआ बाल १६. सिवाय १७. सामने, काम के लिए १८. ईर्ष्यालुओं की आंख की तरह तंग

५

FIGURE 4. First page of poetry from *Deewan-e-Ghalib*, Hind Pocket Books.

its own regional varieties, the poetry collections again gesture to the other face of Hindi and the subsequent widened scope of the Hindi reading public.

Indeed, dominant forms of poetry, such as the ghazal, *shayari*, and the *Rubaiyat*, are freely cultivated within the series, calling into question the strict adherence to the Hindi-Urdu divide that dominated the post-independence discourse. This emphasis, of keeping the poetic text intact with its own register, the act of maintaining poetry "as is," is significant, especially in the context of the Hindi paperback, reflecting Hindi's larger and prior engagement with Urdu. Chapbooks of Urdu ghazals, shayari, Rubaiyat, and songs had been a popular genre of consumption since the nineteenth century.[82] David Lunn shows this in his study of Urdu poetry published in the Hindi journal *Chand*, where "almost every aspect of its presentation of Urdu poetry points toward an aesthetic experience that was emphatically meant to be luxurious and indulgent." Lunn studies the emphasis on this particular kind of "sensuous" Urdu poetry as the formation of what he calls an "alternative canon . . . which transcended the divides of script and the increasing congruence between identifiers based on language and religious affiliation."[83]

Hind Pocket Books followed this larger tradition of publishing Urdu poetry in Hindi commercial space. The publisher here primarily put out Urdu ghazals in transliteration, imbuing this particular form of poetry with distinction. Hind Pocket Books' selection of poets, the canonical Ghalib to perhaps equally popular "Jigar" Muradabadi, reproduces the received Urdu canon in Hindi literature. However, in the context of post-partition India, the number and the care given to Urdu poetry books in the Hind Pocket Books list again calls into question the rejection of Urdu by the Hindi literary establishment as well as by the state. These poetry books were highly successful in the format that promoted bilingualism and encouraged one to read poetry in "as is" form, while easing access to a language for those who may not have been so familiar with, in this case, Urdu. This continuity resonates with practices in Hindi cinema and the space it made for Urdu poetry "as is."[84]

Although it may not be surprising that a popular paperback series would publish ghazals and song collections, what is striking is that the genre of the songbook/ghazal in the Hind Pocket Book collection is one of the most formal representations of genre seen in the series. This emphasis on "seriousness" is, again, a recurring theme of the middlebrow publishing in this book, corresponding to the genre selection that we saw earlier in the chapter. The footnotes explaining individual Urdu words promoted a way of reading that demanded the reader's full scholarly attention. In turn, Urdu poetry was articulated as a "high" or "serious" genre that could be enjoyed only if the readers paid minute attention to both the cadence of the poetry or the meaning of the poem and what the words meant individually. Hind Pocket Books told its readers that Ghalib was within their reach for a rupee, and through that investment, readers would not only gain a gateway into Urdu as language, a poetic culture that they may or may not be unfamiliar with, but also undertake a scholarly exercise that would produce another form of pleasure, one that is gained from an engagement with the "seriousness" of reading.

CONCLUSION

To separately quantify and analyze the different genres and forms that went into the making of the Hind Pocket Books collection produces a more complex understanding of the series as a whole. Although the series conforms to conventions for each genre, presenting them together breaks genre expectations in terms of readership. So, although the novels were often Bengali classics and social romances, the series also featured the seemingly oppositional Progressive and Nayi Kahani writings. Although the company published the ghazal and songbook collections, it took them seriously as poetry. As a whole, the emphasis of the series seems to be on seriousness. Also, as the case of poetry shows, the Hindi Hind Pocket Book is not completely Hindi at all. It is an amalgamation of different languages, genres, and styles. It all came together to form hugely successful and influential publications. Although in this chapter I have discussed only Hindi, Bengali, English, and Urdu texts, the series also carried texts from Punjabi, most notably by Amrita Pritam.[85]

Hind Pocket Books was able to create a direct entry point for books into the household on the basis of a commercial transaction—six for the price of five—with the implicit understanding that this surrender would lead to a meaningful, edifying, and altogether pleasurable reading process. The disparity between contents on offer provides an insight into what the publisher thought the reader would want. First and foremost, the publisher offered a diversity of genres, deliberately urging the reader to gain familiarity with all forms of content: if it has been filtered through the Hind Pocket Book panel, it has passed the judgment of taste, and through its variety, it shall serve to make what Joan Shelley Rubin calls "generalist" readers. Judging from the success of Hind Pocket Books' Gharelu Library Yojana, Hindi middlebrow readers did indeed seek to be "generalist," that is, to know a range of objects, in this case a range of books.[86]

Also, despite various theorists of the middlebrow, from Virginia Woolf to Pierre Bourdieu, having viewed the idea of generalism as a drawback, linking it to the pull of the market and the lack of originality, one need not take their elitist view. The middlebrow, I argue, is a historically relevant category that comes into being not only as a mere act of imitation or even because of the logic of the market. It also functions as a space specifically carved by active demand because, most significantly, it fulfils a particular logic of cultural imagination. The cultural imaginary of the middlebrow demands knowledge of a range that, at first glance, seems to be running counter or in contradiction. However, the impetus is not just on pleasure or aspirational improvement or even subscription to taste; it also lies, as mentioned above, in the need to know. This aspect of "need to know" publishing shall continue in the next chapter, which takes as its focus the weekly *Dharmyug*. Departing from the first two chapters in which I focused on publications from Delhi, *Dharmyug* was published from Bombay and incorporated high literary content into a weekly format.

CHAPTER THREE

Dharmyug

From Dharma to Dharmvir Bharti

Dharamvir Bharti is the only person in this book with a chapter named after him. It is only fitting, then, to start with a history of his life. In a Hindi literary context, though, he certainly does not need introductions: Bharti, much like *Dharmyug*, the weekly periodical that lies at this chapter's heart, was an ever-enduring presence and occupied the lives and minds of Hindi readers, writers, and critics alike. Born in Allahabad in 1926, he died in 1997 in his adopted city, Bombay. In Allahabad, Bharti was devoted to his life as writer. In Bombay, Bharti transferred all energies to editing *Dharmyug*.

The result was, as the weekly's subeditor Kanhaiyalal Nandan states quite simply: "*Dharmyug* was the Number 1 periodical of its times. No Hindi-speaking household could remain content without ordering *Dharmyug* to its home."[1] Published by the Bennett, Coleman and Company (henceforth called the Times Group), based in Bombay (Maharashtra), and best known for publishing the English daily *Times of India*, *Dharmyug* had phenomenal reach: it was historically the only magazine with a reach larger than any other in Hindi in the 1950s and 1960s. In fact, *Dharmyug*'s circulation figures exceeded those of other middlebrow magazines by about twice: according to the Audit Bureau of Circulations figures in 1960, whereas *Sarita*'s subscription figures stood at 30,000, *Dharmyug* had more than 60,000 subscribers, a phenomenal figure for Hindi periodical publishing at the time.[2] After

Dharmvir Bharti took over in 1959, the numbers soared even further, registering more than 100,000 subscribers in 1964. *Dharmyug* toppled English-language sales: the numbers tell us that even the celebrated English-language *Illustrated Weekly of India* of the Times Group, in operation from 1880, trailed slightly behind.[3]

Bharti was not *Dharmyug*'s first editor. Ilachandra and Hemchandra Joshi, who ran *Sangam* (Confluence), a literary magazine from Leader Press, Allahabad (Uttar Pradesh), first edited *Dharmyug*. After the Joshi brothers left, Satyakam Vidyalankar became *Dharmyug*'s editor for a short period.[4] In fact, in the first decade of *Dharmyug*'s life, Bharti was already a prominent writer in Allahabad and, according to Hindi academic and critic Namwar Singh, had already produced his most celebrated modernist works between 1950 and 1955.[5] Why would Bharti, a young, promising Hindi modernist, shift from Allahabad to Bombay to edit *Dharmyug*, invariably leaving a glittering literary career behind? How many of Bharti's literary impulses made their appearance in the magazine? How did Bharti's editorial choices lead to large circulation jumps for *Dharmyug*? Dharmvir Bharti's appointment at *Dharmyug* is central to this chapter. I specifically focus on *Dharmyug* between 1958 and 1961, which best demonstrates this shift.

Why is this shift important to our understanding of middlebrow reading and consumption culture? Here, the *Dharmyug* that Bharti inherited needs close inspection. The magazine's general layout confirms its strong middlebrow foundations. As figure 5 shows, structurally, a typical *Dharmyug* of the 1950s consisted of four main sections. The first section was titled "pictures" (*chitra*). The second section, called "literature" (*katha sahitya*), was followed by a "writings" (*lekh*) section. The final section was a miscellany, loosely titled "attractions" (*akarshan*), carrying a range of articles, such as nonfiction pieces, travel writing, an agony aunt column, a part dedicated to women titled "Women's World" (Mahila Jagat), a film review column, and even an occasional column devoted to publishing photographs of newlywed couples in wedding attire titled, quite simply, "Newlyweds" ("Nav vivahit").

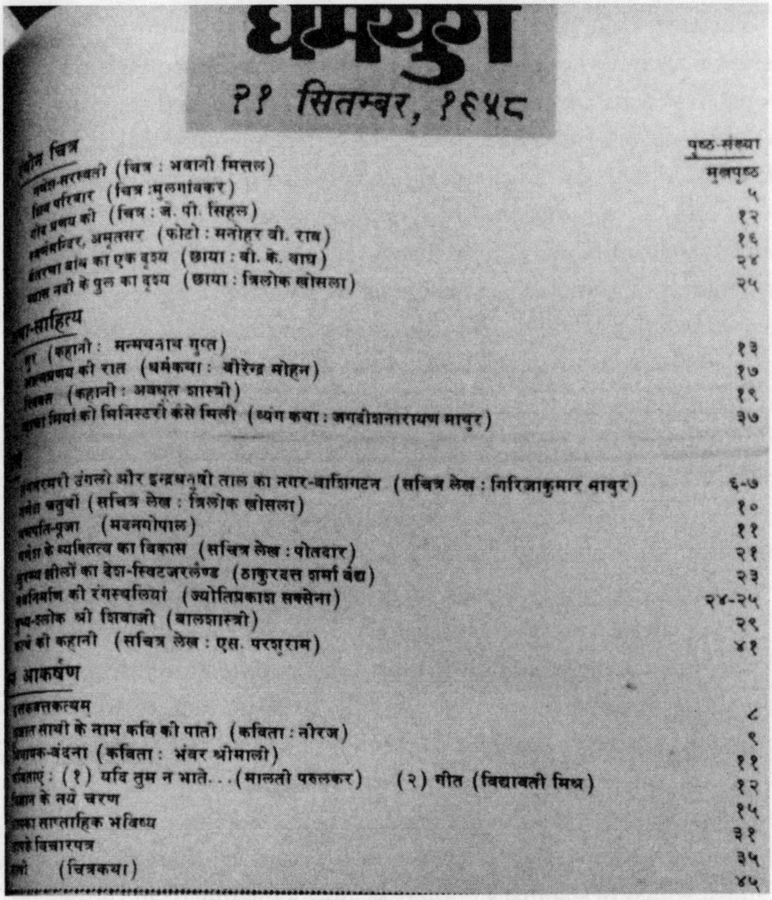
धर्मयुग

२१ सितम्बर, १९५८

	पृष्ठ-संख्या
चित्र	
(चित्र : भवानी मित्तल)	मुखपृष्ठ
परिवार (चित्र : मुलगांवकर)	५
(चित्र : जे. पी. सिहल)	१२
अमृतसर (फोटो : मनोहर बी. राव)	१६
बांध का एक दृश्य (छाया : बी. के. वाघ)	२४
नदी के पुल का दृश्य (छाया : त्रिलोक खोसला)	२५
साहित्य	
(कहानी : मन्मथनाथ गुप्त)	१३
की रात (धर्मकथा : वीरेन्द्र मोहन)	१७
(कहानी : अवधूत शास्त्री)	१९
मियां को मिनिस्टरी कैसे मिली (व्यंग कथा : जगदीशनारायण माथुर)	३७
उंगली और इन्द्रधनुषी ताल का नगर-वाशिंगटन (सचित्र लेख : गिरिजाकुमार माथुर)	६-७
(सचित्र लेख : त्रिलोक खोसला)	१०
पूजा (मदनगोपाल)	११
के व्यक्तित्व का विकास (सचित्र लेख : पोतदार)	२१
झीलों का देश-स्विटजरलैण्ड (ठाकुरदत्त शर्मा वैद्य)	२३
की रंगस्थलियां (ज्योतिप्रकाश सक्सेना)	२४-२५
श्री शिवाजी (बालशास्त्री)	२९
की कहानी (सचित्र लेख : एस. परशुराम)	४१
आकर्षण	
	८
साथी के नाम कवि की पाती (कविता : नीरज)	९
वंदना (कविता : भंवर श्रीमाली)	११
: (१) यदि तुम न भाते... (मालती परुलकर) (२) गीत (विद्यावती मिश्र)	१२
के नये चरण	१५
साप्ताहिक भविष्य	३१
विचारपत्र	३५
(चित्रकथा)	४५

FIGURE 5. Table of Contents, *Dharmyug,* 21 September 1958, Bennett, Coleman and Company.[6]

The weekly's focus on photographs is clearly evident, with the section on "pictures" placed right at the top of the table of contents. The weekly prided itself on printing good-quality photographs, with the titles of stories and other pieces often carrying the subheading "essay with colorful photographs" (*rangeen chitron sahit lekh*). This emphasis is also evident in the *Illustrated Weekly of India*'s attention to photographs and photo-essays.

There was one fundamental catch, though: *Dharmyug*'s photo-essays heavily favored photos of the gods. Bharti once sardonically noted: "When *Dharmyug* first came out, it carried intellectual weight [*baudhik bharipan*] Then when Satyakam Vidyalankar came, he reduced it to calendar art. It published so many photos of Sita, Ram, and Ganesh that they hang in *paan* shops to this day."[7] Bharti immediately set in motion the changes that he wanted made. For one, he reduced this emphasis on religious art and pilgrimage essays. The magazine did not entirely abandon its religious bent but focused more on—and became renowned for—its literary features and travel pieces from both India and the world. After Bharti's appointment, *Dharmyug* turned undeniably literary. Again, when Vidyalankar was editor, the magazine already had enviable circulation. Bharti's changes in the magazine's management, structure, and content increased circulation and readership by leaps and bounds. This was the first time that a Hindi magazine had reached such circulation,[8] which, I suggest, occurred because of a few fundamental reasons. First, while changes in the magazine took place because of strong editorial impulses, the phenomenal circulation growth tells us that readers responded favorably to them. Bharti's *Dharmyug* proved that—sometimes in opposition to (but also very much in conjunction with) Hindu religious images and stories—readers enjoyed consuming, among other things, (ever-growing) existential literature by Kierkegaard and Camus, which destabilizes notions of how, how much, and in what context readers consumed religion. Although religious belonging has been studied as two ends of the spectrum, that is, as secular ideals and in Hindu nationalist contexts, especially in the case of Hindi periodicals both past and contemporary,[9] this easy coexistence model deserves our attention. This is not to praise the "benevolence" of readers who "allowed" alternate discourses in the weekly. For one, those models of religious belonging were always Hindu to begin with. However, *Dharmyug*'s content shift does counter a singular image/idea of a singular Hindu consumer. Middlebrow readers in particular were consuming vastly more diverse materials than credited with.

Second, I suggest that this editorial shift was not merely an ideologically motivated intellectual decision of an editor but also the result of a commercial logic that saw possibilities that lay in production of such a magazine. The Times Group paid to produce, and it paid off to produce this way. *Dharmyug*'s engagement with the world and its literary and intellectual cultures was also the result of the power of scripting these worlds, which, in turn, came from financial resources that the Times Group mobilized for Hindi publishing. *Dharmyug* did not merely "cut and paste" or commission articles on literary and intellectual movements from people associated with them but also paid its own editors and writers to travel so as to report on them, shaping the cultural imaginary of its readers through direct interventions in content. This example shows the power of capital to shape ideas, governed by the publisher's—and, in this case, the publishing house's—financial ability to sponsor and actualize the editor's ideological and cultural vision of the magazine.

Dharmyug's story is, therefore, incomplete without a discussion of the publishing house, one that is much more difficult to trace because of the elusive nature of the Times Group. For such a media house, the information about it is very hard to come by: there exists only one book-length "biography" of the company.[10] However, even it tells the story of the publishing house primarily from the 1980s onward, focusing on the English-language daily newspaper *Times of India* and the way it changed how news was presented. It marks out the "obsessively low profile" of the current vice-chairman Samir Jain: "The photographers of the group are under instructions not to click his pictures for use in the papers. As for other publications and channels, his interactions are so few, with so many years between them, that opportunities to know his story through the popular media are practically non-existent."[11] Jain has often been credited with the birth of "the modern Indian newspaper industry."[12] However, as I indicate, this publishing sense, with a keen eye on the money, was a significant feature of the publishing house even in the post-independence period. And it took incredibly exciting forms in the times of Dharmvir Bharti.

DHARMYUG IN A PRE-BHARTI UNIVERSE: TRAVELS AT HOME, TRAVELS IN THE WORLD

Dharmvir Bharti's criticism of Vidyalankar's time at *Dharmyug*, that "he reduced it to calendar art," holds up to archival inspection.[13] One category of prints and photographs deserves special attention. The 20 July 1958 issue of the magazine, for instance, carries a two-page calendar art print of the Hindu gods Shiva and Parvati (see figure 6).

FIGURE 6. Shiva-Parvati, two-page print. *Dharmyug*, 20 July 1958, Bennett, Coleman and Company.

Shiva occupies the center as one of the three principal deities of Hinduism, with Parvati as his consort. The print also evidences other markers of Shiva that readers could easily identify. Shiva is considered the god of destruction: while the cobra around his neck signifies his power and control over one of the most dangerous creatures in the world, another cobra encircling the linga at the couple's feet signifies Shiva's raw masculine power. Shiva's facial features are depicted as soft, feminine, with his red lips and eyes lovingly looking down toward his consort, who faces straight, her arms and body framed in a mudra, or ritual gesture.

Was this a ubiquitous print of the period ordinarily depicted in social discourse as secular?[14] Shiva was depicted in several forms, and this certainly was one of many. In the context of Ram, another important Hindu deity, Patricia Uberoi warns against a teleology of nationalism in calendar art: "The assumption of a menacing teleology in the advent and velocity of circulation of images of a militant Ram ignores the paradoxes, complexities and circularity of mass print production through the last century. Given the century-long record of the recycling and plagiarism of images from a hybrid range of Indian and foreign sources, a linear history for the contemporary 'militant' Ram imagery, compelling and tantalising though it is, amounts to a travesty of the historical record."[15] Significantly, given the large size of the magazine, the impact of a double-sized A3 (loving) calendar art print of one of the primary gods of Hinduism alongside his consort is a very large and, therefore, striking image.

With the print in mind, the name of the magazine becomes clearer. The word "dharmyug" is derived from "dharma" and "yuga," two root words from Sanskrit. The dictionary meaning of "dharma" calls it "that which is established or firm, steadfast decree, statute, ordinance, law" and as "usage, practice, customary observance or prescribed conduct, duty." Most important, dharma also extends to include "virtue, morality, religion, religious merit, good works."[16] "Yuga," on the other hand, refers to "age," as in "epoch."

It is possible that such an ample, well-colored spread was meant for the reader to preserve, cut, and decorate the home with. The two-page print also does not have any page numbers on it, perhaps to facilitate the cutting and pasting process. Bharti's remark that "it [*Dharmyug*] published so many photos of Sita, Ram, and Ganesh that they hang in *paan* shops to this day" was not speculative, as this was indeed the way in which these prints were put to use, where Gods acted as a peaceful, protective presence in the home.[17]

If some issues had calendar art images of deities, others carried photographs of Hindu holy sites. For instance, one essay in the 3 July 1958 issue published a *dharmakatha* or "religious story" titled "Tap ke kautuki Brahmakumar" or "The mischievous Brahmakumar of austerity," accompanied by a photograph of a "Ram Mandir" in Hinganghat, Maharashtra. The religious story is made contemporary by photographs of religious sites.

Sometimes, these stories appeared unaccompanied by photographs. For instance, the 20 July 1958 issue carried another religious story, "Ek ke amrit peene se kya?" ("What does it matter if one person drinks elixir?"). The stories' bent is edifying. For instance, in the second story, the author directly addresses readers, telling them that change is possible only when everyone comes together and decides to make a collective effort at eradicating ills. Another issue in the magazine carries a *vratkatha* or a "fasting story," which relates to ritual fasting practice. Significantly, the religious story (*dharmakatha*) in the magazine narrates only one religion, Hinduism. I suggest that the presence of the dharmakatha and its corresponding images can be read in continuation of the debates on Hindi journals and periodicals and Hindu nationalism that Vasudha Dalmia, Francesca Orsini, and others have discussed in the context of the late nineteenth and early twentieth centuries, where Hindi journals, invoking questions about Hindi literariness and language, also promoted the ideas of Hindu nationalism.[18] These stories were alien to a middlebrow magazine like *Sarita*. In *Dharmyug*, however, these are clearly defined, prominent features.

The religious photographs, chromolithographs, and calendar art are only some of the many ways in which religion was presented to the magazine's readers. Another means was travel tourism to religious sites, for example, in "A glimpse of life on the *ghats* of Varanasi" ("Varanasi ke ghaton ki jivan jhanki"), in which the entire article praises religious ritualism.[19] The article in question is a two-page photo essay carrying a small introductory paragraph on Varanasi and its *ghats* (riverbanks), with the rest of the space devoted to displaying photographs. The religious imagery in this case is not as conspicuous as it was in other examples. The photo essay ostensibly describes life at the ghats in the form of a travel piece, recording the events occurring there, supposedly from the distant gaze of the unattached tourist. The sacred river Ganga features prominently in each of the five photographs covering two sides of the magazine, with devotees from different parts of the country described in the photographs.

In fact, it is the captions of the photographs that situate the images and deserve comment. One of the photographs is simply titled *Pilgrims on a boat paying respects to the Ganga* (Ganga stuti ka maan karte huye navo mein baithe kuch tirthyatri). In it, a group of pilgrims—male, female, and children—are shown sitting in a boat, with the river Ganga as a backdrop. The captured image could appear to be secular: the pilgrims could be any passengers on any boat on any river. In this sense, it differs from other devotional images of Hindu gods and goddesses offered by the magazine. However, it is the caption that situates the image within the magazine's larger religious discourse. The caption tells us that the river in question is the Ganga, the passengers on the boat are the *tirthyatri*, that is, "pilgrims," and they are performing the *Ganga stuti*, or "praise to the Ganga." Another image in the same piece is titled *Pilgrims giving donations to the beggars sitting at the ghats* (*Ghaton par baithe hue bhikmangon ko daan dete hue kuch tirthyatri*). The temples themselves or the deities residing inside them are not the focus of the photograph but, instead, the backdrop is. The act of almsgiving is framed directly in terms of the pilgrims' religious piety. Finally, the largest and, because of its size, most prominent image on the page—on the top left of the second (and photograph-only) page—is titled "Some devotees from South India bathing in the Ganga" (*Ganga snan karte hue Dakshin Bharat ke kuch bhakt gan*).[20] That the devotees are spelled out as hailing from the South of India is noticeable: no other devotees in the photo essay are described with respect to their region of origin. As mentioned in the first chapter, in the 1950s, the relationship between North and South was particularly factious in the context of the debates on Hindi as the official language of the country and the opposition to it by non-native speakers, especially the states in the South. Linking religious tourism in the North with devotees coming to visit from the South in a Hindi magazine creates the image of quiet solidarity between the two regions. Does the Hindi weekly suggest that religious brotherhood may lead to linguistic solidarity? There may be linguistic discord between the two regions, but the photo essay in *Dharmyug* insinuates that religious brotherhood rises above that discord. A generic, "secular sacred" photo essay on Varanasi acquires direct religious and even linguistic-political connotations through the power of captions on these travel photographs.[21] Again, the magazine accorded Hinduism a central place. By contrast, other religions are conspicuous by their absence. The readers of the Hindi magazine, then, are implicitly framed as Hindu in and by the magazine.

There were travel pilgrimages to the gods, and then there were travels to elsewhere: indeed, *Dharmyug*'s imagination (and coverage) of travel extended much beyond religious sites in India. Travel essays were a common feature of the English-language *Illustrated Weekly of India*, providing visual contexts to the world, aspirational yet accessible. And much before *Dharmyug* and *Illustrated Weekly*, there were many other travelers: A vast body of scholarly material examines both British and Indian travel writing in the colonial and postcolonial periods.[22] Travel accounts were frequently published in book form but often found first light in periodicals.[23] While vividly imbuing these texts with pleasurable descriptions and making them economically viable, travel journeys were also dogged by a variety of other concerns:

they asked questions about the usefulness of travel, its pedagogic functions, who gained access to it, fears about ritual pollution, and so on.

The 17 July 1923 issue of the prominent popular journal *Madhuri* serves as an example. From featuring "Letters from Abroad" (Vilayati Patra) alongside an article on the excavations unearthed from the Harrapan civilization, it contained a variety of travel accounts. While the article presents an in-depth analysis of the excavation sites replete with numerous black-and-white photographs, the letter is a blow-by-blow account of the Paris travels of the writer Sri Narayan Chaturvedi.[24] Other issues featured travels to Geneva and Shimla.[25] In "Letters from Abroad," Chaturvedi vividly describes the sights and sounds of Paris, the strangeness and familiarity of Parisian streets, and, among other things, accidentally running into a fellow Allahabadi, Hemchandra Joshi. Their exchange focuses not only on their surprise upon seeing each other but also directly brings them to a discussion about their beliefs. One tells the other: "You are so orthodox! I had not even dreamt that you would go abroad."[26] The account concludes with the writer shifting to Joshi's hotel and eating food brought from home along with some Parisian shop-sourced fruits and boiled potatoes.[27] This travel essay is in line with the magazine's larger debates on society and jaati, containing leading contributions from Brahmins and Arya Samajists.[28]

Many years later, in the pages of pre-Bharti *Dharmyug*, the world also asserted itself strongly, most prominently, again, through travel essays. A 2 November 1958 issue features photo essays in "Travels to the Gangotri Yamunotri" ("Gangotri Yamunotri ki Yatra"), "Germany's Megacity Berlin" ("Germany ki Mahanagari Berlin"), close-ups of flowers of Mahabaleshwar in an essay simply titled "Mahabaleshwar," as well as "The Experiences of My American Travels" ("Meri Amriki Yatra ka Anubhav").[29] Amid this efflorescence of travel writing, Soviet Russia was ostensibly absent from its pages.[30] However, lives of ordinary American citizens dominate. Recent studies of 1950s South Asian print cultures reveal how Cold War tensions were enacted in literary magazines.[31] Middlebrow magazines like *Dharmyug* also played an active role. These focused travels to America are indicative of a clear choice: celebration of America and its lifestyle.

A photo essay titled "Amrika ka ullasamaya Jivan," loosely translated as "Scenes from America's joyful life," featured in *Dharmyug*'s 3 July 1958 issue. This piece presented contemporary modern scenes from American rural life, featuring snapshots of quotidian professional life such as at a barbershop. Titled "The Countryside Barber" ("Dehat ka nai"), a photograph description reads, "A barber's shop in America's countryside is a very interesting place. Here, hair is cut using modern equipment, and we [also] get to hear very entertaining regional news."[32] This brief description, colored with humor, was aimed at establishing immediate intimacy with the quotidian: American everydayness is just like ours; it can be easily comprehended. The photo essay also focused on American family life. It praised the American family's commitment to *club jivan* ("club life"): "You will rarely find an American household that is disinterested in physical activity or sports."[33] Three photographs appear as accompaniments to this claim. In one image, a female swimming athlete is diving into the water while another image is a close-up of a famous hockey player. The third image is of spectators watching a motorcar race. In addition to being celebrated as vibrant and physically able, the American family also received praise for its other interests in theater, music, and the cinema. The article concluded that America had not only benefited from material gain but had also (admirably) gained enrichment through the cultural and sporting life of its citizens.

Continuing this praise of American life, another photo essay, "From the Courtyard of American Homes" ("Amriki gharon ke anganon se"), carried photographs of American domesticity. First is a full-page photograph of a woman giving two books to her son, who is sitting and playing on the floor (see figure 7). Her daughter is already shown reading at her desk. A child's buggy stands on the right of the image, with a doll tucked inside it. The image portrays conviviality and domestic harmony within "wholesome" and defined gendered

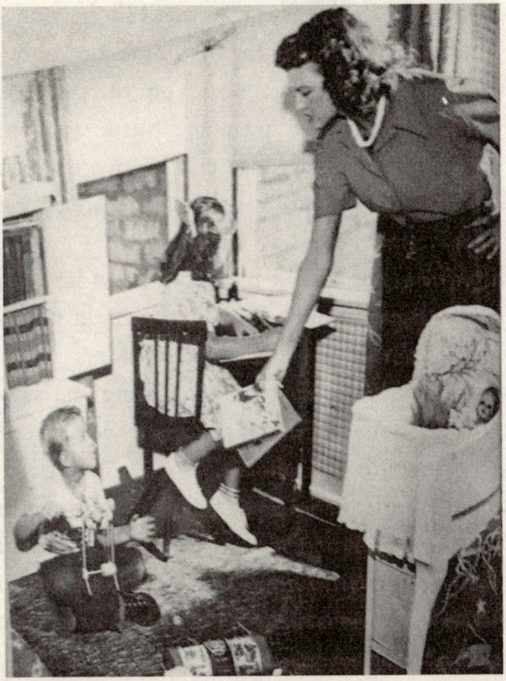

FIGURE 7. "Amriki gharon ke anganon se" (From the courtyards of American homes). *Dharmyug*, 16 July 1958. Bennett, Coleman and Company.

domestic roles—it is the mother in the picture and not the father—as well as gendered activities—it is the son who is at play while the daughter sits at her desk working. The caption reads, "Whether it is India or America, or any other country in the world, women and children provide the grace and hustle-bustle of the home . . . A house where there is no sign of them cannot be called a home." Yet another image shows the daughter helping her mother in the kitchen, with the caption, "Preparing and packing the husband's lunch is part of the daily activity of American wives and mothers. The daughter is helping her mother pack the tiffin. In this way, a mother is preparing her daughter to become capable in household matters."[34]

The article expands on even more similarities between a typical American and Indian home: just as in Indian homes, the man is also the main provider in an American home. His income supports the family and "that is why he lives for his home and only then for the world."[35] Noticeably, the man is absent from the photographs. While the wife and children provide "grace and hustle and bustle" and are featured as the epitome of elegance and beauty, the husband-father figure provides sacrifice and care and, for this reason, presumably, does not need to be shown as a physical entity.

These travel essays became a means of providing security to the reader at home. I understand this as activating a peculiar brand of middlebrow cosmopolitanism, in which readers were exposed to different cultural universes, but by replicating the same structural and hierarchical systems of power that they were used to at home. Preaching a cosmopolitanism of comfort, the article informs its readers that no matter how far one travels to a continent unfamiliar to most readers, one encounters the same pleasurable structures that one is used to at home. In the pre-Bharti imagination of *Dharmyug*, then, the images of a smiling American family can be read in continuation with the religious images of the deities. Both types of images, one devotional and the other inducing curiosity, prescribe a uniformity of hierarchy and provide a narrative of benevolent paternalism that deserves devotion. In one case, the object of devotion is a god, and in the other, it is the male provider.

The use of "cosmopolitanism" here deserves more gloss. Since Immanuel Kant's use of the term, "cosmopolitanism" has lived multiple lives.[36] Kwame Anthony Appiah's first usage of "cosmopolitanism" was to impress transnational solidarities.[37] The term has come to carry a multiplicity of meanings, even to denote failure to reach ideals it had emerged from. Subaltern cosmopolitanism, or the "cosmopolitanism of the poor," lies at one end of the spectrum; on the other, emerging from the Empire, cosmopolitanism is the benevolent face of capitalism.[38] Dipesh Chakrabarty, Carol Breckenridge, Homi K. Bhabha and Sheldon Pollock write: "Cosmopolitans of today are victims of modernity, failed by capitalism's upward mobility, and bereft of those comforts and customs of national belonging."[39]

Dharmyug embodied cosmopolitanism in distinct ways. Its brand of middlebrow cosmopolitanism geared toward promoting a strong sense of belonging in the home and the world, not only through its simultaneous inhabiting of literary and intellectual cultures of the local and the global but, more strategically, also in the *ways* it appeared familiar and nonthreatening to its readers. *Dharmyug* espoused a specific form of cosmopolitan cultural and literary imaginary that promoted two impulses central to the post-independence middlebrow formation: first, fulfilling the consumer's "need to know," that is, the need to accumulate and derive pleasure from a vast variety of literary and nonliterary material through, second, a very essential aesthetic mandate, that is, making the material accessible by basing it in the affective or emotional. Making itself highly aspirational yet approachable, *Dharmyug* took its readers along for the ride. It did so by breaking barriers between literary and nonliterary genres, placing them side by side, whetting readers' appetite to know a range of topics both home and abroad, and grounding its writing in the emotional.

But no cosmopolitanism appears without its exclusions. As other travel pilgrimage essays show, this logic of "at home" in the world had strong foundations in a Hindu idea of home. In this context, another travel piece, titled "Dancing Dervishes" ("Nachne wale darvesh") appearing close on the heels of essays on American life, deserves attention.[40] Written by Jamir Husain Kazmi, this article is significant because it discusses a different religion than Hinduism. Again, photographs lie at the center of the photo essay that focuses on the Sufi dervishes from Lebanon. The subheading of the article itself begins metaphorically, "You must have heard about the cruel naked dance of Lebanon crushing Arab nationalism in the newspapers, but the article presented here talks about how the dancing dervishes are living in very bad conditions."[41] This subhead represents the only time that the article mentions the political event itself. Centered around the cultural practice of the dance, the author explains extensively how dervishes dance in circular motions, also describing the ceremonies surrounding the dance itself. Given the Hindu context and overall tenor of the magazine, this photo essay can be seen as a divergence. However, the form of Islam shown is Sufi Islam, and the country mentioned is Lebanon, not India. And while the two travel articles focusing on America celebrated similarities between India and America, this piece appears to do the opposite: it exoticizes Lebanon, separating it from the cultural and religious Islam that Indian readers would be familiar with. It could be that the unfamiliarity, in turn, creates distance that allows readers to experience pleasure in knowing about a religious-cultural practice that can pass for a purely cultural or even spiritual practice. This representation is borne out by Nile Green's study of Sufism in the 1950s: "In India, certain forms of Sufism (particularly the musical performances and ecumenical shrines of the Chishti brotherhood) were promoted as tolerant forerunners of the multi-confessional secular Indian republic, with their festivals receiving coverage on national television and their history being championed by university teachers."[42] Sufism, therefore, was the "acceptable" face of Islam, and just as Sufi festivals were covered on television, the dance of the dervishes found space in the pre-Bharti *Dharmyug*.

DHARMVIR BHARTI PRE-*DHARMYUG*: LIFE AND TIMES

Before Dharmvir Bharti was *Dharmyug*'s editor, he was one of the most prolific and experimental Hindi writers of the 1950s. His novel *Gunahon Ka Devta* (*The God of Crimes*), published in 1949, is one of the most popular Hindi novels to date.[43] Bharti arguably produced the more celebrated of his modernist writing in the period between 1950 and 1955.[44] *Suraj ka Satva Ghora* (*The Seventh Horse of the Sun*) was published in 1952, and in 1954, he wrote a play called *Andha Yug* (*The Blind Age*), which quickly became a modern classic.[45] Bharti was a celebrated member of Parimal (Fragrance), a literary group in Allahabad that, at its inception, comprised twenty-one core members. Parimal has been loosely defined as a "an alternative to Indian Progressivism."[46]The writer Keshav Chandra Verma, a member of Parimal, remembers that he chose to disassociate himself from the

Progressives because "the Communist Party of India only took steps after looking at what China and Russia decided."[47] It was a group that, as Diana Dimitrova notes, "sought to unite the purposefulness of literature relevant to the Progressivist discourse with more freedom of expression. They were open towards western thoughts and literature and interested in experimenting with new techniques."[48] The Parimal group was well regarded and held over four hundred public literary gatherings over the twenty-five years of its existence. Bharti often participated in the gatherings and read his work to other writers and listeners. Apart from him, other prominent members included Sachchidananda Hirananda Vatsyayan "Agyeya," Prabhakar Machve, and Jagdish Gupta. Most of these authors wrote for *Dharmyug* during Bharti's editorship.

To edit *Dharmyug*, Bharti not only moved from his close social and writerly milieu in Allahabad to the more dispersed one of Bombay, where the Times Group was and still is headquartered, but more important, he also refocused his energies on being an editor rather than a writer. Why did he choose to move away from Allahabad in the first place? Bharti was a lecturer at the Allahabad University and possibly dissatisfied with his position. In his recollections of Bharti, Chandrakant Bandivedekar suggests this: "Despite the reading and writing services available at the university, the place was too limited for a person like Bharti—he needed to reach a kind of place where his multifaceted abilities could be put to good use for society. He got this opportunity in the form of *Dharmyug*'s editorship."[49] Some accounts suggest that Bharti left Allahabad to leave a dissatisfactory marriage, which he hints at in an interview: "The biggest reason was this: there were some life circumstances that led me to leave Allahabad and come to Mumbai; it was a painful exercise for me."[50] In her turn, Bharti's first wife wrote about their marriage and his mistreatment of her.[51]

Parimal, the very literary milieu that Bharti emerged from, was possibly a (major) third reason. Parimal focused on prayogvād, that is, "experimentalism," as an alternative to pragativad, "progressivism." This often led to discord within the group, and Parimal repeatedly came under fire from groups of writers who wished to straddle both grounds and work between different literary spaces. A common critique from this set was that Parimal and, more particularly, its prominent member "Agyeya," did not allow for such easy crisscrossing. The writer Kamleshwar was particularly scathing in his critique of the group.[52] He derided Parimal as "bookish" (*kitabvadi*), particularly blaming Agyeya and his personal obsessions for the fact that the group as a whole could not "progress" and do other kinds of experimental work with their poetry and fiction. Paradoxically, in his opinion, Parimal, the "experimental" group, ultimately became rigid and unbending in its rules about what it considered experimental in the first place. Kamleshwar wrote extensively about how total control was Agyeya's preferred method of administrating the group: "One person's long existing personal tragedy or misfortune unfortunately became the basis of an epoch for Hindi poetry." According to him, Agyeya entirely controlled the group's direction and narrative. Kamleshwar went as far as to compare Parimal to a group of crabs that, in the characteristic fashion of crabs, held on tightly to other crabs, refusing to let them go. In his opinion, Dharmvir Bharti, too, was held against his will: "According to that tradition, the Parimalvadi crabs particularly grabbed hold of Dr. Bharti's leg and did not let him escape."[53]

Kamleshwar's critique of Agyeya (and Bharti) is derived from experience (one can only guess) but also a fixed perspective of memory. Magazine history tells us other stories. For one, Agyeya's own literary as well as editorial journey was multivaried. In an issue of *Pratik* (Symbol), an influential literary magazine that Agyeya edited from mid-1947 onward, in "an open letter from the editor to the Hindi reader," Agyeya castigated all readers who were not literary,[54] yet a decade later, he would find himself working near Bharti's offices, editing *Dinman*, a Times Group newsweekly.[55]

Bharti also made known his own reservations about Parimal's restrictions. Through *Dharmyug* and outside it, Bharti not only straddled Parimal but also wrote and edited outside its boundaries. *Dharmyug* provided a space for him to engage with literary activity more broadly than would have been possible in Allahabad.[56] Bharti's *Dharmyug* accommodated varied perspectives—literary, experimental, or otherwise. It even became a vehicle through which to broadcast literary gatherings. For instance, the 11 April 1964 issue reported a meeting of Parimal attended by a large variety of writers, focusing on, among many others, Kamleshwar's presence!

While some writers criticized Bharti's decision to become editor of *Dharmyug* as a betrayal of literary ideas, others celebrated it in terms of Bharti's own "sacrifice." The writer Surinder Singh recalled poet Ramdhari Singh, known by his pen name "Dinkar," saying, "It was necessary to sacrifice a writer like Bharti to run a magazine like *Dharmyug*."[57] Prakash Hindustani celebrated Bharti's sacrifice to "his own *sahitya seva*" (service to literature) because of his service to *Dharmyug*.[58] While Bharti did continue to write during his editorship, he gave most of his time to the magazine. And it was a lot of time indeed: Bharti retired from the magazine after having served close to thirty years there. Bharti's close involvement with every aspect of the magazine's editorial process included curating readers' letters: he famously answered every letter written to him by readers.[59]

But this book is not a hagiography. By all accounts, Bharti was not a very pleasant man to work with and as editor was particularly disagreeable to be around. *Dharmyug*'s subeditor Prakash Hindustani writes, "Despite being a litterateur and editor, Dr. Bharti's image remained that of a sadist."[60] Working conditions in the office were apparently so dismal that the employees of the Times Group referred to it as the "cancer ward" of the company. Of his time at *Dharmyug*, writer and editor Ravindra Kaliya wrote scathingly that "the atmosphere at the *Dharmyug* offices was so bad that it was impossible to believe that the most popular weekly of India was being produced here; it felt like we were in a bereavement ceremony for eight hours every day."[61]

Also, investigating Bharti's reasons for joining the magazine would only be telling one side of the story. The Times Group was as invested in furthering Bharti's vision as Bharti was invested in working with them. The success that middlebrow publishing enjoyed in the 1950s was possibly a prominent factor for the group to invite Bharti to Bombay. At the same time, the group was not dependent on only one magazine for its literary presence in Hindi. The magazine *Sarika*, edited by Mohan Rakesh, then Kamleshwar, and later Manmohan Saral, occupied that position in magazines of the Times Group. The group had conceived *Dharmyug* as a popular magazine in the same vein as its English-language *Illustrated Weekly of India*. Therefore, the structural model for the magazine, that is, photo essays, short stories, and miscellaneous articles, remained in place with Bharti's editorship. The content and style, however, changed.

CAMUS, KIERKEGAARD, AND *DHARMYUG*: BHARTI'S MIDDLEBROW COSMOPOLITANISM

The 18 September 1960 issue of the magazine carried an article by prominent young writer Kailash Vajpayi titled "Soren Kierkegaard: The Gradual Killing of the Father and the Birth of Existentialism" ("Soren Kierkegaard: Pita ki kramik hatya aur astitvavaad ka janam"). The article contains a short biography of Kierkegaard before focusing more specifically on his theory of existentialism. Vajpayi references a wide range of philosophers such as Friedrich Hegel, Karl Jaspers, Martin Heidegger, and Jean-Paul Sartre. References to philosophy itself are specific and demanding, but Vajpayi begins by telling the story of the death of Kierkegaard's family members and how that affected him: "1834 marks the saddest year of Kierkegaard's life . . . By the way of feminine love, twenty-one-year-old Kierkegaard had only received love from his mother and sister . . . Their deaths finished it [love] off for him forever."[62] The Hindi terms deployed for this are laden with emotion: "feminine love" is written in the text as *stri ka pyaar*, and "finished it off for him forever" is a literal translation of *hamesha ke liye sampat kar diya*. "Stri ka pyaar" also carries direct connotations to romantic love as *stri* can also mean "one's wife" or "one's woman." So death is linked to romantic failure as well. After narrating

Kierkegaard's life story, Vajpayi continues, "One can find the cool touch of death in many places in Kierkegaard's creations."[63] In this way, the idea of death and the theory of existentialism that lie at the center of the article are mediated by the narrative that focuses on the emotional rationale behind Kierkegaard's theory. Only after readers are made familiar with the personal and historical background of Kierkegaard's life are we invited to read about his theory. At one point, Vajpayi quotes Kierkegaard: "Man is not merely a toy of historical and social powers, but the creator of these powers; he is not merely a slave of reason (*vivek*) and principles (*siddhanta*), but defines them himself; he is completely free."[64] Therefore, although Vajpayi accords a disproportionate amount of space within the article to the rather exaggerated narrative of Kierkegaard's life, he is also quick to move on to the birth of existentialism and the central idea of freedom that Kierkegaard expounds. Readers of the article are provided a taste of high theory, with direct quotations from Kierkegaard. In other words, given the subject matter of the article and the title itself, the text is not an unapproachable one in a way that readers feel intimidated or put off but gently leads readers to what Kierkegaard means by existentialism.

This article exemplifies the middlebrow cosmopolitanism that Dharmvir Bharti promulgated at *Dharmyug*. Much beyond *Dharmyug*, the Hindi publishing world was a vibrant one. Literary journals such as Agyeya's *Pratik* and Sripat Rai's *Kahani* were forerunners in practicing a kind of literary cosmopolitanism that, both through their form, editorial content, and author selection as well as translational practices, promoted transnational alliances and cultural imagination.[65] Pre-Bharti *Dharmyug* also promoted itself as equally being the bastion for high literary and intellectual thought. A prominent section of the magazine, titled Sahitya, or Literature, confirms that self-promotion. For instance, the 3 July 1958 issue that contained the "religious story" also carried a serialized short novel called *Kulta* (Wanton) by the celebrated Nayi Kahani writer Rajendra Yadav. The 1959 issues of *Dharmyug* serialized part of Yashpal's now canonical novel *Untrue Truth* (*Jhootha Sach*).[66] Additionally, the issue also published a regular column called A Literary Diary (Ek Sahityik Diary). The special satire issue published 17 July 1958 well represents this diversity of authors writing for, and being written about in, the magazine. The writer Eklavya wrote one of the essays in this issue titled "Irony in the New Poetry in Hindi" ("Nayi Hindi Kavita mein vyangya"), while Kishore Raman Tandon wrote its Urdu equivalent, "Irony in the New *shayari* in Urdu" ("Urdu ki nayi shayari mein vyangya"). Both essays discussed a diverse and celebrated group of writers from different literary strands and movements: Ali Sardar Jafri, Josh Malihabadi, Raghupati Sahay "Firaq" and Sagar "Nizami" in Urdu and Agyeya, Lakshmikant Verma, Bharatbhushan Agarwal, Nagarjun and Satyendra Srivastava in Hindi. The article on irony in Urdu begins, "Just as there have been revolutionary changes in the world, remarkable changes have also taken place in Urdu poetry."[67] Tandon examines different kinds of satire, the first being produced by dissatisfaction with the newly independent nation overwhelmed by corruption, poverty, and capitalism. The writer quotes the poet Josh Malihabadi:

> *Koi mushtari to avaaz de de*
> *Main kambakht jinse-hunar bechta hu*
>
> If there is a customer, please call out to me
> I, wretched soul, sell my talent.[68]

In another subsection titled "Satire of Progressive poets" ("Pragatisheel shayaron ke vyangya"), the poet Raghupati Sahay, also known as "Firaq Gorakhpuri," is quoted extensively.[69] The article on Hindi satire appears on the page alongside the one on Urdu satire and focuses more specifically on the New Poetry movement (Nayi Hindi Kavita). Agyeya's poetry appears here, including one of his most famous poems:

> *Saanp*
> *Tum sabhya to hue nahi*
> *Nagar mein basna*
> *Bhi tumhe nahi aya!*

Ek baat puchhu—(uttar doge?)
Tab kaise seekha dasna
Vish kahan se aya?

Snake!
You couldn't become civilized
To settle in a town
Too you could not
Can I ask you one thing—(will you answer?)
How did you learn to bite
Where did the poison come from?[70]

A one-page article titled "Four Japanese Poems: A Glance" ("Chaar Japani Kavitayein: Ek Drishtipat"), published in the 30 August 1958 issue, provides a further example of literary writing from the pre-Bharti time period. The four Japanese poems in translation begin with a short introduction of the history of Japanese poetry followed by the poems themselves. These poems are first written in the original Japanese that has been transliterated into Hindi, with the Hindi translation appearing next to the Japanese original. As we saw with the Urdu poetry collections published by Hind Pocket Books, publishing text in transliteration itself is not new. However, a Japanese transliteration is novel. Readers are provided a taste of what the Japanese language *sounds* like. The poems themselves are few and may have only tokenistic value, yet their publication gestures to an awareness of literature outside India, though to a lesser extent than other Hindi literary magazines at the time such as *Kahani* and *Chetna*. The emphasis on readers *hearing* Japanese in the article on Japanese poetry is also indicative of the writer's involved engagement with the material.

These examples of catalogs of various writers, along with excerpts from their work, appearing in the magazine before 1959 shows that *Dharmyug* did have a literary commitment even before Dharmvir Bharti took over the editorial helm of the magazine. Satyakam Vidyalankar, the magazine's previous editor, was not producing a diametrically different magazine from that which Bharti would edit. However, when Bharti was hired as editor, the magazine's religious content was "phased out" in favor of more literary articles, short stories, and poetry. Bharti introduced the readers to global intellectual and literary movements. However, the articles were mediated: here, Kierkegaard's high theory was made inviting through a personal biography focused on familial and romantic loss. This is a cosmopolitanism made accessible and approachable, fulfilling the middlebrow function of the "need to know" as well as conforming to and providing a range of pleasures to readers, similar to ones that we have seen through the range of genres that were on offer at Hind Pocket Books through its home postal service.

The 18 September 1960 article on Kierkegaard also defines the magazine's shift from before Bharti's editorship to the changes he instituted afterward. The article opposes any easy understanding of religion. Although religion is not mentioned by name, the article proposes that freedom could be attained in opposition to *siddhanta* (principles) and *vivek* (rationality). Vajpayi evokes Kierkegaard innovatively, quoting him directly: "A person who does not hate either his father, mother, wife, child, brother, sister, or even so far as himself, can never become my student."[71] By the time this direct speech appears in the text, Kierkegaard is someone whom the readers have come to know through his personal life story and, presumably, to sympathize with. Readers are then told that Kierkegaard's prospective student is one who must know how to hate. By the end of the article, then, readers are supposed to reconcile both ideas and understand the basis of this "hate" that Kierkegaard wants his student to have. The question of existence that this statement poses is useful to see in the light of the other articles on religious belonging under discussion until this time, which, if anything, preached the language of benevolence, devotion, and unconditional love.

The same magazine issue carries an exposition on the Beat Generation in America, this time by another well-known young writer, Prabhakar Machve.[72] Machve's article, simply titled "Prabhakar Machve went among the Beatniks" ("Prabhakar Machve gaye Beatnikon ke beech"), is populated with sketches of the poets and artists from the Beat movement whom Machve meets on his travels in America. The article's tone is markedly different from that on Kierkegaard, which treated the theory of existentialism with gravitas. Machve's article is a satire on the beatniks. For instance, one of the subheadings of the article reads "Ye utpatang kavitayein," or "These nonsensical poems." One (more charitable) interpretation of the word *utpatang* is "absurd," pointing perhaps to the tradition of absurdism that the Beat Generation poets Machve meets, as well as Machve himself, may be familiar with.[73] However, as shown in the first, more obvious translation of "utpatang," the poems are also nonsensical. This ambiguous meaning—nonsensical or absurd—is reflected in Machve's description of a visit to a beatnik's house where they showed him an art installation, a *pinjra* (cage) denoting *manushya ki sthiti* (the human condition). While Machve does not mock the installation itself, he does mock the manner in which people are debating about where to place it: "The poor cage was moved around in all eight directions" ("bechara pinjra athon dishaon se ulta pulta gaya").[74] Thus articles concerning literary or intellectual movements in *Dharmyug* are not always discussed in terms of veneration or even plain information to the readers. The writer chooses to present both sides of the beatniks to readers, with a literary style that already picks a position: their poetry can be interesting at times, but some beatniks deserve our mockery. The lighthearted tone of the article again exemplifies the magazine's middlebrow cosmopolitanism in that it offers an approachable and pleasurable route to "world" literature that adds to readers' knowledge.

Another type of article that Bharti immediately instituted was an overview of literary personalities in two parts: through a bibliography enumerating their works, as well as a literary biography or a critical introduction stating their importance within a larger literary history. One such article, "Camus and His Meaningful Literature" ("Camus aur uska sarthak sahitya"),[75] written by the Hindi scholar Dr. Ramswarup Chaturvedi, lists Albert Camus's works along with their years of publication. Unlike in the case of Kierkegaard or the Beat Generation poets, Camus's biography itself was not important to the article. Rather, the article's author solely focuses on his literary work. The first part of the article is indeed a catalog of Camus's works, but that is not its only function. Chaturvedi also goes on to subjectively analyze and recommend the writer to the readers, asking them to start reading him if they have not done so already. At the end of the article, Chaturvedi admits to the difficulty of reading Camus but also states the pleasures that will be made available to the reader after undertaking such an onerous task: "To read Camus is definitely a feeling, that feeling which cannot be forgotten. You might forget his narratives and characters, and it is not as if the count of these is a lot, but the effect of the creation will remain with you, it is so complete and comprehensive that one can hardly begin to analyze it."[76] Therefore, the importance of reading him is romanticized: Chaturvedi emphasizes the *difficulty* of Camus, but the readers are encouraged to engage with him *nevertheless*. Moreover, readers are told that part of the pleasure of reading Camus lies in its sheer difficulty but the feeling derived from such a reading will be priceless. I understand this promise as another attribute of the middlebrow where, as we saw in the second chapter on Hind Pocket Books, readers want to know and expand their understanding of literature through their dependence on the "list." Here, Chaturvedi provides this author "list" to the reader and assures the reader of the future pleasure and satisfaction in anticipation of the difficulty in reading and deciphering the text because of the subsequent benefits that will accrue from it. However, the pleasure derived from the difficulty of reading is an aspect that is infrequently encountered in the middlebrow magazines and paperbacks of the time period, given that the emphasis is on ease of access.

While these articles can be seen as a sign of both insertion of literature debates as well as critical writing within the space of the commercial magazine as a result of Bharti's own intellectual interests, the range of articles offered by the magazine again complicates this narrative. For instance, "The Miracle of Makeup" ("Make up ka chamatkar"), immediately followed the essay published on Kierkegaard. The ease of placement of one following the other serves as another example of the middlebrow because Kierkegaard and Camus are rendered easy and accessible while makeup is ennobled through historical discussion. "The miracle of makeup" carries photographs of many contemporary female actors as well as historical examples of makeup, such as murals of women doing makeup in the ancient city of Khajuraho. The article does not delineate techniques of how to apply good makeup but talks instead about the history of makeup in India: "The tradition of makeup is not new to India."[77] There is, however, one photograph inserted in the bottom left corner of the page that does not belong to the Indian subcontinent but is easily identifiable as an image from Egypt: a bust of the Egyptian queen Nefertiti. To this effect, the article explains that makeup indeed has a "very long" history outside India where Egyptian women colored their lips and eyes, including the queen.[78] So, the magazine in the Bharti period also catered to topics such as makeup but, rather than providing readers the tools or recommendations on how to apply it, discussed instead a longer, more historical underpinning or grounding.

TRAVELS TO THE WORLD, TRAVELS TO THE MOON

Travel writing and photo essays were central to *Dharmyug* even after the editorial shift. The 10 July 1960 issue, for instance, was a "travel special," with one section dedicated to travel pieces. It carried articles on the art of Kangra, titled "Monsoon Clouds: Artworks in Kangra style" ("Aashaar ke badal: Kangra kalam ki kalakriti"); a description of a romantic evening in Venice, titled "A Sad Evening in Venice" ("Venice ki ek udaas shaam"); photographs from the island of Sri Lanka titled "Sri Lanka's paper flowers" ("Sihal dweep ke kagazi phool"); a travel narrative from Fiji titled "Fiji and its naked country" ("Fiji aur uska nanga desh"); and finally, a story essay on Varanasi, "City of Benares: A different style" ("Sheher Banaras: Dusra Pehlu"). Continuing the earlier tradition, these diverse travel narratives attuned the readers of *Dharmyug* to imagine themselves as a part of this larger global cultural landscape. The middlebrow imagination extended beyond the local to the global, mediated by an emphasis on the affective quality of the articles, so that the reader-traveler would feel at home in destinations near as well as far.

What was specifically exciting about these travels was that this was the first time in the history of commercial Hindi magazine publication that such a massive audience base could read debates and reports that were expressly commissioned and written for them. The two articles on America discussed as part of the pre-Bharti *Dharmyug* were written anonymously. Bharti's articles were usually not translated from other languages or other magazines; in most instances, the editor expressly commissioned them.[79] In an interview, Bharti said: "With a bit of courage [*himmat*], I made *Dharmyug* become a magazine bent towards the literary as well as the intellect . . . When the magazine started doing well [*chal nikli*], I put in knowledge, science, everything. I got a report specially written from America about man landing on the moon."[80] Bharti's report on the moon was a feat he felt was worth mentioning. And it was. Much has been written on the "cut and paste" style of journals where they borrowed freely from other journals. This method, very common in the late nineteenth and twentieth centuries, built ease of access, national and transnational solidarities, even slowing and speeding reading practices. In the South Asian context, in a study of M. K. Gandhi's newspaper *Indian Opinion*, Isobel Hofmeyr argues that the "cut and paste" style facilitated what she calls "slow reading," where the "cut and paste" articles gathered from multiple sources encouraged contemplating the reading material rather than quickly scanning the news item.[81]

In the case of *Dharmyug*, the editor rejected these forms of borrowing. Rather than being a reprint of another magazine article from somewhere else, Bharti commissioned the article "specially written from America about man landing on the moon." This may seem minor at the level of content, because content can be collated at the level of commissioning or "borrowing" reports from other publications. However, this *non*-borrowing was one of *Dharmyug*'s selling points: Hindi could travel, Hindi had arrived.

GENRE IN THE TIME OF WAR

Readers traveled far and wide in the magazine, made possible through specific genres, such as the travel essay, literary biography, translated short stories, and the like. However, as we saw in the case of American travel essays, these genres also displayed and activated clear political affiliations. If the late 1950s focused on travels to America, choosing a firm position in the long Cold War, the early 1960s were occupied by another war, the Sino-India war in 1962. The Sino-Indian War was marked by the deployment of a very special genre in *Dharmyug*: that of the *satya katha*, or "true story." The "true stories," as per their name, promised facts about a variety of topics and events. Indeed, the column covered a wide-ranging set of topics: exposés on the construction of dams on the Moon ("Can dams be made on the Moon?"/"Kya Chandrama mein pull banaye ja rahe hain?");[82] covering firsthand accounts of a pilot who flew wild animals on his plane (seasonably titled "Elephants in an airplane flying over the North Pole"/"Uttari Dhruv par Hawaai Jahaz mein Hathi");[83] and even tracing the success of the Beatles.[84]

The column first began on 1 December 1962, inaugurated by the essay "Nehruji's birth anniversary and China's strange gift" ("Nehruji ki varshaganth aur Chin ka vichitra upahar"). The writer, listed as Mukta Raje, declared, "In this issue we are starting a new series of true stories, inaugurated by [exposing] the mysterious conspiracy behind China's unlawful attack on India." The choice of the words "mysterious conspiracy" (*rahasmaya shadyantra*) is telling: the opening words offered both a clinical blow-by-blow reconstruction of this attack and also promised its readers mystery and intrigue. The introduction continued: "Such thrilling events will be explicated which very few people possess the knowledge of." Again, Raje's use of vocabulary is striking: "thrilling events" (*romanchak ghatanaon*) borrows from an already established genre of *romanch*, or "thrill," found in lowbrow magazines, which is the prime focus of chapter four. Here, nationalism is sensationalized.[85]

The writer of the satya katha columns was given as Mukta Raje, a pseudonym: the author was, in fact, Pushpa Bharti, Dharmvir Bharti's wife, who wrote these articles. Ostensibly commissioned specifically by Bharti to write this column, Pushpa Bharti's sensational "true" stories presented themselves as snappy, provocative, declamatory one pagers that left their readers gasping for more: the column always ended with a brief preview of what was to come in the next issue.[86] The satya katha, in turn, was a primary example of where Bharti *did* actually allow for a "cut and paste" style. Pushpa Bharti found these true stories from a variety of sources. What was common to them was her writing style: stories were divided into several sections, each of which ending with a question, with titillating descriptions of its protagonists, specifically focusing on female protagonists. A column, for instance, was provocatively titled "The current conflict between Morocco and Algeria and the Beauty of a Mysterious Palace" ("Morocco aur Algeria ka vartman sangharsh aur rahasyamaye mahal ki sundari"). The "beauty" here referred not to the palace but a beautiful woman who lived there.

It was this genre of the true story that inhabited these varied discourses, which in turn became fixated on covering Chinese spies and spying during the Sino-Indian War. A common theme that emerged across issues was the emphasis on the lives of female Chinese spies. The *satya katha* of the 24 March 1963 issue carried the provocative headline "Communist China's new business—export of beautiful spies?" The article begins with a "previous story": "You may not know that for the past ten years, Communist China has been exporting beautiful girls in large quantities." These girls ostensibly traveled to all corners of the world in the form of brides for unmarried Chinese men, collected military and business secrets, and sent them back to China. This article focused specifically on individual women, naming them as well as publishing their photographs. The implications of focusing on these female spies for the genre are manifold: the author wrote these stories like detective tales, tracing these girls as they left China to make their way into other cities in the world. In the article, these spies do not have conversations with just a faceless state: for readers' voyeuristic interest, their love stories with their husbands are also penned. A section of the *satya katha* describes the first meeting between a spy "most beautiful, with a tight and well-developed body," and her husband, where the husband is equal parts mesmerized and stupefied that he has the good fortune to be this girl's husband.[87]

The intrigue built over these spies continues: the essay ends with a teaser for the next issue: "Now let's go to Kaula Lumpur, the capital of Malaysia, where Irene Ho had spread a horrifying (bhayanak) web of intrigue (jasoosi)."[88] In this manner, the true story as genre featured the affective qualities of thrill, intrigue, titillation, and fast-paced action but also promised its readers certainty: this was the truth, it had happened; however, in its knowability, it could be rationalized and contained.

THE AGE OF DHARMVIR BHARTI (OR WAS IT?)

Dharmyug's journey from being beloved for its religious calendar art, to being celebrated in as one of the "high intellectual" magazines read so widely that it, in many senses, "saved" literature, requires further consideration. Although the literary bastion spoke of Bharti's "sacrifices" for the prosperity of literature, this shift in *Dharmyug* can also be read from the logic of commerce. Middlebrow magazines need to be studied in terms of shifting ideologies but through the lens of the commercialist logic of profit making. It made sense for the Times Group to alter the magazine's content because it also did well for them *economically*.

It is difficult to establish a simple cause-and-effect relationship between Bharti's appointment and the group's financial gain. We cannot, for instance, discount Bharti's cultural mileage that the publishers deployed freely. In addition to his duties as editor, the group also depended on him for managing the Jnanpith, their annual literary award.[89] According to memoirs and personal accounts, however, Bharti himself was deeply invested in this process of making

Dharmyug a commercial success. Talking about his days working for Bharti at *Dharmyug*, Prakash Hindustani noted, "More than the prestige of reporting, Bharti was worried about Bennett, Coleman and Company's money." Bharti is frequently mentioned in literary histories as being a difficult person to work with because of his heavy-handed micromanagement. Hindustani wrote, "He [Bharti] would create such conditions that not only editorial assistants but clerical staff too would be terrified of him."[90] In his memoirs dedicated specifically to recounting his times at the magazine, Bharti's subeditor Kanhaiyalal Nandan mentions that his job was limited to merely shortlisting choices of articles for the upcoming issues and that the overall decision was always taken by Bharti.[91] Bharti would prepare the magazine in advance of publication if he needed to go somewhere in the days during the printing and setting.[92]

Other editors spoke of Bharti's deep commitment to adhering to management's restrictions and guidelines. Ravindra Kaliya, another subeditor at the magazine, noted that while *Dharmyug* reached literary heights, "The process of 'marvarikaran' had slowly begun." According to Kaliya, "marwarikaran," or the Marwari-ization of the magazine, meant that a "seth," loosely translated in this context as a Marwari businessman, could not be represented as an exploiter in the magazine. In his memoir, Kaliya wryly noted, "The editorial department would keep getting such instructions. One did not know if the editor himself had set these regulations or he got these instructions from somewhere. The English departments were free from these frustrations."[93] Of his time working at the magazine, Manmohan Saral wrote of the rift between another subeditor, Kanhaiyalal Nandan, and Bharti, where the former even ran a signature campaign against him in a bid to improve the work conditions at the magazine.[94]

Contextualized further from the viewpoint of the group's management at large, *Dharmyug*, one of the many Hindi magazines published by the Times Group—prominent of which was the more literary magazine *Sarika*—while paying its editors and writers well, was not on a par with English magazines. Nandan recalls a meeting, led by Mohan Rakesh, of all Hindi editors of *Sarika* from 1962 to 1963, called to discuss a raise in their salaries. Disappointed by the disparity in salaries between employees working for English- and Hindi-language publications, the Hindi editors wrote a letter requesting an audience with the Sahu Jain family, owners of the group. Nandan recalls how all the editors were flown from Bombay to Calcutta at the company's expense to meet Shanti Prasad Jain, the proprietor, so as to register their protest and demand a salary raise. However, once everyone was gathered, Jain refused to negotiate with the editors. After the refusal, only Rakesh resigned from his position in protest.[95] Although this story is little more than an anecdotal reference in Nandan's memoirs, it is significant to note that the Times Group also invested in *Dharmyug,* financing travel trips for its writers and editors. The magazine straddled journalistic ground in this manner, where its own subeditors were sent to various locations and commissioned to write about their travels abroad. For instance, Manmohan Saral, another editor under Dharmvir Bharti, traveled to London, Paris, the Soviet Union , America, Scandinavia, Netherlands, and Germany while under the employment of the magazine.[96] The editor and the group were in constant negotiation, sometimes accommodating, sometimes rejecting concerns. In this way, the cosmopolitan middlebrow world of *Dharmyug* came alive.

CONCLUSION

This chapter differs from others in this book in one fundamental way: it does not focus on the short fiction that *Dharmyug* published with the same concentration, instead being structured around the magazine before and after Dharmvir Bharti became editor. I concentrate on Bharti as editor, placing him squarely as an actor in a dynamic commercial publishing market. Returning to the first chapter where I discussed Vishwa Nath's role in *Sarita,* if one compares Vishwa Nath and Bharti as editors, it might appear that I argue for an editor-cum-publisher (Vishwa Nath) in opposition to, or in comparison with, an editor (Bharti) appointed by a commercial enterprise, who not only is disconnected from the publishing business but is also a well-established modernist writer. However, the picture that ultimately appears for Dharmvir Bharti is this: he was as connected to the publishing process as was the family-run publishing enterprise itself, mediating style of the content for the readers. Crucially, we see how, for the Times Group, this content made commercial sense: quite simply, it yielded larger circulation and revenue. Thus I create a larger conversation in terms of commercial publishing history in the post-independence period, engaging in a dialogue not only with intellectual and literary ideologies of commercially successful magazines but also, crucially, with market concerns. Commercial middlebrow magazines of the 1950s and 1960s question easy divisions between "literariness" and "marketability."

The next chapter further complicates the history of commercial publishing that I have examined thus far by introducing another element to the story: that of lowbrow publishing. I study three magazines—*Maya* (Magic), *Rasili Kahaniyaan* (Juicy Stories), and *Manohar Kahaniyaan* (Pleasing Stories) to discuss the characteristics and themes of conflict that middlebrow magazines from the time period excluded from their pages.

CHAPTER FOUR

Romanch and the 1950s

The World of Genre Magazines

While three chapters in this book focus on Delhi (*Sarita* and Hind Pocket Books) and Bombay (*Dharmyug*) as prominent midcentury publishing centers, the story of post-independence publishing in Hindi would be incomplete without situating Allahabad as a publishing location. As the capital of the United Provinces of Agra and Oudh (later named the United Provinces and current day Uttar Pradesh) until 1920, Allahabad functioned as a major colonial administrative hub. Located only some hours away from Varanasi, Allahabad was also an important Hindu pilgrimage center and a key nucleus of Hindi publishing.[1] A rich history of literary and nationalist publishing is inextricably tied to Allahabad's Indian Press. It published the Hindi monthly *Saraswati*, which, under Mahavir Prasad Dwivedi's editorship, arguably set the tone for the standardization of *khari boli* (upright tongue) as Hindi.[2] Other journals, *Grihalakshmi* (Wealth of the home), *Stridarpan* (Woman's mirror), and *Chand* (Moon), also flourished within the city. Allahabad was a significant Hindi literary center in the 1940s and 1950s, with several leading modernist and progressive writers living, writing, and thriving there.[3]

This chapter sheds light on another rich and dynamic aspect of Allahabad's publishing history: as a center of popular publishing and genre fiction. Here, I focus on *Maya* (Magic), *Rasili Kahaniyaan* (Juicy stories), and *Manohar Kahaniyaan* (Pleasing stories) published by the enormously successful Mitra Prakashan and Maya Press. Mitra Prakashan and Maya Press, established by K. M. Mitra and his brother-in-law B. N. Ghosh for publishing and printing works, respectively, put out several enormously popular genre fiction standalone titles under its two series. Titled the "Manohar Series" and "Maya Series," respectively, they were often advertised together and included a range of novels and short story collections. Priced at twelve annas per book, offerings were as diverse as anyone's literary imagination could be: the series sold the classic nineteenth-century Urdu novel *Umrao Jaan Ada*, the nineteenth-century British novel *David Copperfield*, as well as novels by well-known contemporary writers: among them Khwaja Ahmed Abbas's *Andhera Ujala* (The shadowy light), which, as its advertisement promised, "will show you the true picture [vastavik chitra] of cinema," and Bhairav Prasad Gupta's short story collection *Farishta* (Angel), which "will encourage/stimulate healthy entertainment alongside advancing life and developing character." However, celebrating (or even revealing) authorship was not the case with all novels. For instance, some were advertised without author names but promised thrills: a novel titled *Yam ki Chhaya* (The shadow of yama) guaranteed "mystery and romance" (*rahasya aur romance*), *Doctor Shekhar* was billed as a "thrilling detective novel" (*romanchkari jasoosi upanyas*), and *Maut ki Malka* (Mistress of death) stressed that "the novel is as thrilling as the book's name is terrifying."[4]

The three magazines—*Maya*, *Rasili Kahaniyaan*, and *Manohar Kahaniyaan*—from these houses were ephemeral periodicals, with a few extant copies still existing. Ironically, I found them while thumbing through copious volumes of periodical records at Allahabad's Hindi Sahitya Sammelan (Society for Hindi Literature), an institution that prides itself on promoting Hindi as national language and, accordingly, carries precious manuscripts, nationalist papers, and other periodicals.[5] There, in between numerous visits, electricity cuts, mandatory termite treatments, and the helpful, nonjudgmental assistance of spectacular library staff, I read through many bound volumes of these magazines, meticulously preserved against the ravages of time.[6] We can only guess at the years these magazines were first published. One thing is definite: the publishing house and press were in business much before this, especially *Maya,* which ran (in a different, more literary form) for decades before I pick up the story in the 1940s.[7] The publishing house and printing press, too, have since closed. Subject to heavy litigation, the family rarely makes any public statements or gives interviews. Some clues do help us construct a partial story of beginnings. Litigation documents reveal that Mitra Prakashan and Maya Press were established as private limited companies in 1953.[8] According to Audit Bureau of Circulation records, *Maya* and *Manohar Kahaniyaan* certainly flourished, with circulation figures ranging between 41,000 and 60,000 subscribers throughout the 1950s.[9] Matching *Dharmyug*'s 1960 circulation figures, *Manohar Kahaniyaan* peaked its decadal circulation figures at an enviable 65,000 subscribers in 1959.[10]

Manohar Kahaniyaan matched *Dharmyug*'s circulation figures, but neither it nor *Maya* and *Rasili Kahaniyaan* were middlebrow publications. Until here, my focus has been middlebrow publishing, but in this chapter I examine the publication of genre fiction, an equally significant segment. Through a close reading of short stories, I find that these magazines facilitated conversations that middlebrow magazines often either ignored or did not address. Indeed, Hindi middlebrow magazines' primary emphasis on aspirational narratives meant that they also ignored other central questions: poverty and unemployment, poor living conditions and the lack of privacy, fissures drawn across religious belonging, desire and the pressures of the joint family. *Maya, Rasili Kahaniyaan,* and *Manohar Kahaniyaan* actively aired these fears, desires, and complex realities that emerged from post-1947 Indian individual and social experiences. Using fear and uncertainty to peg their stories, these magazines unsettled readers' expectations and, wittingly or unwittingly, unraveled the aspirational narratives we have witnessed thus far. In a way, by challenging the middlebrow aesthetic that concentrated on aspiration and consumption, genre magazines carried short stories that provided alternative moral universes to readers.

At the same time, to propose that these alternative moral universes were set to achieve specific or ostensible political intentions of publishers, editors, or writers would be to, perhaps, oversell and in doing so underrepresent this world. However, these short stories exposed fears and insecurities: of domesticity that led not to an ideal resolution but rather to an alienation and unhappiness; of the inability to achieve the privacy of domestic or married life in a very public, crowded domestic space such as the chawl; of the problem of licensing and rationing that affected the people standing in the long ration queues; and of the difficulty of resolving Hindu-Muslim suspicions after the cataclysmic events of the Partition. These were tangible concerns affecting the post-independence Indian population. Shortages and rationing of food and cloth were some of the major problems the new nation faced. Developmental policies immediately following 1947 depended on the citizens' duty to support the nation's food development goals, where, Benjamin Siegel shows, "the new state urged its citizens to give up rice and wheat, whose imports sapped the nation of the foreign currency needed to forward a plan of industrial development."[11] Taylor C. Sherman focuses on the "Grow More Food" campaign that pushed the "developmentalist" argument of growing food further, in which "the Indian National Congress party and opposition groups were torn over the question of whether development ought to be pursued using the newly acquired instruments of the bureaucracy or through the old mechanisms of popular action outside of the state."[12] In addition to food and other scarcity, another concern was the trauma from the carnage of the Partition and the inability to write about it. With the passing of the Special Marriage Act in 1954 and the Hindu Marriage Act in 1955, marriage remained one of the hotly debated institutions in the 1950s.[13]

The magazines under consideration recognized that everyday citizens—who were their readers and consumers—felt these questions palpably. They employed varied genres such as detective fiction, melodramatic romances, thrillers and mysteries, ghost and horror stories, and what I call "fictions of melodramatic poverty," that is, stories in which narratives of poverty were laden with pathos and other heightened emotions that made the reader sympathize with the plight of the impoverished character. Short stories in these magazines employed such techniques as hyperbolic language, melodrama, and fast-paced action and plotting, often featuring extramarital affairs, numerous murders, and sharp shifts in the protagonists' fortunes. At first glance, it might seem that these peculiar formal elements and characteristics undermine the point of the whole story. However, Derek Littlewood and Peter Stockwell's frame of "affective genres," which "classify the emotional response or affect," provides a convincing critical counterpoint.[14] Affective genres, that is, the very way in which these stories were written, were conducive to raising serious worries and uncertainties that, perhaps, could not be aired otherwise.

I propose *romanch* as the frame through which we can better and more comprehensively understand the functions performed by these stories. The dictionary definition of "romanch" suggests the "curl or thrill of the body hair" and "thrill (of ecstasy or of horror)" which relates to feelings of "dread but excitement."[15] This affective duality of "dread but excitement" is paramount to understanding romanch's function. The romanch in these stories expresses physical feelings resulting from unpleasant emotions of fearful uncertainty, which, because of the way it is represented, also provides the pleasurable feeling of excitement. Romanch, in short, is the fearful excitement arising from the nonrestoration of a moral universe. The stories in *Maya, Rasili Kahaniyaan*, and *Manohar Kahaniyaan* provided readers with thrilling plot twists, depictions of criminality within the domestic space, the excitement of dabbling with the ghostly, the horrific, and the unknown. Yet, at the same time, the romanch also arose because readers would not meet with a satisfactory resolution at the end of the narrative. In other words, the physical reaction of romanch, of the thrill that comes from "curl or thrill of the body hair," hair standing on end, helped temper the dread arising from the very real, social, psychological concerns that were not aired in other ways in the lowbrow magazines—and not at all in middlebrow magazines.

STRUCTURE AND GENRES

In the third chapter, we saw a hierarchy in production quality between *Dharmyug* and *Sarita*. Comparable to the paper quality of Hind Pocket Books paperbacks, *Maya, Rasili Kahaniyaan,* and *Manohar Kahaniyaan* were printed on particularly poor-quality newsprint paper (*lugdi*). This difference is even more visible in the quality of photographs. While *Dharmyug*'s full-page glossy photographs were attractively spread out over many pages, in contrast, apart from the cover page (and even that, sparingly), these magazines carried no photographs at all. What these publications *did* carry in profusion were sketches. Consider a lugdi magazine with sketches vis-à-vis a glossy magazine with photographs and high-quality chromolithographs: Could this have specific connotations in terms of the magazines' material consumption? *Dharmyug* was most definitely a collectible object, and its many full-length photographs and chromolithographs of the gods could possibly adorn the home. On the other hand, did the paper quality here signal that these magazines were meant to be instantly disposable? The other lugdi book object, Hind Pocket Books paperbacks, were saved from this fate through their heavy emphasis on creating a library. Unfortunately, no reader responses could be gleaned to substantiate the afterlife of these magazines.

Another revealing difference lies in magazine structures. Although middlebrow magazines fashioned themselves as digests offering a range of nonfiction and fiction pieces that extended to all members of the family, *Maya, Rasili Kahaniyaan,* and *Manohar Kahaniyaan* did not carry multiple offerings, editorials, or even readers' letters. Anything apart from stories was expunged. Space was clearly at a premium: most issues did not even carry a table of contents on a separate page, choosing instead to fit it at a corner of the first page (see figure 8). Short stories were the beginning and end of these magazines' repertoire.

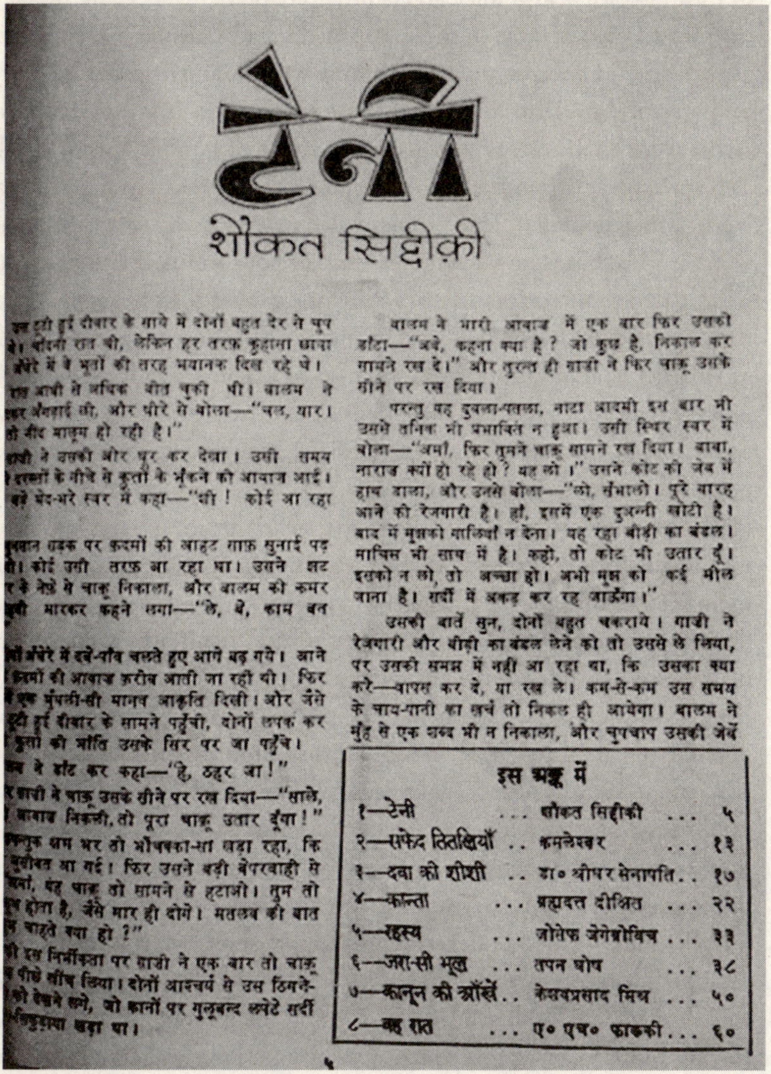

टेनी

शौकत सिद्दीक़ी

बालम ने भारी आवाज़ में एक बार फिर उसको डाँटा—"अबे, कहना क्या है? जो कुछ है, निकाल कर सामने रख दे।" और तुरन्त ही गाज़ी ने फिर चाकू उसके सीने पर रख दिया।

परन्तु वह दुबला-पतला, नाटा आदमी इस बार भी उससे तनिक भी प्रभावित न हुआ। उसी स्थिर स्वर में बोला—"अमाँ, फिर तुमने चाकू सामने रख दिया। बाबा, नाराज़ क्यों हो रहे हो? यह लो।" उसने कोट की जेब में हाथ डाला, और उससे बोला—"लो, सँभालो। पूरे बारह आने की रेजगारी है। हाँ, इसमें एक दुअन्नी खोटी है। बाद में मुझको गालियाँ न देना। यह रहा बीड़ी का बंडल। माचिस भी साथ में है। कहो, तो कोट भी उतार दूँ। इसको न लो, तो अच्छा हो। अभी मुझ को कई मील जाना है। सर्दी में अकड़ कर रह जाऊँगा।"

उसकी बातें सुन, दोनों बहुत चकराये। गाज़ी ने रेजगारी और बीड़ी का बंडल लेने को तो उससे ले लिया, पर उसकी समझ में नहीं आ रहा था, कि उसका क्या करे—वापस कर दे, या रख ले। कम-से-कम उस समय के चाय-पानी का ख़र्च तो निकल ही आयेगा। बालम ने मुँह से एक शब्द भी न निकाला, और चुपचाप उसकी जेबें

इस अङ्क में

FIGURE 8. Table of Contents, *Manohar Kahaniyaan*, March 1959, Maya Press.

Because paratexts are lacking, the criteria and manner of selection of these stories is also unclear. As other chapters—especially the one on Hind Pocket Books—show, copyright had become a prominent aspect of middlebrow publishing, and writers and translators were duly given copyright credits. In these magazines, it is unclear how rights were obtained for stories from a range of famous authors such as Kamleshwar, Upendranath Ashk, and Saadat Hasan Manto, if they were obtained at all.[16] This problem also reappears when we examine short stories that were published as translations from other languages. More often than not, translators were not credited. At the same time, the presence of esteemed editors at the helm of these magazines, such as Bhairav Prasad Gupta, who went on to become editor of the high literary magazines *Kahani* (Story, 1954) and *Nayi Kahaniyaan* (New Stories, 1959), indicates that rights and prices of stories may have been negotiated with the original writers.

What really sets these magazines apart from others we have met in this book, however, is their range of genres: detective fiction, melodramatic romances, thrillers, mysteries, ghost stories, "weird fiction," and fictions of "melodramatic poverty," that is, where narratives of poverty are laden with pathos and other heightened emotions.[17] Except for melodramatic romance, these genres strictly remained outside the cultural imagination of the middlebrow magazines as well as the Hind Pocket Books series. As we have seen, middlebrow publishing and, subsequently, readership actively allowed for flexible movement, but *only* between highbrow and middlebrow genres. Indeed, only during exceptional moments—and after several explanatory justifications—did middlebrow publishing allow what it ordinarily excluded, as seen in the decision by Hind Pocket Books to publish romance writer Gulshan Nanda.[18] During the period, however, Hind Pocket Books also typically kept detective fiction, thrillers, mysteries, and horror outside its bounds. These were genres that the publisher D. N. Malhotra felt were "limited to action and no substance."[19]

Armed with their heady cocktail of genre fiction, the three magazines I discuss here were not the first periodicals of their kind.

In fact, each genre that blossomed in *Maya*, *Rasili Kahaniyaan*, and *Manohar Kahaniyaan* has its own history of pejorative precedents. Certain terms like *ghasleti* (inflammatory), *ashlil* (vulgar), *sasta* (cheap), *ganda* (dirty), and *lokpriya* (popular) were already associated with genre fiction in Hindi in the late nineteenth and early twentieth centuries.[20] Charu Gupta shows how several genres, such as "erotic sex manuals, popular romances, entertaining songs, texts offering advice on sexual relationships," were often consumed under the overarching discourse of obscenity.[21] These umbrella terms have evolved both out of Hindi publishing and literary history's neglect and derogatory treatment of such literature and literary practices, condemning what was a vibrant, popular book market with its specific "horizon of expectations."[22] Even the less derogatory among these words, like "cheap" or "popular," do not convey the specificity of genre fiction, which constituted the bulk of these magazines.

As previously noted, another crucial point of distinction in genre magazines can be seen in terms of its absences. Readers' voices are largely absent, except for a reader submissions column on true stories called The Moment of Thrill (Romanch ki vo ghari) that I discuss at greater length later in this chapter. Editors, too, did not have a strong presence within the magazines, with editorial comments missing from their pages. This important structural decision gives the impression that the magazines did not (at least actively) encourage readers' comments on short stories and special issues. All these factors give an appearance of surreptitiousness and urgency: magazines produced on quick turnaround and meant for fast consumption.

ADVERTISEMENTS AND THE DEFINITIONAL PARADOX

An advertisement in the March 1955 issue of *Sarita* condemned certain categories of advertisements it termed "vulgar, ugly, and misleading."[23] What these advertisements were, however, the magazine left to readers' imaginations. This assurance, though, enacts yet another point of difference. All magazines studied in this book thrived—both visually as well as financially—on their advertisement spaces. However, stark differences existed in brands and products advertised as well as in the layout of advertisements. *Sarita* and *Dharmyug* featured prominent or full-page advertisements that marketed well-respected and, in most instances, internationally known brands, such as Dettol, Lux, HMV, and Ponds, often featuring prominent actors and actresses or other happy and healthy-looking models and promising readers a successful, invigorating, and unapologetically consumption-oriented life. Through these advertisements, readers kept themselves up-to-date with the latest beauty, health, and skin and hair care products on the market.

By comparison, lowbrow magazines carried text-heavy advertisements. Additionally, products from large brands are missing from the three magazines under consideration. Although they carried some advertisements for beauty products like shampoos and soaps, these were decidedly from comparatively smaller manufacturers, such as the Calcutta Chemical Co. Ltd. (see figure 9). Bigger brands are conspicuously absent. It is unclear whether bigger brands chose

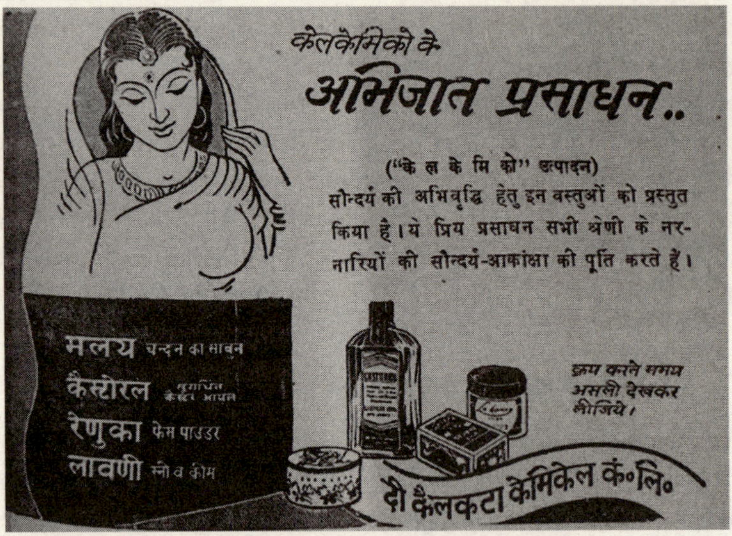

FIGURE 9. Advertisement for the Calcutta Chemical Co. Ltd. *Maya*, April 1952, Maya Press.

not to advertise their products in the lowbrow magazines, or if the publishers themselves chose not to pursue advertisements from them.

Instead, what we do find are full-text advertisements for infertility and children's tonics, advertisements that had been in circulation from the early twentieth century.[24] "For infertile women—an easy solution for giving birth," reads one such advertisement that appears several times in the magazines. In this full-page ad, a certain Ratanbai Jain guarantees "my sisters" that her medication will definitely work. The price for this cure is also listed: a hefty five rupees and twelve annas.[25] In another full-page advertisement that also appears frequently, Prem Pyari Agarwal addresses her "dear sisters" (see figure 10), telling them about how she miraculously found a cure for her irregular menstrual cycle and leukorrhea: "By god's grace I am now the mother of many children", she confidently asserts.

While remedies against infertility comprise the majority of the full-page advertisements, other concerns also appear periodically. Another advertisement, this time for family planning, is titled "Birth control (family planning)." By noting that "Pandit Jawaharlal Nehru, Lady Mountbatten, Shri K. M. Munshi, Shri A. P. Jain (who) have sent letters of appreciation and commendation" to this company for its work, the advertisement boasts of being in line with both colonial and early postcolonial governmental policies as well as public discourse around family planning.[26] Another dominant focus is on tonics to produce healthier and thriving children. One advertisement for such reads: "Faldhara: only strong children can make a bright nation" ("Faldhara: balvan santan hi desh ko ujjval bana sakti hai").[27] Also, the majority of the advertisements themselves are precise and clinical and offer direct solutions to specific problems. In terms of "respectability," then, advertisements in these magazines did not cross boundaries of the illicit, sensual, or sexual. In a sense, the advertisements themselves can be viewed as pseudoscientific manuals focusing predominantly on healthy living and reproductive health.

Despite the emphasis on women's and children's health, no advertisements directly addressed men's (sexual or otherwise)

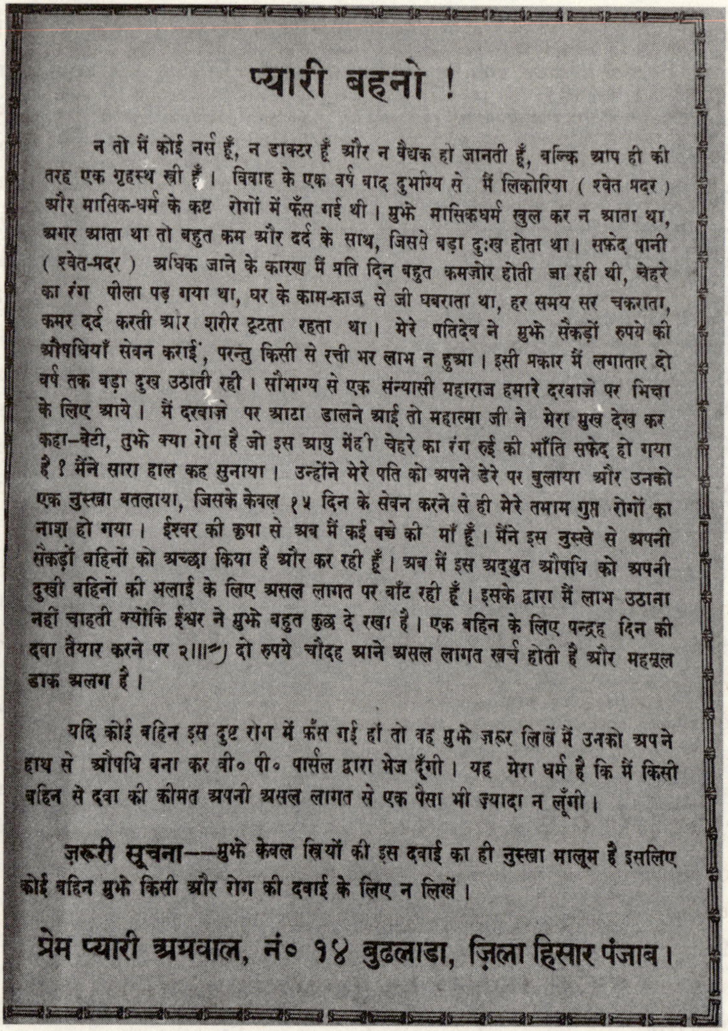

FIGURE 10. "Dear Sisters!" *Rasili Kahaniyaan*, March 1946, Maya Press, 93.

health. Charu Gupta notes that although discourses of the early twentieth century argued for sexual abstinence, restraint, and sex only for procreation, the advertisements set alternative frames: "Advertisements for aphrodisiacs were printed in large numbers in many 'respectable' newspapers and magazines, especially from the early twentieth century . . . [These] whetted the appetite and fantasies of Hindu males, [and] offering unattainable pleasures proved to be extremely popular."[28] Even Agyeya's famed *Pratik* featured what Alok Rai terms "some advertisements for a rather different kind of book," such as promises of "putraprapti ka marg," or the "path to achieve sons."[29] In lowbrow genre magazines, however, men's sexuality or sexual appetite is not invisible: it was definitely an important aspect of the stories themselves. However, the advertisements do not invoke these desires. The focus of the advertisements suggests that the magazine's readership was construed as primarily female.

ROMANCH AND THE SHORT STORY

The stories within the genre magazines stand out in their complex peculiarities, whose constituent formal elements include the spectacle, macabre details, quick turns of events, and frequent murders, with stories often ending in revenge. These genres—detective fiction, melodramatic romance, thrillers and mysteries, horror and fictions of melodramatic poverty—are "affective genres," primarily deployed to arouse an "emotional response or effect."[30] The "emotional response" here is of "romanch," the feeling of dread yet excitement.

I invoke the word "romanch" from the magazines' own vocabulary. *Maya*'s only interactive section titled "Romanch ki vah ghari" (The moment of romanch) asked its readers to narrate stories that made the heart tremble (*dil kamp uthta hai*).[31] As stated earlier, "romanch" translates to the "curl or thrill of the body hair," and the "thrill (of ecstasy or of horror)" relates to feelings of "dread but excitement" (see figure 11).[32] The magazine offered to pay between (a decent) three to (a whopping) fifteen rupees for readers' real-life stories: "Send us a true story from your life in a maximum of forty lines . . . The incidents should be from your own life."[33]

These true-life stories were *romanchak* indeed. A column featured a female reader's entry about how her ex-lover, long dead, appeared in her room the night before she was getting engaged to another man. This ex-lover told her that he had a present for her. This "present" was

रोमांच की वह घड़ी

हर आदमी के जीवन में एक या अधिक ऐसी घटना या दुर्घटना जरूर घटती है, जिसे याद कर दिल कांप उठता है, रोमांच हो आता है। आदमी इन घटनाओं को आजीवन नहीं भूल पाता और मन-ही-मन यह कामना करता रहता है कि कोई वैसी घटना फिर उसके जीवन में ही नहीं, बल्कि दुश्मनों के साथ भी न घटे। इन घटनाओं का हमारे जीवन में कोई-न-कोई महत्व अवश्य होता है, साथ ही इन घटनाओं को पढ़-सुन कर दूसरे भी कुछ सबक सीख सकते हैं। उदाहरण के तौर पर, मान लीजिये, आप कहीं प्रवास पर ठगों के चक्कर में फँस गये या किसी रात अचानक नींद खुलने पर आपने देखा कि आपके घर में चोर घुस आये हैं, या रात को किसी सुनसान जगह में आपने ऐसा कुछ देखा कि आप डर गये—आदि ऐसी सच्ची घटनायें हर आदमी के लिये बहुत दिलचस्प तथा शिक्षाप्रद होती हैं।

ऐसी घटनाओं के लिये हम अगले मास से 'माया' में कुछ पृष्ठ सुरक्षित रखना चाहते हैं। आप अपने जीवन की कोई ऐसी सच्ची घटना अधिक-से-अधिक चालीस पंक्तियों में ठीक-ठीक लिख भेजें। 'माया' के हर अंक में ऐसी कुछ घटनायें हम बराबर छापेंगे और उन पर तीन रुपये से पन्द्रह रुपये तक पुरस्कार भी देंगे। घटनायें आपके अनुभव की ही हों। लिफ़ाफ़े पर आप 'रोमांच की वह घड़ी' जरूर लिख दें।

—सम्पादक

FIGURE 11. "Romanch ki vah ghari," *Maya*, October 1952, Maya Press.

her current fiancé's head that had been severed from his body: "I saw that it contained Kishor's severed head."[34] Horrified, the reader fainted. When she regained consciousness the next day, she found herself surrounded by family members. Her fiancé had indeed died. Another reader recounted the fear she had experienced when, on a hunting expedition, she heard lions circling the tent all night. Describing the dread, the reader wrote, "I shivered. My entire body shuddered. I started sweating."[35] She was terrified of being at the hunting lodge, even more so when she heard an animal scratching under her bed. She screamed, only to find that the animal was a harmless dog.

How do we read these true stories of terror—of a horrible ghostly visit that does come true for the contributing reader, and of a fearful, fretful night with a significantly less fearful ending for the second reader? These conflicting feelings of dread in different forms like fear, terror, uncertainty, and ambiguity that come together in romanch complicate a somewhat simplistic notion of genre as "formula fiction" or "prose of low resolution."[36] Margrit Pernau, Helge Jordheim, Imke Rajamani, and others have argued for the need to historicize emotions, arguing that emotions are not static but rather denote different social and psychological states in different periods.[37] Following from this, rather than merely examining formal aspects of the text and dismissing them as lowbrow, it is far more useful to investigate the range of emotions depicted. Pernau et al. also note that the first disciplines that investigated emotions (albeit in Eurocentric criticism), "foreground the bodily and involuntary reactions which accompany emotions."[38] Romanch as "bodily and involuntary reactions which accompany emotions" provides an important frame, where conflict is only always partially resolved in the narratives, with the story providing no neat solutions. These are, as Steve Neale argues, stories where elements of genres "are always in play rather than simply replayed," occurring across a range of tales.[39]

Women

We can see this take place most poignantly in romanch's treatment of female protagonists. Through these characters, stories often complicate templates of moral resolutions for both the 1950s in general and middlebrow magazines in particular. Take, for instance, the short story "Coffee" ("Kafi"). Written for *Maya* by Vimla Phadke, a writer who is absent from any mainstream literary histories but features frequently in the magazine, "Kafi" opens with a detailed description of Manju, a clerk working in an office. Manju is not only an ordinary-looking woman but also, at the age of thirty, already looks middle-aged: "Her life had no kind of pleasure in it! Her face always seemed to have a kind of weariness. Circumstances had turned her middle-aged before her time."[40] Manju is in love with a fellow clerk named Upendra. He wants to return her affections but cannot because of financial difficulties and familial obligations: first, he has to get his sister married. Lest we settle into the lull of this unrequited romance, the author introduces the first twist in the story: Manju discovers that her deceased grandmother has left her a substantial fortune. Now she is free: she can leave her job and has the means to marry anyone she likes. Manju broaches the subject with Upendra, but he vehemently opposes, not wanting her to think that he would marry her out of greed.

Manju's change in fortunes brings new romance. After Upendra's refusal, she falls in love with Abhay, a photographer. Manju prefers Abhay's flamboyance to Upendra's quiet energy: "One day, he landed up at Manju's home. And just in the next few meetings, he was able to charm Manju. It was as if Abhay knew some magic. Upendra disappeared from Manju's mind, as if she did not even know him." Manju and Abhay get married. What seems like a romantic love triangle turned resolution suddenly takes a sinister turn. While Manju is blissfully in love, Abhay starts controlling her finances. At the same time, Manju starts having recurring dreams of his death: "She would always dream of Abhay's corpse soaked in blood. She would feel that he was calling her with his outstretched, blood-soaked arms and that she was running toward him to be caught in his embrace unhesitatingly . . ."[41] Has a lover's neurosis taken over her dreams? Abhay's moodiness makes Manju even more unsettled, and she suspects him of infidelity.

The story overturns any expectations when Manju decides to search through Abhay's things. What she finds is truly horrifying: her husband is, in fact, not Abhay but a man named Kalicharan. In the past, he has married and murdered countless women, escaping with their inheritance. At this point, a story that presumably started as a melodramatic romantic love triangle suddenly escalates into a fast-paced sensational thriller. From being a happily married woman, Manju is now a betrayed woman terrorized by fear. The narrative shows Manju completely shaken by this knowledge, manifesting the physical sensations associated with romanch: "Her hands and legs swelled up [*hath pair phul gaye*]. Her body started shaking [*uska sharir kampne laga*]."[42]

The readers now follow Manju's attempts at escape. At one point, she manages to run outside the house and then entreats an old man to go fetch Upendra from town—it is unclear where the story is located—so that he can free her from Abhay's grip. Until then, Manju has managed to pretend that she does not know who Abhay really is. Here, readers are wrapped up in the pleasurable knowledge that Manju has a plan that only they, and not Abhay, are aware of, which leads to a sense of dramatic irony, a necessary condition for melodrama.[43] This irony, however, is quickly undercut by narrative tension: Abhay coerces Manju back home and then tells her that he is going to kill her. The readers travel with Manju in fear for her life.

The climax, however, again unfolds as a complete surprise. Manju asks if she can, as a last request, make Abhay some coffee. In the next scene, Manju not only confesses that she knows all about his criminal behavior but also that *she* has killed two previous husbands for their property by mixing a strong *jaribooti* (root) in their coffee. The significance of story's title—"Coffee"—is revealed to us. Maybe Manju, caught in a desperate position, is ingeniously making up a story to buy time? The plot thickens: Manju declares that she has not only killed two husbands but has also murdered an abusive lover in the same way. The same fate befalls Abhay. He dies. The serial killer, then, is murdered by another serial killer.

Readers are treated to yet another twist when Upendra enters the scene. Manju wraps her arms around him, screaming, "Help me! This is not Abhay but the famous murderer Kalicharan." Kalicharan ostensibly dies of natural causes: "Kalicharan's eyes had gone cold. He could not do anything to anyone. Forensic investigation revealed that Abhay's death had been caused by a heart attack."[44] Manju has not been caught and can rebuild her life with Upendra. However, one wonders whether Manju will live with Upendra peacefully or if he will be her next victim.

Even though the narrative does not directly disclose Manju as Kalicharan's murderer, the open-endedness of the conclusion calls readers' attention to moral questions around murder, self-defense, and revenge. The narrative builds Kalicharan as a flat character, one who has murdered several innocent victims. However, it leaves two crucial questions entirely up for debate: Was this murder in self-defense? And a more complicated question to answer: Are Manju's previous murders justified? Even if we are to justify Manju's avatar as a woman seeking revenge (she does mention an abusive past lover), how are we to understand the conclusion? The narrative leaves that unanswered as well. Upendra might be Manju's renewed romantic interest, or he might be in grave danger. For the story's purposes, Upendra is a mere prop. This prop is not only necessary to maintain the good-evil binary between Upendra and Kalicharan: Manju makes Upendra feel like she is an innocent victim and that he has "saved" her. However, the irony is not lost that, for all practical purposes, Manju performs the role of a helpless victim and provides Upendra with a false sense of heroic masculinity by falling into his arms when he comes to "rescue" her. The story completely derails any expectations of a romantic love triangle or, even later, that of the thriller but also subverts expectations of femininity. If we return to earlier models and types of femininity in the book, we find that we cannot easily prescribe here the gender normative roles attributed to female characters in the middlebrow *Sarita*, *Dharmyug*, and Hind Pocket Books publications. Here, these roles are more fluid, and the female protagonist takes violent measures to ensure her own safety or, perhaps, to commit more crimes.

Another story that complicates readers' expectations of the female protagonist is "Paap ka arambh" ("The beginning of sin") by Upendranath "Ashk." Unlike Vimla Phadke who finds no place in canonical Hindi literary history, Ashk was then, and still is, a well-regarded writer. "Paap ka arambh" is a story of extramarital infidelity, jealousy, and, most significant, a wife's loneliness. It is narrated from the point of view of a young wife. Already at the very beginning of the story, she discovers that her husband, a teacher, has been having an affair with the school headmistress. At this point, the wife is a picture of absolute abjection. Soon, however, she confronts her husband about the affair. At this point, he denies it. When he finally does acknowledge it, he is so livid that he tells the wife to pack her bags and go back to her parents' house. The wife turns even more abject: "But I couldn't have left a home when it was on fire. Only god knows what he kept saying to me. He kept swearing expletives at me and kept packing my bags for me. He kept my trunk out but I wouldn't move beyond the doorway. At that time, my state was that of a child's, who has been told off and will neither play herself nor would let anyone else play."[45] The scene, however, shifts rapidly: the wife's elderly servant advises her to stop feeling dejected. Instead, she should take her life back in her own hands and should work to inspire jealousy: "If only Masterji [the husband] were to know that you are also beautiful and that someone is ready to die for you, he would be yours." While this appears like a classic response to marital infidelity, what the maid says further is worth noting: "Even if he is not yours, [trying this] will be better than dying. You are not so innocent that you don't even see what I am saying. After all, will dying solve your problem?" What presented first as a manipulative solution is imbued with new meaning: the servant insists that even if her husband ultimately leaves her, the wife should take control of her own destiny. In the short story, the wife's *uddeshya* (aim) has been transformed. Here, service of the husband or, alternatively, the patriarchal nation is replaced by service to strengthen the woman's own selfhood. Because of the maid's advice, the wife decides to focus not on educating her husband but rather educating herself. "I will tell him that I am not one of those simple, weak, and cowardly women who will continue to remain at the feet of men, who will remain docile at everything that the man does, be it right or wrong."[46] She starts taking greater care of her appearance. More significant, she begins to focus on her education that Balwant, a private tutor, imparts to her.

As she starts taking care of her appearance and education, she become a desirable subject but also a *desiring* subject again. She notices that, although this has no effect on her husband, Balwant notices her makeover. At this point, it seems that the wife was missing not her husband's affections in particular but rather an outlet for her own desires. In a dramatic scene, in direct expression of desire, the wife drinks from her tutor's cup, shocking him as well as herself:

> I said, "I am thirsty too."
> "So go and drink."
> "Who will get up and go?" Saying that, I looked at him once and picked up the glass that he had used and brought it to my lips.[47]

This moment is dramatic because, to Hindi readers, the idea of quenching one's thirst is a set trope, synonymous with the quenching of sexual desire. If the narrative leading to this moment was beset with coy sexual tension between the two parties, it becomes utterly clear to both readers as well as the tutor that, for all practical purposes, the wife has expressed direct desire for him, a man other than her husband. Balwant and (the still unnamed) wife begin an affair.

Readers live in suspense together with the first-person narrator, who feels guilty about having the affair but is nevertheless happy and excited that her desires are being met. The next dramatic moment in the story emerges when the husband discovers the wife's affair after he finds them sitting intimately close to each other. The husband, however, remains passive: "But he didn't say anything, just looked at me and then went back. My heart was beating wildly."[48] He moves out. As the story had begun with the wife's narration of her loneliness, the fact that it was her infidelity that finally ended the marriage must rattle her. However, exchanges between husband and wife after their separation is banal; they only meet to exchange information. At this pivotal moment, the narrative, as well as the wife, turn quiet. Another wave of independence mixed with sadness hits the narrator. If the husband has gone, there is nothing holding her back from leaving. After the wife decides to leave, Balwant comes to fetch this still unnamed narrator. They decide to stay for the night at one of the hotels near the railway station before departing for a new life in the morning. The narrative brims with the emotional tension (romanch), where the wife both feels happy starting a new life and also heavy that her marriage has failed. The story ends when the wife and her lover cross paths with the husband and *his* lover in front of their respective hotels, without exchanging a word, in utter silence: "They passed by us and went into the Dilkhusha [Happy Heart] Hotel, and we crossed them and entered Pavitra [Pure] Hotel!"[49]

"Anagnorisis" is the word Greek tragedy uses to describe the moment of a tragic, life-altering recognition. Steve Neale uses the term "agnition," stating that it is this recognition, the understanding or coming to it always a little too late, that lies at the heart of melodrama. At this moment, Neale argues, melodrama reduces the audience to tears because matters could have been resolved but ultimately cannot be. Neale discusses this in context of cinema, where the protagonists exchange looks across the street. The camera employs techniques such as the point of view shot and the eyeline match to establish a missed connection, making the audience aware of the pain both protagonists are feeling. The audience is meant to feel the pain even more intensely on account of the fact that the protagonists refuse to communicate it to each other: "The spectator is powerless not so much before each situation, the state of affairs at any one point in the film, but rather in relation to the course the narrative will take, whether the state of things changes or not."[50]

"Paap ka arambh" includes both these key melodramatic conventions. This story ends with another melodramatic complication: What do we make of an ending that does not keep to moral order? Melodrama is most commonly used to fulfill what has been termed "nostalgia for an ordered ontology," often articulated with a reinforcement of morality, an "incessant struggle against enemies, without and within, branded as villains, suborners of morality, who must be confronted and expunged, over and over, to assure the triumph of virtue."[51] Here, however, the pain—and romanch—also appears from the disruption of the story's moral universe. The wife could have suffered while her husband had an affair. Instead, she chooses to have an affair herself. As is the case with several such stories in these magazines, *particularly* when the fiction does not keep to the moral order, it takes on the garb and the techniques of genre fiction evoking romanch. In his seminal work on melodrama, Peter Brooks argues that melodrama does not merely release tension but also invites the reader to think.[52] This story's melodramatic conclusion challenges the reader's view of what constitutes the "sin" (*paap*). Does the sin begin with the husband or the wife? Because the wife is the narrator and we are introduced first to her loneliness, then to the husband's infidelity, and consequently her suicidal state, the story introduces linear causality, drawing us closer to the wife's plight, which arguably leads her to having an affair, making us sympathize with her state of mind. The story's underlying fear of domestic instability becomes apparent. Ultimately, readers are provided with alternatives to imagined resolutions that, elsewhere, are mainstays of middlebrow magazines.

Not all stories of domesticity in the lowbrow magazines are about disillusionment. "Paru," written by Kamla Phadke for the March 1952 issue of *Maya*, is about the comedy arising from a modern domestic crisis regarding the employment of a cook. The narrator-protagonist places a prominent advertisement in the local newspaper to find a replacement for her cook. Her friend warns her about the futility of doing this—most cooks will not respond simply because they cannot read: "After having read the advertisement in *Dainik Jyoti*, my friend said to me: 'Do you think that literacy has improved so much in our country that a cook will read your advertisement and, then, send you a letter of interest on top of it? You're being very silly.'"[53] Throughout this conversation, assumptions of class and literacy are made visible. Both women belong to modern nuclear families. The narrator lives with her husband alone. Because of her class entrenchment, the most natural thing for her to do is to place a newspaper advertisement to find a cook. This brand of self-reflexive humor about class position runs throughout the text. One wonders what this humor is in service of: Does the writer ironically reflect on how the modern, educated, and well-meaning woman is perhaps disconnected from realities of everyday domestic life?

The cooks who do respond to the advertisement just as quickly leave the narrator's employ: one (male) cook gets booked for gambling, and the narrator suspects the second one (again, male) of harboring what she calls "communist" ideas. She bases this assumption on what the cook, a passionate supporter of the kingdom of Travancore, told her a few days before he suddenly disappeared: "The kingdom of Travancore will never die. It is a different case from other kingdoms . . . We will never tolerate this evildoing by the Congress."[54] The humor here generates from the narrator's absolute ignorance about political leanings: she has mistaken a royalist for a communist. Other political events and references dot the story, serving as instruments of humor—at each time the narrator completely misinterprets political references and seems to make all statements in earnest. The humor derived from this can cloak another indictment: not only is the modern, educated, and well-meaning woman perhaps disconnected from everyday domestic life but is also, at the same time, disengaged from the outer political world. Indeed, the authorial stance here is brutal, as complications of both inner and outer workings of life elude the modern woman.

After the second royalist-communist cook departs, the quest for a new cook begins. In yet another series of misunderstandings, the third candidate is mistaken for royalty. The couple (the wife is joined by her husband this time) soon comprehend their mistake but only after they have already respectfully seated the cook and poured her tea. This confusion sets the scene of domestic comfort and harmony within the nuclear family. The couple does not take itself too seriously: "After [the cook's] departure, he [the husband] said with some anger, 'What do you do! We ended up being so embarrassed because of your advertisement!' Although, afterward, reminded of this event, we got stomach aches because of laughing so hard."[55] When the narrator finally finds someone, a beautiful young cook named Paru, the tone of the narrative changes. Tension and manipulation replace banter and repartee. The narrator tells us that she finds that Paru cannot cook well, nor can she clean, but is extremely desirable to the opposite sex. For this reason, both her husband and his friends like Paru. The narrator notes that the husband's friends start visiting the narrator's home more often than previously only to flirt with Paru. In a semi-comical mode, the narrator describes her helplessness; since she cannot serve the guests bad food, she takes to cooking herself while Paru gets the credit for it. The narrator is in a double bind, jealous of the attention that Paru gets but, at the same time, unable to dismiss her, precisely because people will gossip that she let go a good cook just because she happened to be beautiful. The author here conveys the narrator's fear of being talked about or made fun of. Although the narrator is seemingly modern and independent, she cares equally about her reputation as a competent homemaker. Ironically, as the narrator herself tells us, she also works at a nonprofit organization for the upliftment of women.

However, refusing to be defeated, the narrator hatches a scheme to get rid of Paru once and for all. She actively encourages a young driver's attentions toward the cook, allowing her to go and see a film with him. She also convinces her that the driver would be a good match for her. The narrator is thrilled when Paru finally marries him: marriage would mean Paru would need to quit her job. The moral of the story is this: the only way to preserve a happy marriage is through another marriage. The narrator's own marriage and social standing are threatened enough for her to transform from a social activist to fervently plotting her cook's marriage. She goes to great lengths to describe the delight she feels when Paru gets married. This turns to gloating, as we can see in her conversation with guests who have come home for dinner after the cook's departure: "'Haven't you heard? Our Paru got married only a few days ago.' Saying this in front of my husband and our guests makes me very happy. However, after hearing this, the guests sulk. It is entertaining to see this."[56] Albeit written in the comic mode, this story, too, is governed by fear, most significantly of loss of class position and its prescriptive forms of idealized femininity that bind even the most modern women, ones who place advertisements in newspapers in their search for a cook. The narrator has triumphed, but not without appearing jealous, petty, and, in her spare time, reduced to cooking food for unwanted guests and plotting marriages for beautiful women.

Men

Although most of the stories in these magazines are narrated from the perspective of female narrators/protagonists, social standing and the fear of losing it are concerns of male narrators/protagonists as well. These men often suffer from difficulties arising from poverty, social anxiety, and expectations of masculinity. This section analyzes two of the short stories that encompass what I call fictions of melodramatic poverty, that is, stories in which poverty is charged with great pathos and invites the reader's sympathy. The protagonists of these stories struggle with the difficulties accruing from their weak economic and social position, and while these stories have different outcomes, the "romanch" or fear and dread here arises from the inability to control their everyday living conditions.

In "Naked voices" ("Nangi avaazein"), written by canonical writer Saadat Hasan Manto and published in the November 1952 issue of *Maya*, the need for privacy in a cramped living space while maintaining a need for physical and sexual intimacy with one's partner are the primary concerns of Bholu, the story's protagonist.[57] Written in the third person, the narrative opens with Bholu's eagerness to get married. He tells his friend Ramu in desperation: "I am also a human being. For God's sake, I cannot sleep at night. It has been twenty days since I slept . . . Please tell brother (*bhaiya*), he should start making preparations for my wedding, else, I swear to God, I will lose my mind."[58] Here, Bholu equates being "human" with getting married. Very strong overtones of sexual tension dot the conversation above, and readers are made alert to his sexual frustrations: Bholu has not slept for twenty days, he desperately needs a wedding and, by extension, a wife, and without these conditions, he will lose his mind. Soon, through the extended family network, Bholu finds a suitable bride. However, inexplicably at this point, Bholu's living circumstances start to make him uncomfortable. Bholu lives in a chawl (poor tenement): his "home" is just a bed in a room full of beds that are occupied by other bodies that can always be heard if not seen. In short, there is no room for privacy.

In his first excitement, Bholu decides to make his bed a private space for himself and his future bride: he installs four posters around the bed and hangs curtains on them, making the space self-contained. However, as the date of the wedding draws closer, Bholu's excitement transforms into dismay, despair, and fear. He can constantly hear other couples' sexual activity all around him, and the "naked voices" haunt him. The romanch in the story is derived from the fear of being heard during sexual intimacy. He is terrified that his own intimacies will become a public spectacle. Here, fear is expressed through his anxious questions: "Will he also produce such sounds? . . . Will people around us also hear our sounds? . . . Will they also spend their nights being awake, just like he is? If someone peeked in and saw, what would happen then?" Bholu begins to dread the upcoming nuptials. The ideal that Bholu was aspiring to has now turned him neurotic. After the marriage date is set, Bholu's neurosis reaches a crescendo and becomes even more painful: "Is a curtain made from jute even a curtain? Then, people are spread on all sides of the bed. Even the slightest whisper will reach others' ears in the dead of the night . . .

How can people lead such naked lives?" The story maps Bholu's mind as it darts back and forth. Even after he has married the girl, who he thinks is very beautiful and desirable, he cannot bring himself to be intimate with her. Unable to resolve his dilemma between desiring his wife and having the privacy necessary to initiate sexual intimacy, Bholu ultimately rejects her. After a very short period, he tells her to go back to her parents' house. The lack of intimacy also cannot be kept private: soon, rumors circulate in the chawl that Bholu sent his wife back home because he was sexually disinterested, with the implicit assumption that he is impotent. In other words, to the home's inhabitants, the information about lack of intimacy is as significant and exciting as the sounds confirming it. Bholu himself hears the rumors, which is perhaps the moment that drives him mad: "Now Bholu wanders around the bazaar completely naked. Whenever he sees jute hanging, he tears it apart in tiny pieces."[59]

Impotence arising out of the shame and fear of unveiled intimacy lies at the heart of the narrative. Bholu's neurosis is born the moment he has to initiate intimacy in a semipublic space. The unsettling ending in the form of stark and literal naked madness raises the larger question regarding what it means to be the urban poor. The short story can be read as part of a whole series of stories focusing on homelessness or living on footpaths—or in crowded chawls—that indict the newly independent state for failing to cater to its citizens' basic needs.

The second story also shows disapproval of the state's inability to provide. The 1950s, a decade marked by food and other shortages, had a strict "control" system in place that required people to stand in queues all day to obtain basic necessities like food and oil from the government's ration shops. The story "Black market" ("Kala Bazaar") by Madhukar Kher (*Maya*, 1952) narrates Ram Snehi's fight against the corruption inherent within the government's "control" system. Narrated in the third person, the story follows Snehi, an ordinary daily wageworker. He becomes aware of the "black market" after his wife tells him about how she has to bribe officials to get rations. Livid,

Snehi decides to protest against this corruption. He takes a day off work and stands in line all day to get cooking oil. Snehi refuses to pay the bribe even when the grocer prompts him. Standing in line takes its toll, and the narrative describes Snehi's physical fatigue in great detail. But Snehi expects it to have his reward at the end. Readers step into a world where Ram Snehi seeks justice, where he seeks to combat the system through his individual battle. The daily wageworker's protest ends when grocers hang the sign *tel khatam* (oil finished) at the counter. Ram Snehi has to return home empty-handed. The control system was an indispensable part of everyday middle- and lower-class life. William Gould writes: "Corruption became a discourse for representing the injustices and disqualifications of a range of communities pushed to the periphery of India's dominant national narrative, be they displaced refugees or urban poor. But also, from the point of view of governments, the policing and control of the dispossessed created the notion of social chaos, around which the idea of local corruption could be naturalized."[60] The story's end was bound to strike a chord with the readers, with a rhetorical question, perhaps on the mind of many: "He was unable to sleep at night. His body was paining. He was thinking, is this fair or unfair?"[61]

This conundrum had no easy resolutions. Clearly, the new Nehruvian nation-state was failing its citizens. Ram Snehi's main concern, that corruption was consuming subsidies, can be articulated in another way. If, as Benjamin Siegel argues, "India's leadership proposed a vision of citizenship wherein rights derived from the completion of responsibilities, and wherein preferences were to be subsumed in the name of development," this story rejects such a narrative because this "completion" is accompanied not only by scarcity but also by corruption.[62] Ram Snehi may be a daily wageworker, but clearly, this was not the dilemma of one; it engulfed the entire nation. Yet although such a situation would have resonated with the experience of the middle classes, middlebrow fiction certainly did not articulate this situation. Food and commodity scarcity, as well as the material and emotional suffering that arose from it, formed the "other," which the middlebrow publications did not want to be weighed down with. These problems instead found expression in the stories here.

"Othering": Representation of Muslim Characters

Muslim authors and characters were absent from the middlebrow publications, and even in my sample of lowbrow magazines I could locate only two stories that had Muslim characters, both of which are discussed below. In this respect, middlebrow and lowbrow Hindi publications overlap—explicitly and implicitly, these magazines work as Hindu spaces. Muslim characters show up in lowbrow genre magazines in ghost or "weird" stories. "Mirror" ("Aaina"), written by Basant Kumar Mathur and published in *Maya*'s June 1947 issue, is a story of a man's inexplicable fascination with a mirror in his house. This mirror periodically shows him "weird," otherworldly images: "In just two to four minutes, those clouds settled in two places. Then I started feeling as if two eyes were staring at me. A shiver ran through my spine. In just a few moments, the image of a beautiful woman appeared inside the mirror. Her long, black hair was a little unclear, but in that fog, I could clearly see her eyes—lotus-like, beautiful eyes." Clearly, the narrator is fascinated with the beauty of the ghostly image that lies beyond the mirror. Even though he wants to, he cannot will himself away from the image. To the narrator, who is equal parts allured and repelled, the female ghostly form is both horrifying yet tantalizing. This is where the romanch lies: the image is ghostly and terrifying, but the woman in the mirror is beautiful, with the narrator sexualizing her. He describes the woman's eyes as ones expressing unfulfilled desire: "Those two eyes were very alive. They had an amalgamation of excessive love (*utkirsht prem*), unquenched desire (*atript vasna*), fear (*bhay*), womanly pride (*nari sulabh garv*), and softness."[63]

As time goes by, the narrator also sees a man inside the mirror. The ghost story is presented in the form of a diary with date entries about each sighting of the woman alone and of the couple together. For the narrator, the images are dreamlike, as if he is viewing them in a cinema hall; he often repeats that what he sees is "cinema-like," or *cinema ke parde ki bhanti*.[64] His involvement with the mirror produces very real physical effects of romanch: "I have been having a headache since the morning, a burning sensation in my eyes, and my body is tense. Surely, my condition is related to the mirror."[65]

What is the allure of the otherworldly, the spectral? I argue that, in this case, the supernatural makes it easy for the narrator to talk about sensuality or sexuality. The female form is admired but through the mirror. It soon emerges that the woman in the mirror is none other than the Mughal emperor Aurangzeb's daughter Zeb-un-Nisa and the man in the mirror is her lover Azam Khan, who Aurangzeb had banished from the palace. While this incident may not be historically accurate, there is indeed a legend according to which Aurangzeb's daughter Zeb-un-Nisa hid her lover in her bedroom in a cauldron, and knowingly, Aurangzeb ordered that fire be set to the cauldron, killing her lover. The story ends thus: "The *Quila mohalla* [the fort and neighborhood], mirror, Shahzaadi Zeb-un-Nisa—everything seems like a dream. But what is my relationship to this incident? Why did this mysterious incident only appear to me? Perhaps one of you can give me an answer?"[66] Alongside pondering this question, wondering why the narrator had these visions, one can approach it through another similar, connected question: Why did the narrator choose Zeb-un-Nisa's story? Zeb-un-Nisa has been recovered in more recent scholarship as a prominent member of Aurangzeb's advisory circle and a poet.[67] Romance, a common-enough genre, is inflected with the historical ghost story. While explicit descriptions of physical intimacy abound in these magazines, because of its sheer absence, the idea of romantic relationships between Hindus and Muslims is seen to be taboo. Therefore, perhaps, the only way to narrate the sexual attraction for the "other" is when it is "othered" even further, in this case, beyond a mirror in another, more distant and acceptable, or even desirable, Muslim world. In other words, a story about a time gone by that cannot return renders the material safe. The added love story between the two star-crossed lovers makes it yet more palatable and enjoyable. The ghost story becomes a pleasurable yet terrifying, exciting, and titillating romanch encounter.

The second story featuring Muslim characters is not supernatural or ghostly but one of friends divided by religion and partition violence. "The embrace of death" ("Mrityu ke bahupaash mein"), written by Shyam Sundar Goyanka in *Rasili Kahaniyaan*, is a story of two friends from a neighborhood who until recently have lived in complete harmony. Abbas, the Muslim friend, is rather agitated, while Prakash, the Hindu friend, is seen addressing him kindly:

> "Forgive me, brother . . . Forgive me . . . ," Abbas choked. Clouds of regret crashed against his heart and he started to cry.
>
> "Stop, brother, stop, what will come of crying? It was my own fault, I am reaping my own karma."[68]

The readers soon become aware that Abbas has come to visit Prakash at the hospital. Prakash has sustained burn injuries over his face, also losing his eyesight, from an acid attack during the recent Hindu-Muslim riots that he had participated in. At this stage, several paragraphs into the narrative, the readers then slowly become aware that it was, in fact, Abbas himself who threw acid on Prakash's face! The story at this point is beset with tension, with Prakash stoically reminding Abbas of their mutual friendship before the riot and a flustered Abbas repeatedly asking Prakash for his forgiveness. While Prakash cries in pain, he also takes hold of Abbas's hand, telling him he has completely forgiven him. Already brimming with romanch, with the guilty Abbas being physically unable to hold on to Prakash's hand, the climax is particularly horrifying: Prakash lures a guilty Abbas to stay with him in the hospital to take care of him for the night, only to throw acid on him! The story ends abruptly with Abbas's face scarred and *him* blinded. While throwing acid over him, Prakash says this to Abbas:

> Take heart. It's burning a lot. Why are you biting me like an animal? What will get out of cutting me, my friend? Do you think that I'll survive this and go to jail for hurting you?
>
> After saying this, Prakash took the bottle of acid and drank it.[69]

How is one to interpret fear and horror in the above story? The narrative technique used by the writer—Goyanka was not recorded in any mainstream literary histories—is one of leading readers from one revelation to another, much like a detective story. Readers are invited to investigate the tension's buildup, being handed shocking revelations at every turn. The ultimate climax is beyond anticipation, throwing readers into complete confusion. A gradual increase in what seemed to be forgiveness is overturned by a climax that instead proffers revenge. The story then also becomes a story of revenge against the "other." The binary between good and evil is maintained. At one level, readers "know" that Prakash actually has cause to attack Abbas. However, this binary is complicated, because readers also know from the very beginning that Abbas feels extremely guilty about the violence he inflicted on Prakash. When Abbas is made to believe that Prakash has forgiven him, he cries: "You're an amazing person . . . I am unable to repay the debt of your friendship."[70]

How is one to read the "other" in this story? The fear experienced while reading the story is from the Muslim character's perspective, as is the guilt, which is important to keep in mind. The story, then, is not only one of revenge: the genre is primarily that of thriller, and revenge is coincidental to perhaps necessitate an acceptable closure. However, the underlying conflict between friendship and betrayal also becomes a very important lens through which to read the story.

CONCLUSION

On a hot and humid afternoon in 2022, I found myself standing in the backyard of Allahabad's iconic Bharati Bhawan Library that opened to the main road named after it. Some wholesale potato sellers had set up shop in front, the atmosphere was muggy and electric. The head librarian had invited me outside for a chat: together, we drank some (very sugary and tiny) tea. He asked me to close my eyes and imagine Chowk, the chaotic overactive neighborhood we were in now, in its splendor more than a hundred years ago at the turn of the twentieth century. Look ahead, picture where Madan Mohan Malaviya once walked, he said, referring to the library's cofounder and also eminent Congressman and Hindi nationalist. Further up ahead, you can see where Jawaharlal Nehru was born, he gestured toward a jam-packed road, presumably at the Meerganj house that no longer exists.[71] Other indistinguishable and fervent hand gestures pointed to different roads that led to other distinguished writers: Dharmvir Bharti used to come here, Harivansh Rai Bachchan walked there. Everyone who was anyone was within walking distance or walked the distance to this once great institution which now was the heart of a thriving sabzi mandi (vegetable market).

Before literary Allahabad began emptying out and writers moved to Delhi or Bombay, it was a city brimming with political ferment and literary intent. Allahabad was one of the first cities where coffeehouse culture came into being in India—you could always find some writer or the other sitting with his coterie discussing the future of literature (and forging it) in the process. Some people left, some died, but, at the same time, many pockets of publishing from Allahabad continued to flourish. This chapter delineates that history. The editors of the genre magazines were *also* part of the Allahabad coffeehouse space, though the head librarian did not bring them up, nor are they mentioned in any written or oral histories of Hindi literature. For instance, Chandrama Prasad Khare, one of *Sarita*'s first employees, recalls that before he left Allahabad and found a better-paying job with Delhi Press, he was an integral part of Maya Press.[72] For Khare, the move to Delhi was important: it represented professional growth. In the larger milieu of publishing, dynamics were shifting to the new capitals of production, circulation, and, most significant, thought. The geographies of publication were shifting, and so were the profiles of the publishers. While magazines of this chapter stood their ground majestically for years, they, too, found themselves moving. Delhi Press bought the rights to *Manohar Kahaniyaan* in 2008.[73]

CONCLUSION

Who's Afraid of Manmath Nath Gupta?

We first met Manmath Nath Gupta as author of yearly book reviews at *Sarita*. I contrasted Gupta's yearly reviews with the magazine's other book reviews and advertisements, contending that his arguably created a more critical space where readers were encouraged to read new literature analytically. His yearly reviews were another way through which the magazine forged middlebrow tastes: readers were consumers, producers, and critics. However, apart from this role as reviewer and arbiter of taste at *Sarita*, Manmath Nath Gupta also plays a significant role in the argument I make for publishing in the post-independence period in general. In the late colonial period, Gupta had been a prominent revolutionary: he was imprisoned for fourteen years after taking part in the Kakori train robbery on 9 August 1925. After independence, he became a member of the Communist Party of India; he wrote an influential book on progressivism and took part in the lively literary debate between progressivism and experimentalism.[1] Yet, in addition to his political activism and literary criticism, Gupta was also a prolific author of fiction and wrote not only for *Sarita* but also for *all* the other middlebrow publications discussed in this book.[2] Of course, he also authored works for lowbrow publications.[3] Finally, he wrote for literary magazines like *Kahani*.[4] How do we situate Manmath Nath Gupta at the intersection between such varied spaces?

Existing written and oral accounts of Hindi literature in the 1950s point to a deeply divided field—not only on political and ideological grounds but also on literary grounds between literary and commercial magazines.[5] This is what emerges from Agyeya's critical view of *all* existing Hindi readers, dismissed for not being literary enough but also from the view that modernist writer Dharmvir Bharti "sacrificed himself" (or, alternatively, betrayed literary ideals) when he went to work for the Times of India Group in Bombay as *Dharmyug*'s editor. There was also the silence in writers' memoirs about having ever published in magazines like *Sarita* or *Maya*.[6]

Instead, Manmath Nath Gupta's example shows that (a) most writers published pretty much everywhere, particularly if they were trying to earn a living through writing. (b) Much like England at the time, best-selling commercial magazines sought out literary pieces, which, as Pierre Bourdieu astutely notes, could become more reader-friendly and change complexion according to the venue they appeared in.[7] Thus, as we saw in chapter four, even a Manto story could fit within the paradigm of romanch.[8] (c) Distinctions still existed, even among literary and middlebrow magazines, and writers were careful to gear their works accordingly. Manmath Nath Gupta wrote different fiction for *Dharmyug* from what he wrote for Hind Pocket Books. (d) In this context, the middlebrow marks the coming together in the same magazine space or book list of writers who are normally considered literary and others who never figure in literary histories but were clearly popular at the time, like Vimla Luthra. (e) Again, as Manmath Nath Gupta's example shows, middlebrow magazines did not patronize their readers but acknowledged their interests and their call to democratize language, literature, and taste. (f) The post-independence world of Hindi writing and publishing was an intensely dynamic one and is best understood through a version of Robert Darnton's "communication circuit," that is, as equally constituted by writers, publishers, and readers.[9] While conventional literary histories focus on writers, critics, and debates, I have focused on publishers-editors, magazines, and book lists as spaces and on readers, trying to insert their voices and agency. In fact, in each chapter I have concentrated on some aspect of Darnton's circuit: the readers in *Sarita*, the publishers in Hind Pocket Books, the editor in *Dharmyug*, and the printing and production quality and the *absence* of editorial and readers' voices in the lowbrow magazines.

This book is the first comprehensive attempt at systematically exploring the world of Hindi middlebrow publishing and reading in the post-independence period. It has extended to middlebrow magazines the attention that has so far been accorded only to literary or women's publications, treating them as texts that interact with the culture which produced them and which they produce and places "where meanings are contested and made" and where readers made sense of their lives.[10] My reconstruction has made five key interventions in the larger field of South Asian literary and cultural history. First, my book reorients our understanding of Hindi as a language in this period. Whereas in the context of post-1947 India and the Constituent Assembly debates Hindi was viewed as overbearingly nationalist and Sanskritized and was claiming the status as the national language at the expense of the other Indian languages and its own regional varieties, my study illuminates how Hindi in middlebrow magazines functions as a nonnormative and democratizing medium, providing a space for ordinary readers to express the right to a language that they would understand and enjoy. And although writers Bharatendu Harishchandra and Mahavir Prasad Dwivedi have been hailed as the makers of modern Hindi and the fashioners of the Hindi public sphere, this book has highlighted the overlooked role of *Sarita*'s Vishwa Nath and Hind Pocket Books' Dina Nath Malhotra as important editor-publishers, towering personalities, and entrepreneurs who dramatically widened the scope of the Hindi reading public. They both came from family backgrounds in printing and publishing and explored publishing first as a *commercially* viable venture but equally saw themselves as visionaries who exercised editorial command.

Second, I have used the Hindi magazine archive to reevaluate the middle classes, their consumption habits, and their place within the history of cultural taste in the post-independence period. The 1950s have been approached largely from the perspective of planning, policy, and the Partition, but they were also a period when middle-class selves were reimagined and rearticulated in differentiated and layered ways. Consumption has been a recurring concern and narrative within this book, and I have discussed consumption both through the materiality of the magazines and their contents but also through advertising of unabashedly consumer objects in the magazines, showing the segmentation within advertising in Hindi publishing.

Third, reading against the grain of criticism that has focused on literary magazines, I have made a case for studying reading for pleasure. Hindi middlebrow magazines and paperbacks offered a wide range of material that encouraged an eclectic and wide-ranging everyday reading habit and that urged readers to find themselves on the pages of the magazines. This is why I have focused on "everyday" reading and how the middlebrow commercial magazines unsettle our notions of literary language and "literariness." Reading the advertisements alongside short stories has shown the usefulness of approaching the post-independence period in terms of the individual's "service to the self" within the framework of the family. For this reason, readers have been a central consideration in this book.[11] Hindi middlebrow readers, who have largely been unaccounted for in academic scholarship, were confident readers who embraced the idea of themselves as creators and consumers rather than serving a large nationalist purpose.

Fourth, connected to the previous point, I have shown that middlebrow publishing is one of the primary sources through which to understand the aspirations and consumption habits of contemporary middle-class Indian women. Pre-independence journals already offered a variety of reading material to women, yet they articulated reading in terms of "service" to Hindi, literature, and the nation, calling on women to conform to "women's duty." *Everyday Reading* has emphasized the importance of women's desires both within the imaginative world of short stories as well as columns and readers' letters, but also of women as readers and consumers. In fact,

Sarita, Hind Pocket Books novels, and the lowbrow magazines gave more space to women than *Dharmyug* did. The growing importance of women as consumers of books and magazines meant that the publications carried letters as well as short stories, articles, and opinion pieces from women. However, it is significant to note that the publisher-editors I studied focused on men and women as readers alike, but the publisher-editors themselves were male.

Last, *Everyday Reading* also reevaluates "middlebrow" and "lowbrow" as conceptual categories, arguing that taste is not as neatly stacked along a single hierarchical axis, as literary historians of Hindi—or Bourdieu—would have us believe. My conceptualization of the middlebrow, though still relational, is less hierarchical than Bourdieu's. The confident Hindi middlebrow of the 1950s and 1960s was internally diversified but also had overlaps: cosmopolitan *Dharmyug* could mingle with the democratic and modern *Sarita*, alongside the wide-ranging and more Urdu-friendly Hind Pocket Books. *Everyday Reading* effectively expands the boundaries of "literariness," "modernism," and "cosmopolitanism" in the 1950s and 1960s, positing that middlebrow publishing partly participated in all these debates cogently and wholeheartedly. This leads us to reconsider how we remember literary centers. Bombay is often celebrated as the center of Hindi film and, in more recent scholarship, as the hub of literary modernism, yet I have shown that, through *Dharmyug*, it was equally significant as a hub of middlebrow cosmopolitanism.[12] Allahabad is celebrated in Hindi literary and cultural histories, yet it was also a commercial hub of lowbrow literature.

Middlebrow magazines like *Sarita* and *Dharmyug* and publishers like Hind Pocket Books have been the main focus of my project. Through libraries, personal collections, and publishers' offices and holdings, I have mined archives as systematically as possible. In far more comfortable (read "air-conditioned") spaces like central and institutional libraries in Delhi, I also came across a wide variety of literary and highbrow magazines, but these have not been the focus of this book. Equally, I felt it important to examine some genre magazines like *Maya, Rasili Kahaniyaan,* and *Manohar Kahaniyaan* so as to gauge how much they overlapped with or departed from middlebrow magazines.

I came to the study of middlebrow magazines and publishers through publishing history: the book emerges from research questions I first asked when writing my dissertation at the University of Delhi, examining the unexpectedly good production quality since 2009 of the contemporary novels of Hindi master crime writer Surendra Mohan Pathak, published by Raja Pocket Books. I examined how changes in production altered the writer's reputation from a pulp novelist to a reputable author, as well as the implications of such on the way crime fiction is understood in Hindi publishing in the twenty-first century.[13] Investigating pulp fiction in the twenty-first century led me to ask questions about what "pulp" meant in the larger history of commercial publishing in Hindi, only to find that it had not yet been investigated with respect to the post-independence period. Apart from Prabhat Ranjan's essay on Hind Pocket Books, I could not find any history that had previously engaged with this question.[14] This realization led me to think about the birth of the paperback in Hindi and Dina Nath Malhotra's towering presence and self-canonization, which forms the core of the second chapter of this book.

I began with *Sarita* and its editor-publisher Vishwa Nath, who also edited several other commercially successful English-language magazines such as *Caravan* and *Women's Era*. When V. S. Naipaul wrote on *Women's Era* and his meeting with Vishwa Nath, who was by then in his late seventies, he admitted that he did not think that he would find himself being captivated by women's magazines in India. Yet *Women's Era* caught his attention because it "acknowledged the conditions in which its readers lived." The magazine did not patronize women. Naipaul wrote: "People who don't need this kind of advice don't need *Women's Era*. And the people who need the advice are never rebuked or ridiculed. The faults are never written about as the reader's faults. They are other people's faults, faults the reader might have observed; there is always some story or fable to soften the correction. *Women's Era* invites its readers to a special, shared world. The editorial tone is one of concern, almost love."[15] Naipaul's insight into *Women's Era* and Vishwa Nath as editor in the 1990s holds true for my analysis of *Sarita* and Vishwa Nath as editor in the 1950s. I have shown that, through their structure, content, and style, the publications under consideration in this book not only created cultural imaginaries and milieus for their middle-class readers but also did so always by "acknowledging" them. Readers, in turn, loved the publications. Returning to the first example in the first chapter where we saw Babulal Ahir and his sister-in-law fighting over a magazine, like Ahir, readers across North India faced a similar daily relationship with the magazine: they wanted to read it, and they wanted to read it immediately. *Everyday Reading: Hindi Middlebrow and the North Indian Middle Class* is my attempt to answer how this happened and why.

Notes

INTRODUCTION: MIDDLEBROW

1 Amarkant, "Hatyare," 109.

2 The most recent example of this study can be found in Menon, *Planning Democracy*.

3 Some notable examples include Balasubramanian, *Toward a Free Economy*; De, *A People's Constitution*; Roy, *Beyond Belief*; and Berry, "Lakshmi and the Scientific Housewife."

4 For more on Nehru's foreign policy, see Kennedy, *International Ambitions of Mao and Nehru*, and McGarr, "After Nehru, What?"

5 See Pandey, "Prose of Otherness," for his articulation of the complicity of the state archive in projecting the partition experience as inexplicably aberrational stands at the center of the discourse. Much more-recent work has also focused on the state's complicity in the forceful eviction of Muslims from the so-called secular state. See Khan, *Great Partition*, and Zamindar, *Long Partition*, and their study of permits given to refugees to travel to their new state, chosen ostensibly by them but in many cases having been forced to migrate by the state.

6 Some stellar works studying this gendered experience of partition violence include Butalia, *Other Side of Silence*; Kaur, *Since 1947*; and Menon and Bhasin, *Borders and Boundaries*.

7 A large body of literary and academic work is dedicated to the representation of partition in both literature and film. See Kumar, *Narrating Partition*; Saint, *Witnessing Partition*; and Mehta and Mookerjea-Leonard, *Indian Partition in Literature and Films*.

8 See, for example, Dwyer and Patel, *Cinema India*; Vasudevan, *The Melodramatic Public*; and M. Prasad, *Ideology of the Hindi Film*.

9 Some notable examples include Orsini, *Hindi Public Sphere*; Nijhawan, *Women and Girls*; C. Gupta, *Sexuality, Obscenity, Community*; and A. Ghosh, *Power in Print*.

10 Orsini, *Hindi Public Sphere*, and Nijhawan, *Women and Girls*.

11 Roy, *Beyond Belief*. The most visceral examples of this can be found in Nehru's food campaigns. Benjamin Siegel discusses it in the context of food shortages and national campaigns that stressed, among many things, missing meals and

eating "substitute foods" in place of staples like rice and wheat. See *Hungry Nation*.

12 For scholarship on the nationalization of Hindi from the nineteenth century onward, see Dalmia, *Nationalization*; A. Rai, *Hindi Nationalism*; and Sadana, *English Heart, Hindi Heartland*.

13 Orsini, *Hindi Public Sphere*, and Mody, *Making of Modern Hindi*.

14 Some notable examples for Hindi include Mani, *Idea of Indian Literature*; C. Gupta, *Gender of Caste*; and Orsini, *Hindi Public Sphere*. See also, in particular, Mani, "Feminine Desire Is Human Desire."

15 The only other study is in Hindi, Ranjan's slim essay "Lugdi Sahitya ke Andhere Ujale."

16 Audit Bureau of Circulation, accessed through email message Pawan Kumar Lingwal to author, 24 September 2015, and *Press and Advertisers YearBook*.

17 See Darnton, "'What Is the History of Books?' Revisited," 495.

18 See Gupta and Chakravorty, *Print Areas*, *Movable Type*, and *New Word Order*. See also Orsini, *History of the Book*, for a comprehensive overview of the discipline in India.

19 See Dalmia and Kumar, *Balabodhini*.

20 Mody, *Making of Modern Hindi*.

21 Orsini, *Hindi Public Sphere*, 25.

22 Orsini, 268.

23 Orsini, 270.

24 Orsini, 284.

25 Beetham, *Magazine of Her Own?*, 2.

26 Lathan and Scholes, "Rise of Periodical Studies."

27 Allen and van den Berg, *Serialization in Popular Culture*, 2.

28 "Exchange Rate, 1945–1971," Reserve Bank of India, https://www.rbi.org.in/commonperson/English/Scripts/FAQs.aspx?Id=1877.

29 For more on this in a nineteenth-century context, see Stark, *Empire of Books*, and R. Chatterjee, *Empires of the Mind*, who tie these questions to the very successful Naval Kishore Press and Oxford University Press, respectively.

30 I tried to find direct references to subsidies provided by the Indian government but came across only paper subsidies or sanctions being filed in the annual yearbooks. Often, however, government subsidies in publishing were obtained through personal connections. For instance, Hind Pocket Books managed to obtain some subsidies from Prime Minister Jawaharlal Nehru as well as establish post offices in the office compound. See Rajya Sabha TV, "*Guftugu* with D N Malhotra."

31 See, in particular, Dalmia, *Nationalization*; Orsini, *Print and Pleasure*; Stark, *Empire of Books*; Ashk, *Hindi sahitya ka maukhik itihaas*, vol. 3.

32 Ashk, *Hindi sahitya ka maukhik itihaas*.

33 Gyanranjan, "Vagabond Nights," 315.

34 R. Sharma, "Architecture of Intellectual Sociality," 276.

35 A. Rai, *Hindi Nationalism*, 67.

36 For more on the Marwari connection with Hindi, see Parsons, "Bazaar and the Bari," and Mukul, *Gita Press*. For more on the Marwari community in Calcutta, see Hardgrove, *Community and Public Culture*.

37 "Penguin Random House Acquires Respected Hindi Publisher Hind Pocket Books."

38 Punch quoted in Pollentier, "Configuring Middleness," 42.

39 See Woolf, *Death of the Moth*. This letter was written in response to J. B. Priestley's review of her novel *To the Lighthouse* in the *Evening Standard* paper in 1932. For more on this debate, see Baxendale, "Priestley and the Highbrows," 74.

40 Woolf, *Death of the Moth*, n.p.

41 Bourdieu, *Distinction*, 250.

42 Gonzalez, "A Contemporary Look at Pierre Bourdieu's 'Photography,'" 129.

43 Bourdieu, *Distinction*, xii, quoted in Pollentier, Configuring Middleness," 37, 38.

44 Bourdieu, *Distinction*, 81.

45 Bourdieu uses the term "legitimate culture" in scare quotes often in his body of work to explicate the mediations between taste and class as well as to define the highbrow's position within the hierarchy of taste.

46 Pollentier, "Configuring Middleness," 43.

47 Rubin, *Making of Middle/brow Culture*, xix, xviii, xix.

48 Radway, *Feeling for Books*.

49 In their 2016 essay, Cecilia Konchar Farr and Tom Perrin note, "In the twenty-six years between 1982 and 2008, eighteen scholarly monographs with the word 'middlebrow' in the title were published; by contrast, in the six years from 2009 to 2016, at least twenty-four such volumes have either been published or are in production, with seven in 2015 alone." See their "Introduction."

50 Chartier, "Laborers and Voyagers," 52.

51 For instance, *Maya*, June 1952, 43, carried a half-page advertisement for *Dharmyug*, specifically its *varg pahelī* or crossword puzzle series.

52 Fernandes, *India's New Middle Class*, 7, 8.

53 Newbigin, *Hindu Family*, 43. Hindu Undivided Family is a separate taxable entity defined as a "person" under Section 2 (31) of the Income Tax Act 1961: "a family which consists of all persons lineally descended from a common ancestor and includes their wives and unmarried daughters. An HUF cannot be created under a contract, it is created automatically in a Hindu Family."

54 Fernandes, *India's New Middle Class*, 9, 13.

55 Varma, *Great Indian Middle Class*, 37. See also Desai, *Mother Pious Lady*.

56 Haynes et al., *Towards a History of Consumption*; Haynes, *Emergence of Brand-Name Capitalism*; S. Joshi, *Fractured Modernity*. In *Passionate Modernity*, Sanjay Srivastava's definition of consumption as "a process of objectification" also proves useful here. He writes of consumption as "object or activity [that] becomes simultaneously a practice in the world and a form in which we construct our understanding of ourselves and in the world" (4). Srivastava also examines

post-independence magazines but in the context of what he calls "footpath modernity": Srivastava's city is the "unofficial city" (143); in this book I work within "official" city and consumption culture.

57 Certeau, *Practice of Everyday Life*, 167.

58 The only other study is in Hindi, Ranjan's "Lugdi Sahitya ke Andhere Ujale."

59 Malhotra *Dare to Publish*, 62; Rajya Sabha TV, "*Guftugu* with D N Malhotra."

60 Shekhar Malhotra, interview, 3 August 2015.

61 Audit Bureau of Circulation, accessed through email message from Pawan Kumar Kingwal to author, 24 September 2015, and *Press & Advertisers YearBook*.

62 Between 1950 and 1955, *Maya* and *Manohar Kahaniyaan* averaged circulation figures of 45,590 and 44,746, respectively. Pawan Kumar Lingwal, email message to author, 24 September 2015.

CHAPTER ONE: SARITA AND THE BIRTH OF MIDDLEBROW PUBLISHING

1 Letters to Editor, *Sarita*, January 1950, 6. All translations from *Sarita*, and the other Hindi sources in this book are my own.

2 The semiannual circulation figures provided by the Audit Bureau of Circulations archives show that *Sarita*'s circulation grew from 10,901 subscribers per month in 1952 to 29,002 in 1960. Lingwal, email to author, 24 September 2015.

3 See Orsini, *Print and Pleasure*; Yang, *Bazaar India*.

4 For a debate on the nationalization of Hindi from the nineteenth century onward, see Dalmia, *Nationalization of Hindu Traditions*, and A. Rai, *Hindi Nationalism*. In terms of the debates around Hindi as possible national and official language, the post-independence period was a particularly tumultuous one. See also Das Gupta, *Language Conflict and National Development*. The section "Language Rivalry after Independence" records how "Hindustani" was already being contested by what he calls "Hindi leaders" from as early as 1947 (131). The first leaders in the Constituent Assembly who supported the move included P. D. Tandon, Govind Das, Sampurnand, Ravi Shankar Shukla and K. M. Munshi (131). For a larger decadal overview of the language debates in the parliament in the 1950s, see Cohen, "Negotiating Differences."

5 Naipaul, "Women's Era," n.p.

6 "Exchange Rate, 1945–1971," Reserve Bank of India, https://www.rbi.org.in/commonperson/English/Scripts/FAQs.aspx?Id=1877.

7 Orsini, *Hindi Public Sphere*; Nijhawan, *Women and Girls*, and R. Sharma, "Words in Motion Pictures."

8 Orsini, *Hindi Public Sphere*, 25. See the introduction to *Everyday Reading* for a more detailed history of pre-independence journals.

9 For more on the Dwivedi period, see Mody, "Literary Self-Determination."

10 Mandhwani, "Communism, Congress."

11 Vishwa Nath, "Sarita Pravah," *Sarita*, March 1958, 141.

12 Orsini, *Hindi Public Sphere*; Mody, *Making of Modern Hindi*.

13 For more on Gandhi and his usage of Hindustani, see Gandhi, *Thoughts on National Language*; Lelyveld, "Words as Deeds: Gandhi and Language"; and Lelyveld, "Fate of Hindustani."

14 The reader, Sadashiv Tailang, wrote, "I can't comparehend what language *Sarita* is written in even after having read it. Truth be told, *Sarita* is not a completely Hindi, Urdu, Marathi or English magazine. Although it is a Hindi magazine, it uses the English 'full stop' rather than the Hindi '*purna viram*.' Can you clear my doubts about this?" See *Sarita*, April 1949, 6.

15 Letters to the Editor, *Sarita*, April 1949, 143.

16 Letters to the Editor, *Sarita*, August 1951, n.p.

17 "1001th Issue," *Sarita*, January 1997, 21.

18 In fact, Vishwa Nath and other writers' essays written against organized religious practices were compiled in the form of nine booklets titled *Sarita Mukta Reprints*. This essay collection was still in print in 2017.

19 Indu Shekhar, "Dharm ke naam par!," *Sarita*, May 1949, 18.

20 Shekhar, 18. Sati is the practice of a woman's self-immolation at her husband's funeral pyre.

21 This reformist tone is most visible in the case of article's discussion of the practice of sati, which Indian social reformists actively campaigned against in the nineteenth century, with the colonial authorities banning the practice in 1829.

22 Parvati Mishra, "Nari jivan mein shringara ka mahatva," *Sarita*, May 1948, 64.

23 Mishra, "Nari jivan mein shringara ka mahatva," 64.

24 *Sarita*, October 1949, 41.

25 *Sarita*, November 1960, 208.

26 Santoshnarayan Nautiyal, "Upar ki amdani," *Sarita*, December 1949, 47.

27 G. Rai, *Hindi Kahani ka Itihaas*, 402. This statement has been translated from Hindi by the author.

28 See Roadarmel, Theme of Alienation, and Mani, "Gender, Genre," for an overview of the Nayi Kahani. See also the introduction by Yadav, *Ek Duniya Samanantar*.

29 G. Rai, *Hindi Kahani ka Itihaas*, 441.

30 Two stories for *Sarita* by Rakesh and Yadav are discussed in a later section of this chapter.

31 Vishwa Nath wrote this in response to a question posed by Dwarkaprasad Agarwal, a reader who asked the editor about why he insists on everyone buying their own copy of the magazine since *Kalyan*, the other magazine that he subscribed to, says, "*Kalyan* has a prayer: We request our customers to be open hearted and let their brothers and sisters read this magazine." *Sarita*, May 1957, n.p. *Kalyan*, published by Gita Press from Gorakhpur, was an incredibly successful religious magazine. See Mukul, *Gita Press*.

32 *Sarita*, May 1949, 61.

33 The editor, in fact, replied to this letter, saying, "We always try to ensure that all creations in *Sarita* are written in an easy, clear language, because of which many

'Champions of literature' (*sahityik maharathi*) are irritated with *Sarita*. However, we will pay more attention to this." Letters to Editor, *Sarita*, June 1949, 10.

34 Letters to Editor, *Sarita*, January 1953, n.p.

35 Letters to Editor, *Sarita*, March 1949, n.p.

36 Letters to Editor, *Sarita*, July 1949, n.p.

37 *Pratik* was launched in 1947 under the editorship of Sachchidananda Hirananda Vatsyayan "Agyeya." Agyeya was one of the leading literary figures of the time who pioneered the Nayi Kavita or New Poetry movement. He was also a proponent of the Prayogvād or experimental turn in Hindi writing. See Rosenstein, *New Poetry in Hindi*, and A. Rai, "Reading *Pratik* through Agyeya."

38 Letters to Editor, *Sarita*, November 1949, 6.

39 Letters to Editor, *Sarita*, December 1949, 6.

40 A. Rai, "Reading *Pratik* through Agyeya," 23.

41 Letters to Editor, *Sarita*, December 1949, 6.

42 Letters to Editor, *Sarita*, February 1950, n.p.

43 "Naye Ankur," *Sarita*, January 1952, n.p.

44 In addition, the vast critical narrative on the Nayi Kahani does not consider the possibilities of how genre is inflected within the alternative urban space of the magazine, especially since multiple Nayi Kahani writers wrote for numerous commercial magazines such as *Sarita* and *Dharmyug*. Therefore, although one finds snippets of writers' associations with magazines, the critical narrative has not yet accounted for the literary writer's space within these profitable middlebrow magazines.

45 A *rākhi* is a ceremonial thread that a sister ties to her brother during the festival of Raksa Bandhan as a mark of trust, who, in return, pledges to protect her.

46 "Pat, *Pathakon ki samasyayein*," *Sarita*, March 1953, 95.

47 However, it is not as if *Sarita* only represented arguments toward these ideas. For instance, an article titled "The Development of Individuality within the Family" argues against a nuclear family or the idea of love marriage itself. Sushma Nirdesh, the writer of the piece, makes a historical case for a joint family, arguing that this idea has evolved from the need for protection, "collective effort (*sammilit prayatna*) and cumulative wealth (*sankilit dhan*)" and that the nuclear family emerging from marriages based on love does not conform to this need. She argues further that "the worst problem with love marriage is that young men and women pay attention to their feelings of love when they are making the choice. However, they forget the world's norms at that time." *Sarita*, May 1949, 50.

48 The editor replied to this letter immediately, noting that everyone needs pots and pans made from mud and that "even millionaires do not pay money for things they buy in hand. All of government officials' work is carried on loan, because their salaries are exhausted within the first eight to ten days of the month." Letters to Editor, *Sarita*, June 1949, 12.

49 Letters to Editor, *Sarita*, May 1950.

50 An article titled "Makeup to What Extent?" (Makeup kis seema tak?) is again an example of how women at home and outside are examined from a similar lens and the work ethic of both groups is equally acknowledged. Although the article didactically warns women not to put on too much makeup, it is not written from a moral perspective. Rather, this point is argued from the perspective of the amount of time that makeup deserves, since both women at home and at work can only dedicate a limited amount of time to it: "If you do not have any other work to do, then you can spend the adequate amount of time on makeup. However, housewives do not have much time to spare. The time of women who work in school and at offices too is necessarily precious. Such women should definitely become adept at putting on makeup in the least amount of time. You should be aware of what takes the most of your time while dressing." *Sarita*, April 1950, 81.

51 Orsini, *Hindi Public Sphere*, 270, 274.

52 Nijhawan, *Women and Girls*, 18.

53 Nijhawan, 4.

54 For instance, Nijhawan states, "The periodicals that had first addressed women, girls, and children as separate audiences collapsed these gendered divisions and began conceptualizing women and girls and men alike as future citizens of an independent nation." Nijhawan, 21.

55 Letters to Editor, *Sarita*, March 1949.

56 For more on religious chapbooks and almanacs, see Orsini, *Print and Pleasure*.

57 Brooks, *Melodramatic Imagination*, 21. The turn to melodrama in Hindi cinema is best illustrated by Ravi Vasudevan's *Melodramatic Public*, valuable for turning the lens of melodrama in the direction of popular cinema and nuancing the responses of the Indian spectators to both melodramas and spectacles.

58 The writer signed the story by her first name but was in fact the well-known Nayi Kahani writer Usha Priyamvada.

59 This switch from the Hindu undivided family to the nuclear family comes from a larger social history. Eleanor Newbigin builds a case for the emergence of the post-devolution middle-class subject because of pressures from "Hindu merchants and urban professionals," stating that, "in this way, the Hindu legal 'joint' family was 'made' at precisely the moment that multi-generational family units were coming under pressure." See "Post-Colonial Patriarchy?," 132.

60 This brings into perspective an interesting debate around the Hindu Code Bill that was raging when the story was written, with popular film representations like *Mr. and Mrs. 55* (1955) foregrounding it. There is no clarity in the story about the legality of the couple's separation. The wife just leaves, and the husband remarries.

61 Usha, "Man aur Hath," *Sarita*, January 1953, 63.

62 Vimla Kapur, like Usha, frequently wrote for the magazine. However, she finds no mention in larger literary histories.

63 Vimla Kapur, "Kachche Dhage," *Sarita*, June 1950, 33.

64 About the "openness" of the average Indian household, Verma writes: "You see the body being displayed everywhere in this country. Others might find a contradiction in such shameless exhibitionism in a closed and inhibited society like ours, but we have got quite used to it. Eyes peep from one house into another. No tender personal secrets can be hidden from the greedy and prurient gaze of the neighbours. From the morning bath to sleep at night—every act is performed in public view. Families may be rigid in their concepts of status and position but their daily lives are like the pages of an open book." See "Returning to One's Country," 65.

65 *Sarita* frequently commissioned Vimla Luthra, lost from literary histories, to write. She most notably wrote *ekanki*, "one-act plays," during the 1950s. An early example is *The Washerman's Coming* (*Dhobi ka Aagaman*, January 1949), a humorous short play about a couple whose morning routine is thrown into complete disarray because the washerman reaches their house earlier than usual to ask for clothes. Another, titled *The Arrangements for the Engagement* (*Sagai ka prabandh*, June 1949), again involves the family thrown into absolute confusion on the day their daughter is supposed to be introduced to her fiancé. A discussion of one of her English-language plays can be found in Mandhwani, "Communism, Congress."

66 Vimla Luthra, "Kala ke Davedar," *Sarita*, January 1952, 22.

67 Lutgendorf, "Making Tea in India," 12, 15.

68 Shukla, *Naukar ki kameez*, 17.

69 Rakesh, "*Seemayein*," 29, 30.

70 Rakesh, 32.

71 Rakesh, 33.

72 Rakesh, 33.

73 Usha Saksena, "Lal Chunar," *Sarita*, December 1951, 19.

74 For more on *stridhan*, see Diwan, *Modern Hindu Law*.

75 The February 1950 story is titled "Vachan," written by a female writer, Fareeda Bedi. The story is set in Kashmir and opens with the villagers discussing the fate of a respected elder, Kaneej Bibi, who is edging toward death. She calls the villagers to hear what she has to say. The story then goes into flashback where we are told that she had given her child away to make ends meet. After this confession, which is laden with melodrama, the woman dies. This is the only story that I could source in *Sarita* that openly discusses poverty. See chapter four for more on what I call the lowbrow genre of "melodramatic poverty."

76 "Hindi ki chuni huyi pustaken," *Sarita*, January 1952, n.p.

77 "Hindi ki chuni huyi pustaken."

78 Radway, *Feeling for Books*, 170.

79 Naya Sahitya, February 1951.

80 Manmath Nath Gupta, "Pichle Varsha ka Hindi Sahitya," *Sarita*, January 1960, 26.

81 In the early 1960s, Gupta wrote the novels *Jaal* (Trap) and *Dishaheen* (Directionless) for the Hind Pocket Books list.

82 Gupta, "Pichle Varsha," 26.
83 Gupta, 54.
84 The writer of the diary is not mentioned by name, but Chandrama Prasad Khare told me that he penned this diary. Chandrama Prasad Khare, interview, October 2015.
85 "Sahityik Diary," *Sarita*, February 1960, 150.
86 "Sahityik Diary," *Sarita*, January 1960, n.p.
87 "Letters to Editor," *Sarita*, February 1950, n.p.

CHAPTER TWO: HIND POCKET BOOKS

1 Rajya Sabha TV, "*Guftugu* with D N Malhotra."
2 Although no major critical work on Nanda has been published until this book—perhaps more an indication of Nanda's perception and legacy as a middlebrow writer—film criticism and encyclopedias have taken stock, albeit in cursory fashion, of Nanda as a scriptwriter. Nanda was especially well known for his collaborations with Hindi director-producer Yash Chopra. See Dwyer, "Mumbai Middlebrow," and Usman, *Rajesh Khanna*. For a pioneering study of Gulshan Nanda's extremely successful reception in China, see Jia, "Trans-Asian Popular Aesthetics."
3 Malhotra, *Dare to Publish*, 196.
4 *Dīvān-e-Ghalib*, back cover. It is difficult to point to the exact edition of the *Dīvān-e-Ghalib* because, while I found multiple editions of the same book in the company archives, the exact edition numbers were missing.
5 For instance, on Facebook Live, Meera Johri, Malhotra's niece and the proprietor of Rajpal & Sons, links Hind Pocket Books's success to her father Vishwanath. See "Vishwanath, Prakashan Rajpal."
6 See this book's introduction for an extensive discussion of these concerns.
7 Malhotra, *Dare to Publish*, 62, and Rajya Sabha TV, "*Guftugu* with D N Malhotra."
8 Chander, *Ek Gadhe ki Atma Katha*, back cover.
9 Malhotra, *Dare to Publish*, 153.
10 Malhotra, 113.
11 S. L. Keswani, "Paper Production and Its Availability."
12 Nath, interview.
13 Malhotra was also awarded the gold medal for his master's at Punjab University. See Mishra, "Indian Man Waits Six Decades."
14 Malhotra, *Dare to Publish*, 150.
15 Most histories of publishing from the postindependence period focus on school textbook publication as the most profitable publishing venture. Refer to Singh, "School Level Text Books." Amrik Singh also called for partial nationalization of textbooks because of pricing wars: "The problem at the primary level is that print runs are very high. If private initiative is allowed access to it, and is allowed free play, the prices will definitely go down" (205).

16 While nationalization of textbooks has not yet been a subject of any full-length study, the National Book Trust was established in 1957 under the Ministry of Education as an autonomous body. A large number of studies have been conducted on the production of school textbooks in India versus that in Pakistan, with particular focus on nationalist manipulations of history. See S. Joshi, "Contesting Histories and Nationalist Geographies." See also Malhotra, *Dare to Publish*, 97.

17 As already mentioned, *Sarita* was priced at one rupee as well. It was difficult for a book to be priced so low, as Malhotra himself attested in his *Guftugu* interview: in the first publication round, each book earned him only a meager profit margin of three to four paise. Rajya Sabha TV, "*Guftugu* with D N Malhotra."

18 Hind Pocket Books and Rajpal & Sons do not have any combined conclusive list of their publications, but certain writers such as Krishan Chander were contracted by both businesses to be published at the same time. See the interview with Salma Sidiqqui, Chander's wife, by Liaqat Jafri Poonchi, "Guftugu with Salma Sidiqqui."

19 However, the major reason for Rajpal & Sons publishing in hardback was not just that the individual reader at large still preferred hardbacks but also keeping in mind the institutional reader: for instance, the central library subscriptions, a major source of funding, demanded hardback editions. Shekhar Malhotra, interview, 3 August 2015.

20 The Audit Bureau of Circulations, a voluntary body of publishers that focused on circulation auditing, was formed in 1948. Many publishing conferences and conventions also took place during the 1950s, which Malhotra himself was part of. Malhotra, *Dare to Publish*.

21 Malhotra, "Publishing of Paperbacks."

22 Malhotra, *Dare to Publish*, 113.

23 Rajya Sabha TV, "*Guftugu* with D N Malhotra."

24 Malhotra, *Dare to Publish*, 187.

25 Shekhar Malhotra, personal interview.

26 Some publishing histories mention Hind Pocket Books as the first paperback publications in Hindi, but no major critical work has been conducted on Hind Pocket Books apart from Prabhat Ranjan in his pioneering essay, "Lugdi Sahitya ke Andhere Ujale." My translation.

27 Read the introduction in this book for more on Nayi Kahani writers. Chapter one also carries a section on the short stories written by the authors for *Sarita*.

28 While I have not generated systematic data to support this claim, informal interviews as well as correspondence with the first-generation readers of Hind Pocket Books and their families revealed a similar sentiment that the Home Library Scheme allowed these readers to have a library of their own for the first time. My own maternal grandmother was an avid reader and collector of these paperbacks until she shifted home from Delhi to Gurgaon, when she had to let her library go.

29 In that regard, Penguin is hailed as the first publisher of the modern paperback. Not only did Penguin publish different genres such as scientific information and intellectual nonfiction alongside fiction, which had been the mainstay of other paperbacks before, but it also made the paperback easily available at unconventional points of distribution, such as Woolworth's. See McCleery, "Return of the Publisher."

30 See "A Story Book Book Story."

31 Emili Edward Moreau first established A. H. Wheeler stalls in 1877 in Allahabad. The book stalls quickly grew to become very successful and spread across North and North West India. In 1937, when Moreau left India, he sold the company to Tinkari Kumar Banerjee. The company is still run by the Banerjee family. The name "Wheeler" is still synonymous with reading and rail journeys, with about 258 railway bookshops to its name in 2011. R. Chatterjee, "Five Centuries of Print." For a comprehensive history of Wheeler, see Prasad, "Railway Bookselling and the Politics of Print in India."

32 Malhotra, in Rajya Sabha TV, "*Guftugu* with D N Malhotra."

33 For instance, Abigail McGowan moves away from the nationalist history of consumption of Khadi, spun cloth, and Gandhi caps "to a history of how people interacted with goods more generally—who chose, bought, and utilized shoes or umbrellas" (33). McGowan argues that in this time period, although they were still uncertain of how to approach these commodities, women were slowly becoming active consumers. See "An All-Consuming Subject?" In another essay, McGowan maintains that while women were slowly becoming in charge of household budgets and purchases, they often saw this as an additional burden. See her "Modernity at Home." The reluctance of the consumers to reach for the book perhaps arises both from this inability to process the book as a consumable object and simultaneously coming to terms with it, particularly in the case of women as readers.

34 Malhotra, *Dare to Publish*, 187.

35 Ranjan, "Lugdi," 83.

36 Sharon Murphy has extensively researched the reading habits and the lending libraries for East India Company soldiers in the nineteenth century and Priya Joshi has examined the history of British books in Indian libraries, yet very limited research has been conducted on how books reached readers in the twentieth century. Francesca Orsini's research on the Bharati Bhawan in the time period between 1920 and 1940 shows that although novels were commonly borrowed, readers bought songbooks. See P. Joshi, "Reading in the Public Eye"; Murphy, "Libraries, Schoolrooms, and Mud Godowns"; and Orsini, *Hindi Public Sphere*.

37 However, Prabhat Ranjan estimates the figure at 545,000 subscribers. Ranjan, "Lugdi," 83.

38 Malhotra, *Dare to Publish*, 220; Rajya Sabha TV, "*Guftugu* with D N Malhotra."

39 As Francesca Orsini and Charu Gupta show, the Hindi popular market space, from as early as the late nineteenth century onward, was already replete with

instances of cheaply produced novels, self-help literature, and other hugely successful religious chapbooks such as *chalisas* and *brahmasas*. See Orsini, *Print and Pleasure*, and Gupta, *Sexuality, Obscenity, Community*.

40 Radway, *Feeling for Books*, 170. See also Rubin, *Making of Middle/brow Culture*.

41 Scherman, in turn, found inspiration in another major twentieth-century American mass production phenomenon: the Ford production line. Radway, *Feeling for Books*, 171.

42 Johri, "Vishwanath, Prakashan Rajpal."

43 Matthew Arnold derided the middle classes in Victorian England as "philistines" taking over the process of cultural production and consumption. According to Arnold, the middle classes, ill-equipped to be tastemakers, had suddenly emerged as the largest consuming class in England at an alarming rate. See Rapple, "Matthew Arnold's Views on Modernity."

44 This kind of aggressive marketing strategy can be studied most clearly in the case of cold drink product placements. Since the 1990s, cold drink companies have connected with food chains, department stores, schools, and universities in order to pair the cold drink with another product. Over time, this pairing has become so successful that consumers are unsure if they desired a cold drink in their food combo in the first place, taking it as a given. See Mukerjee, "Coca-Cola's Branding Strategies in India."

45 Shekhar Malhotra, interview, 23 September 2015.

46 Malhotra, *Dare to Publish*, 188.

47 In his 23 September 2015 interview with me, Shekhar Malhotra—Malhotra's son and current owner of Hind Pocket Books—also recalled that Rajendra Yadav once insisted that Hind Pocket Books drop Mannu Bhandari as author. D. N. Malhotra decided to drop Yadav from the series and retain Bhandari instead.

48 The novel is touted on the front cover as "Against society's discrimination! This is the story of a strong girl's resolve . . ."

49 Hansraj, *Sankalp*, back cover.

50 Y. Sharma, *Ek Swapna Ek Satya*, back cover.

51 Refer to Orsini's *Print and Pleasure* in which she discusses how popular Bengali detective fiction was one of the major ways through which detective fiction entered the Hindi market, that is, in translation.

52 See Ruth Vanita's detailed introduction to her translation of a short story collection by Sharma "Ugra" titled *Chocolate, and Other Writings*.

53 See Sil, *Life of Sharatchandra Chattopadhyay*, and Ranjan, *Kothagoi*.

54 Chander, *Ek Gadhe ki Atma Katha*, back cover.

55 Ashok K. Shah, under the pen name "Pratik," wrote his PhD thesis on Guru Dutt's novels, published as *Upanyaskar Guru Dutt: Ek Anusheelan*, 27.

56 According to Pratik, Dutt once recounted an anecdote involving an income tax officer who assessed Dutt's income at thirty-four thousand rupees from his novel writing, a huge amount for the time period. Dutt justified this income by denying extravagance: apparently, he had spent all his income on air flight expenses

during the year, a mode of transport he was forced to take because of his many work commitments that came as a result of writing. Shah "Pratik," *Upanyāskār Guru Dutt*, 28.

57 Shah "Pratik," *Upanyaskar Guru Dutt*, 42. Some of his other publishers during the 1960s included Ritambhar Prakashan, Makarand Prakashan, Bharati Sahitya Sadan, and Umesh Prakashan.

58 See Malhotra, *Dare to Publish*, and his list of best-selling authors.

59 Vasudevan, "Shifting Codes," 109.

60 Dwyer, "Fire and Rain," 12.

61 This does not include the Progressives' continued and strong relationship with the Hindi film post-independence. Many leading Progressives such as Khwaja Ahmed Abbas, Krishan Chander, Sahir Ludhianvi, and Rajinder Singh Bedi worked extensively in the Hindi film industry in the capacity of writers, songwriters, and directors. See Abbas's autobiography, *I Am Not an Island*, for an insight into his life as a filmmaker and writer.

62 In her interview with me in November 2015, Rachel Dwyer talks of the use of melodrama in this manner through exteriority, which is placing narrative and feelings onto external objects. This form of exteriority was common in Mehboob's celebrated social films such as *Andaaz* (1949), *Amar* (1954), and *Mother India* (1957). See Francesca Orsini's introduction to the *Oxford India Premchand* for a detailed history of how Premchand ushered in social realism in Hindi.

63 See Kapur, "Mythic Material in Indian Cinema," 23.

64 Vasudevan, *Melodramatic Public*, 320.

65 Dutt, *Lalsa*, 74, 76, 85.

66 Virdi, "Reverence, Rape," 254.

67 See Abbas's autobiography, *I Am Not an Island*, for an insight into Abbas's life as a filmmaker and writer. He also wrote *Andhera Ujala* (Darkness and light) and *Pyaar ki Pukar* (The call of love) for Hind Pocket Books.

68 Jalil, *Liking Progress, Loving Change*, 328, 329.

69 *Amar Vani*, front cover.

70 Goyalinka, introduction to *Atma Rahasya*, by James Allen, 2.

71 Varma, introduction to Smiles, *Mitavyaya*. I was unable to locate the first edition of the text, although the 1927 edition insists that, although a new introduction was added, no changes were made to the text itself.

72 For instance, Asa Briggs theorizes Smiles's 1859 *Self-Help* against the other two major works published that year, namely, John Stuart Mill's *Essay on Liberty* and Charles Darwin's *The Origin of Species* and notes that Smiles's work should not be reduced as a peculiarity but be judged with regard to the intellectual climate of the time period, all of which signaled a bent toward self-reliance for the sake of the collective good. See "Samuel Smiles: The Gospel of Self-Help."

73 Varma, introduction. This sentiment finds echoes in M. K. Gandhi's articulations on poverty, in which he stated that poverty also existed owing to the lack of any trusteeship model in place. He called this trusteeship model "Ramrajya," which,

he insisted, could only be attained if a hierarchical father-son relationship existed between the rich and the poor, the ruler and the ruled, based on ability. See Sarkar, "Gandhi and Social Relations."

74 Theosophy had attained massive popularity through Helena Petrovna Blavatsky's and Henry Steel Olcott's efforts from the late nineteenth century onward through their move to India. See van der Veer, *Imperial Encounters,* and Viswanathan, *Outside the Fold,* for a history of theosophy in India.

75 Allen, *Safalta ke aath sadhan,* back cover.

76 Allen, *Safalta ke aath sadhan,* 2.

77 Allen, "Eight Pillars of Prosperity."

78 For more on song booklets, see Ravikant Sharma's unpublished thesis "Words in Motion Pictures."

79 Kshemchandra 'Suman,' *Hindi ke Sarvesreshtha Prem Geet.*

80 Pandit, preface to Ghalib, *Deewan-e-Ghalib,* 3.

81 Pandit, preface to Muradabadi, *Jigar ki Shayari.*

82 Orsini, *Print and Pleasure.*

83 Lunn, "Denying Difference," 140, 143.

84 In the introduction to his unpublished thesis, Ravikant Sharma talks of the Hindi-Urdu symbiosis in Hindi cinema and particularly examines Harish Trivedi's critique of Mukul Kesavan's essay on Islamicate cultures in Hindi cinema. See Sharma, "Words in Motion Pictures."

85 In the titles that I worked on, Pritam has four works to her credit: *Kasam* (Promise), *Nina, Aasoo* (Tears), and *Band Darvaza* (Closed doors).

86 Rubin, "Self, Culture, and Self-Culture in America," in her *Making of Middle/brow Culture.*

CHAPTER THREE: *DHARMYUG*

1 Nandan, *Kahna Zaroori Tha,* 12.

2 Audit Bureau of Circulations, Lingwal, email message to author.

3 Circulation figures collated from Press & Advertisers Year Book, India News & Feature Alliance (INFA), 1964. Founded by Durga Das, editor in chief of the *Hindustan Times,* this alliance was formed in 1959. The exact circulation figure provided by the yearbook are 107,788 for *Dharmyug. Illustrated Weekly* trailed behind *Dharmyug* at 100,743 subscribers.

4 Dharmendra Gupta also recalls that the Joshi brothers went back to Allahabad to revive *Sangam* but failed to do so. See *Laghu Patrikayein aur Sahityik Patrakarita,* 22.

5 Prakash, "Dharmvir Bharati."

6 The table of contents of the magazine comprised only a part of the page. Usually positioned on the top left of the A3-size page, the contents were surrounded by advertisements. These have been cut in the image.

7 Bandivedekar, "Patrakar Bharti," 181. "Paan" refers to betel leaves popularly chewed as a digestive and to serve as a mouth freshener.
8 In the circulation figures that I was able to access, the only other magazine in North India able to match these figures was *Shama*, an Urdu magazine. In 1960, according to Audit Bureau of Circulations, its circulation was at 70,423, higher than *Dharmyug* for that time (Lingwal, email message to author). For more on *Shama*, see Sharma's unpublished thesis "Words in Motion Pictures."
9 For instance, in addition to Rai, *Hindi Nationalism*; Mody, *The Making of Modern Hindi*; Orsini, *The Hindi Public Sphere*, see Mukul, *Gita Press*, for more on Hindu nationalist publications like Gita Press's *Kalyan*.
10 Malhan, *TOI Story*.
11 Malhan, 17.
12 Subramanian, "Supreme Being."
13 Bandivedekar, "Patrakār Bharti," 181.
14 For more on post-independence calendar art, see Uberoi, "From Goddess to Pin-Up," and Jain, *Gods in the Bazaar*.
15 Uberoi, "'Unity in Diversity?,'" 197.
16 Monier-Williams Sanskrit-English Dictionary, s.v. "dharmyug."
17 A prominent example of this can be found in Christopher Pinney's *Photos of the Gods*, in which he prominently features a wide-ranging and complex history of calendar art from the late nineteenth century and offers what he calls a "history made by art" (8). He coins the term "corpothetics" to describe the devotion to these seemingly cheap images, writing, "'Corpothetics' entails a desire to fuse image and beholder, and the elevation of efficacy . . . as the central criterion of value" (194).
18 See the introduction for a detailed discussion of the debates around Hindi journals of the pre-independence period and their links to Hindu nationalism.
19 *Dharmyug*, 3 August 1958, n.p.
20 *Dharmyug*, 3 August 1958, n.p.
21 I borrow this term from Shobhana Bhattacharjee's "secular sacred pilgrimages" that take place post-partition. See "Indian Travel Writing," 134.
22 For a summary overview, see Bhattacharjee, "Indian Travel Writing"; Majeed, *Autobiography, Travel and Postnational Identity*; and more recently, Majchrowicz, *World in Words*.
23 Majchrowicz, *World in Words*, 61.
24 Narayan Chaturvedi, "Vilayati Patr," *Madhuri*, 17 July 1929, 751–57.
25 This was not limited to just popular magazines like *Madhuri*. *Vishwamitra* (Friend of the world) took its readers on both a whopping thirteen-page-long journey to Budapest and a (slightly shorter) expedition to the islands of the Philippines. Mahamaya Prasad Singh, "Budapest ki Sair," *Vishwamitra*, February 1935, 514–27, and Sri Vishwambhar Nath Sharma, "Narmundka Sikar," *Vishwamitra*, February 1935, 568–674.

26 Narayan Chaturvedi, "Vilayati Patr," *Madhuri*, 17 July 1929, 756.
27 Chaturvedi, "Vilayati Patr," 756.
28 See Orsini, *Hindi Public Sphere*, 187.
29 "Gangotri Yamunotri ki Yatra," 6–7; "Mahabaleshwar," 33; and "Meri Amriki Yatra ka Anubhav," 24–25, all in *Dharmyug*, 2 November 1958.
30 For more on the Cold War, Nehru's nonalignment, and the effects on publishing, see McGarr, *Cold War in South Asia*.
31 Mandhwani, "Communism, Congress"; Orsini, "Literary Activism"; Zecchini, "Meanings, Forms and Exercise of 'Freedom.'"
32 "America ka ullasmaya Jivan," *Dharmyug*, 3 July 1958, n.p.
33 "America ka ullasmaya Jivan."
34 "Amriki gharon ke anganon se," *Dharmyug*, 16 July 1958, n.p.
35 "Amriki gharon ke anganon se."
36 In terms of denoting transnational solidarities, the term "cosmopolitanism" has been most prominently used by Immanuel Kant, who espoused cosmopolitanism as a necessary moral theory to establish what Martha Nussbaum calls "an ambitious program for the containment of global aggression and the promotion of universal respect for human dignity" (28). See Kant's "Universal History with a Cosmopolitan Purpose," and Martha Nussbaum's essay "Kant and Cosmopolitanism."
37 Appiah, *Cosmopolitanism*.
38 For another, comprehensive account of "cosmopolitanisms" in the plural, see *Cosmopolitanisms*, edited by Bruce Robbins and Paulo Lemos Horta, particularly their introduction (1–20) and "The Cosmopolitanism of the Poor" by Silviano Santiago (21–39).
39 Chakrabarty, Breckenridge, Bhabha, and Pollock, introduction, 6.
40 Jamir Husain Kazmi, "Nachne wale darvesh," *Dharmyug*, 3 August 1958, 21.
41 Kazmi, "*Nachne wale darvesh*." The Lebanon crisis the article refers to was the result of the unrest between Lebanon and Egypt that escalated because of the unwillingness of Lebanon's president to break diplomatic ties with the West in the aftermath of Great Britain's attack on the Suez Canal, a civil conflict between Muslims and Moranite Christians in 1958. See Abu Khalil, "US Intervention in Lebanon."
42 Green, *Sufism*, 216.
43 For an English-language translation and introduction to the novel, see Saxena, "Falling Stars," 340–41.
44 Prakash, *Dharmvir Bharati*.
45 See Chinmay Sharma's unpublished thesis "Many Mahabharatas" for a more detailed analysis of the play in his chapter titled "Modernist Interventions in the Mahabharata."
46 Dimitrova, *Other in South Asian Religion*. For more on Parimal, see K. Verma, *Parimal*, and Schomer, *Mahadevi Varma*.
47 K. Verma, "Parimal banam pragatisheel andolan," in *Parimal*, 16.

48 Dimitrova, *Other in South Asian Religion.*

49 Bandivedekar, "Patrakar Bharti," 174–88.

50 D. Bharti, *Dharmvir Bharti se Sakshatkar*, 34.

51 In Allahabad, Bharti was married to Kanta Kohli. She wrote a revealing novel based on their relationship and divorce, scandalous for its time. See Kohli, *Ret ki machhli.*

52 Kamleshwar also held the long and distinguished career of being an editor of several magazines, which included *Vihaan* in the early 1950s, *Nayi Kahaniyaan* (1963–66), *Sarika* (1967–78), *Katha Yatra* (1978–79), *Ganga* (1984–88), *Ingit* (1961–63), and *Sri Varsha* (1979–80). Besides these, he also remained editor of the Hindi dailies *Dainik Jagaran* (1990–92) and *Dainik Bhaskar* (1996–2002) and worked at Door Darshan in the capacity of additional director general from 1980 to 1982.

53 Kamleshwar, *Adharashilayein*, 111, 110.

54 According to Agyeya, the first *pathak*, or "reader," is "concerned with spiritual welfare"; the second pathak "associates Hindi magazines with reading suitable for women"; the third "seeks entertainment"; and the fourth reader is "the Progressive chap," someone for whom Agyeya holds much disdain. The final reader is the "person who seeks to purify Hindi" (23). At this moment, Agyeya did not identify with, or respect, any of the categories of readers that he enumerated. Instead, he wanted to create a sixth, more literary reader. *Dharmyug*'s "middlebrow cosmopolitanism" charted a different, more democratic path. Read from this position, it was the sort of magazine that created the disreputable reader for Agyeya and would fall into the multiple categories that he enumerated and rejected. This section on Agyeya and readers is translated by Rai in "Reading *Pratik* through Agyeya," 23.

55 "Bhumika," *Agyeya Rachna Sagar*, 28.

56 Keshav Chandra Verma, however, provides us with another version of the Bharti-Parimal-Progressive story. In his memories of Parimal, Verma wrote that the group was flexible about its progressive leanings and that Bharti was one of the members who suffered not at the hands of Parimal but rather at those of the Progressive Writers Association, which he then had to leave because it sought to interfere with his writing: "Bharti used to be one of the most important writers of the Progressive association. However, they protested against it when his writings started carrying the 'Bharti stamp' [ankush]." Verma, *Parimal*, 15.

57 Singh quoted in Hindustani, "Dr Dharmvir Bharati."

58 Hindustani, "Dr Dharmvir Bharti."

59 See Saral, "Dharmyug ka Samay."

60 Hindustani, "Dr Dharmvir Bharti."

61 Kaliya, *Ghalib*, 131.

62 Vajpayi, "Soren Kierkegaard: Pita ki kramik hatya aur astitvavad ka janm," *Dharmyug*, 18 September 1960, n.p.

63 Vajpayi, "Soren Kierkegaard," n.p.

64 Kierkegaard quoted by Vajpayi, "Soren Kierkegaard," n.p.
65 Orsini, "Literary Activism."
66 The English translation, by Yashpal's son Anand, has a very nonliteral title: *This Is Not That Dawn*. *Untrue Truth* is my very literal translation.
67 Kishore Raman Tandon, "Urdu ki nayi shayari mein vyangya," *Dharmyug*, 17 July 1958, 6.
68 Tandon, "Urdu ki nayi shayari." Many thanks to Maryam Sikander for her help with translating this couplet.
69 Raghupati Sahay (1896–1982) was known by his pen name Firaq Gorakhpuri. Celebrated as one of the most accomplished Urdu poets of the period under study, he was awarded the Padma Bhushan (a civilian award) in 1968, the Sahitya Akademi Fellowship in 1970, and the Times Group–instituted Jnanpith Award in 1969. For a general introduction to "Firaq," see Kanda, *Masterpieces of Urdu Ghazal*.
70 Eklavya, "Nayī Hindī kavitā me vyanga," *Dharmyug*, 17 July 1958, 7.
71 Kierkegaard quoted by Vajpayi, "Soren Kierkegaard," n.p.
72 Prabhakar Machve was again a well-known litterateur. Jawaharlal Nehru appointed him the head of the Sahitya Akademi in 1954, from which he retired in 1975. See his memoir *From Self to Self*.
73 Prabhakar Machve, "Prabhakar Machve gaye Beatnikon ki beech," *Dharmyug*, 18 September 1960, n.p.
74 Machve, "Prabhakar Machve gaye."
75 Ramswarup Chaturvedi, "Camus aur uska sarthak sahitya," *Dharmyug*, 8 January 1961, 21.
76 Chaturvedi, "Camus," 21.
77 "Make up ka Chamatkar," Dharmyug, 18 September 1960, 23.
78 "Make up ka Chamatkar," 23.
79 Nandan, *Kahna Zaroori Tha*.
80 Bandivedekar, "Patrakar Bharti," 181.
81 For more detailed analysis of the "cut and paste" method of publishing, see Hofmeyr, *Gandhi's Printing Press*, and Mukhopadhyay, *Required Reading*.
82 Mukta Raje, Satyakatha, *Dharmyug*, 8 July 1962, 24.
83 Raje, Satyakatha, *Dharmyug*, 22 July 1962, 24.
84 Raje, Satyakatha, *Dharmyug*, 29 March 1964, 7 April 1964, 24.
85 Raje, Satyakatha, *Dharmyug*, 1 December 1962, 24.
86 Sahapedia, "Pushpa Bharati in Conversation."
87 Raje, Satyakatha, *Dharmyug*, 24 March 1963, 25.
88 Raje, "Satyakatha," *Dharmyug*, 24 March 1963, 50.
89 The Jain family established the Jnanpith Award in 1961 with the support of many prominent literary personalities such as Harivansh Rai Bachchan, Ramdhari Singh Dinkar, Jainendra Kumar, Jagdish Chandra Mathur, and Prabhakar Machve. Rajendra Prasad, the first president of India, was also approached and chaired the first committee. See "Shanti Prasad Jain," obituary, *New York Times*.

90 Hindustani, "Mere sampadak Dr Dharmvir Bharti."
91 Nandan, *Kahnā Zarūri Thā*.
92 Kaliya, *Ghalib*.
93 Kaliya, 129.
94 Saral, "Dharmyug ka Samay."
95 Kaliya, *Ghalib*, 129.
96 Saral, "Dharmyug ka Samay."

CHAPTER FOUR: ROMANCH AND THE 1950S

1 For a history of the Belvedere Press in Allahabad that published sant orature, see Orsini, "Booklets and Sants." See also Mukul, *Gita Press*.
2 See Orsini, *Hindi Public Sphere*; R. S. McGregor, "Rise of Standard Hindi."
3 See Mehrotra, *Last Bungalow*, for a succinct history of literary writing communities in Allahabad. See also the introduction as well as chapter three of this book for a discussion of the Parimal literary group.
4 All quoted material from the advertisement for the Manohar Series, *Maya*, June 1952, 2. An anna was one-sixteenth of a rupee, making 12 annas come to three-quarters of a rupee or roughly twenty cents. "Exchange Rate, 1945–1971," Reserve Bank of India. https://www.rbi.org.in/commonperson/English/Scripts/FAQs.aspx?Id=1877.
5 For a brief history of Hindi Sahitya Sammelan, see Mandhwani, "Hindi Library."
6 At some archives I was not so lucky. For instance, I did find many of these magazines in jumbled stacks at Allahabad's Bharati Bhawan Library. Unfortunately, silverfish and other insects had gotten through the better part of them before I could. At my touch, the paper crumbled and turned to dust.
7 It is unclear when the first issue was published, but the September 1931 issue gives us some clues. The then editor (and founder), Kshitindramohan Mitra Mustafi, wrote an open letter to readers lamenting that *Maya* had been closed for a long period of time due to lack of funds. He also blamed its closure on publishing the "National Issue" ("Rashtriyank") which came under fire from the Press Ordinance (82–84). I could trace this to the Press Ordinance of 1930, which "reintroduced many of the features of the hated 1910 Press Act." Christopher Pinney, "Iatrogenic Religion and Politics," 46.
8 Deepak Mitra v. District Judge, Allahabad, 1999 SCCOnline All 609.
9 *Maya* and *Manohar Kahaniyaan* averaged circulation figures of 45,590 and 44,746, respectively, between 1950 and 1955. Audit Bureau of Circulation data from Lingwal, email message, 24 September 2015.
10 Lingwal, email.
11 Siegel, "'Self-Help,'" 977.
12 Sherman, "'Grow More Food,'" 572–73.
13 Similarly, the Hindu Succession Act, the Hindu Adoptions and Maintenance Act, and the Hindu Minority and Guardianship Act came in effect in 1956,

further codifying the family in terms of property relations. Uberoi, "Legislating the Family." These bills caused furor in the parliament, even leading to B. R. Ambedkar's resignation. Protesting against the bill as it stood, Ambedkar said, "If you mean to give liberty—and you cannot deny that liberty in view of the fact that you have placed it in your Constitution and praised the Constitution which guarantees liberty and equality to every citizen—then you cannot allow this institution to stand as it is" (92). See Keating, *Decolonizing Democracy.*

14 Derek Littlewood and Peter Stockwell discuss three ways through which genre can be classified, that is, affective, stylistic, and discursive. Stylistic genre relates to the "style or technique in which the director has expressed the narrative." The discursive genre relates to the "subject matter or narrative emphasis." The affective genres include horror, comedy, romance, thriller, or tragedy. See Littlewood and Stockwell, *Impossibility Fiction*, 178.

15 McGregor, *Oxford Hindi-English Dictionary*, s.v. "romanch."

16 Kamleshwar, "Safed titliyan," *Manohar Kahaniyaan*, March 1959, 16–17; Upendranath "Ashk," "Paap ka arambh," *Maya*, June 1952, n.p.; Sa'adat Hasan Manto, "Nangi avaazein," *Maya*, November 1952, n.p.

17 The term "weird fiction" is attributed to H. P. Lovecraft, who defines it as "relative insignificance of all human life when measured on the scale of cosmic infinity." Emma Dawson Varughese utilizes the term "weird fiction" to discuss fantasy in India (termed *bharatiya fantasy*), which, she writes, "foregrounds the numinous and instances of 'awe,' especially in relation to superhuman beings and, by extension, the flouting of natural law." Varughese, *Genre Fiction of New India*, 22. See also Joshi, "Establishing the Canon of Weird Fiction."

18 For more on Nanda, see the chapter three in this volume. See also Malhotra, *Dare to Publish.*

19 Malhotra, *Dare to Publish.*

20 See C. Gupta, *Sexuality, Obscenity, Community*; Ashk, *Hindi sahitya ka maukhik itihaas*, 3:59; G. Rai, *Hindi Kahani ka Itihaas* .

21 C. Gupta, *Sexuality, Obscenity, Community*, 50.

22 See Jauss, *Toward an Aesthetic of Reception.*

23 *Sarita*, March 1955, 61.

24 For a detailed account of advertisements in the early twentieth century, see C. Gupta, *Sexuality, Obscenity, Community.*

25 "Exchange Rate, 1945–1971, Reserve Bank of India. https://www.rbi.org.in/commonperson/English/Scripts/FAQs.aspx?Id=1877.

26 More recent histories include Sreenivas, *Reproductive Politics*, and Ahluwalia, *Reproductive Restraints.*

27 *Maya*, January 1947, n.p.

28 See C. Gupta, *Sexuality, Obscenity, Community*, 43.

29 A. Rai, "Reading *Pratik*," 25.

30 Littlewood and Stockwell, *Impossibility Fiction*, 147.

31 Romanch ki vah ghari, *Maya*, October 1952 , 85.

32 McGregor, *Oxford Hindi-English Dictionary*, s.v. "romanch."
33 Romanch ki vah ghari, 85.
34 "Premi," *Maya*, December 1952, 103.
35 "Sher," *Maya*, December 1952, 101.
36 Wood, *Lolita in Peyton Place*, 44.
37 See Pernau et al., *Civilizing Emotions*.
38 Pernau et al., 3.
39 Neale, "Melodrama and Tears," 16.
40 Vimla Phadke, "Kafi," *Maya*, n.d, 17.
41 Phadke, "Kafi," 18, 19.
42 Phadke, 25.
43 Neale, "Melodrama and Tears," 7.
44 Phadke, "Kafi," 29.
45 Upendranath "Ashk," "Paap ka arambh," *Maya*, June 1952, 33.
46 Ashk, "Pap," 37.
47 Ashk, 37.
48 Ashk, 39.
49 Ashk, 40.
50 Neale, "Melodrama and Tears," 11.
51 Maniquis, "Review of *The Melodramatic Imagination*," 485.
52 Peter Brooks locates melodrama not only as a genre but also as an "imaginative mode." Brooks contends that melodrama is necessary mode "in which polarization and hyperdramatization of forces in conflict represent a need to locate and make evident, legible and operative those large choices of ways of being which we hold to be of overwhelming importance even though we cannot derive them from any transcendental system of belief." Brooks, *Melodramatic Imagination*, viii.
53 Kamla Phadke, "Paru," *Maya*, March 1952, 37.
54 Phadke, "Paru," 37.
55 Phadke, 38.
56 Phadke, 47.
57 As mentioned before, this raises questions about copyright because it does not seem likely that Manto himself gave the story to the magazine for publication.
58 Manto, "Nangi avaazein," *Maya*, November 1952, 79.
59 Manto, "Nangi avaazein," 80, 81.
60 Gould, "From Subjects to Citizens?," 44. Elsewhere, Gould tellingly writes that "the history of anti-corruption in early Independent north India can be characterized as an exercise in optimism, which gradually gave way to a sense of hopelessness." See Gould, *Bureaucracy, Community and Influence*, 16.
61 Madhukar Kher, "Kala Bazaar," *Maya*, 1952, 162.
62 Benjamin Siegel, "Self-Help," 980. See also Chapter 2 of Vijay Joshi's *India's Long Road* for an overview of the planning policies of the Indian government which predominantly focused on control such as "state intervention in markets" as well as "the dominant role of the public sector" (19).

63 Basant Kumar Mathur, "Aaina," *Maya*, June 1947, 2, 3.
64 Mathur, "*Aaina*," 5, 7.
65 Mathur, 4.
66 Mathur, 7.
67 Krynicki, *Captive Princess*.
68 Shyam Sundar Goyanka, "Mrityu ke bahupas mein," *Rasili Kahaniyaan*, 68, n.d.
69 Goyanka, "Mrityu ke bahupas mein," 68.
70 Goyanka, 66.
71 Moitra, "Triangle River Tango."
72 Khare, interview.
73 "Delhi Press Acquires 'Manohar Kahaniyan' and 'Satyakatha' Magazines," *exchange4media*, 4 September 2008, https://www.exchange4media.com/media-print-news/delhi-press-acquires-manohar-kahaniyan-and-satyakatha-magazines- 32347.html.

CONCLUSION: WHO'S AFRAID OF MANMATH NATH GUPTA?

1 M. Gupta, *Pragativad ki ruprekha*.
2 I found that Gupta wrote the novels *Trap* (*Jaal*) and *Directionless* (*Dishaheen*) in the Hind Pocket Books list that I examined. In the 13 July 1958 issue of *Dharmyug*, Gupta wrote an ironic story or *vyangyakatha* called "Life and poetry" ("Jivan aur kavya").
3 The November 1947 issue of *Maya* carried an article titled "Kakori Train Dacoity," excerpted from the upcoming "romanchkari" book by "Mr. Manmath Nath Gupta, the erstwhile prisoner in the Kakori Case," 84–87.
4 Gupta wrote the short story "Epoch" ("Zamana") in the July 1954 issue, "Knife" ("Chhuri") for the September 1954 issue, and "Justice" ("Nyay") in the January 1955 New Year's special issue.
5 These stratifications were practiced not only by readers but also by writers: *Dharmyug* was feted and celebrated by writers. It held a special place in the memories (and memoirs) of its writers. Perhaps the most evocative expression of this lies in an essay by prominent modernist New Story (Nayi Kahani) writer Mannu Bhandari. Bhandari writes movingly about temporarily moving from her marital home to her faculty accommodation at Delhi University to concentrate on finishing her first novel. The result, *Aapka Bunty* (Your bunty), was first serialized in *Dharmyug* in 1970. Bhandari, Ek sahityik tukka.
6 A notable exception is Kamleshwar, who recounts his days of penury in Delhi when he had to borrow money for, among other things, cigarettes. He writes, "I started doing translation work for Delhi Press and *Sarita Sahitya Mandal*. I had a dear friend, Naresh Bedi, who worked for Delhi Press as well my dear friend and classmate, Chandrama Prasad Khare. He was in some reputable post in Delhi Press. Life didn't quite start running, but it at least started functioning." See Kamleshwar, "Ti Haus," 76–77.

7 Bourdieu, *Distinction*, 81.

8 In chapter four we saw how literary writers like Upendranath Ashk and Kamleshwar wrote for, or were published in, lowbrow magazines.

9 Darnton, "What Is the History of Books?," 67.

10 Beetham, *Magazine of Her Own?*, 5.

11 There is no study comparable to G. Rai's *Hindi sahitya par pathakon ki ruchi ka prabhav*, which ends with the 1920s.

12 Zecchini, *Arun Kolatkar and Literary Modernism*; Nerlekar, *Bombay Modern*.

13 Findings have been published in Mandhwani, "From the Colloquial to the 'Literary.'"

14 Ranjan, "Lugdi Sahitya ke Andhere Ujale."

15 Naipaul, "Women's Era" (e-book).

Bibliography

INTERVIEWS

Dalmia, Vasudha. Interview by author, Delhi, 7 November 2015.

Dwyer, Rachel. Interview by author, London, November 2015.

Khare, Chandrama Prasad. Interview by author, Delhi, October 2015.

Lingwal, Pawan Kumar. Email message to author, 24 September 2015.

Malhotra, Shekhar. Interview by author, Delhi, 3 August 2015, 23 September 2015.

Mehta, Ramesh. Interview by author, Delhi, 23 July 2017.

Nath, Paresh. Interview by author, Delhi, 2 November 2015.

HINDI MAGAZINES

Sarita, 1945 to 1960.

Dharmyug, 1958 to 1961.

Maya, 1945 to 1960.

Rasili Kahaniyaan, 1945 to 1960.

Manohar Kahaniyaan, 1945 to 1960.

HIND POCKET BOOKS TITLES

Allen, James. *Safalta ke aath sadhan*. Translated by Mahavir Adhikari. Delhi: Hind Pocket Books, n.d.

Chander, Krishan. *Ek Gadhe ki Atma Katha*. Delhi: Hind Pocket Books, n.d., ca. 1958.

———. *Ek Gadhe ki Vapsi*. Delhi: Hind Pocket Books, n.d.

———. *Ek Gadha Nefa mein*. Delhi: Hind Pocket Books, n.d.

Dutt, Guru. *Lalsa*. Delhi: Hind Pocket Books, 1968.

———. *Mamta*. Delhi: Hind Pocket Books, 1962.

Ghalib. *Deewan-e-Ghalib*. Delhi: Hind Pocket Books, n.d.

Gupta, Manmath Nath. *Dishaheen*. Delhi: Hind Pocket Books, n.d.

———. *Jāl*. Delhi: Hind Pocket Books, n.d.

Hans, Manas, ed. *Amar Vani*. Delhi: Hind Pocket Books, 1959.

Hansraj. *Sankalp*. Delhi: Hind Pocket Books, n.d., ca. 1958.

Muradabadi, Jigar. *Jigar ki Shayari*. Delhi: Hind Pocket Books, n.d.

Pandit, Prakash, ed. and trans. *Aaj ki Urdu shayari*. Delhi: Hind Pocket Books, n.d.

Pritam, Amrita. *Aasoo*. Delhi: Hind Pocket Books, n.d.

———. *Band Darvaza*. Delhi: Hind Pocket Books, n.d.

———. *Kasam*. Delhi: Hind Pocket Books, n.d.

———. *Nina*. Delhi: Hind Pocket Books, n.d.

Sharma, Yagyadutt. *Ek Swapna Ek Satya*. Delhi: Hind Pocket Books, n.d., ca. late 1950s.

"Suman," Kshemchandra, ed. *Hindi ke Sarvasreshtha Prem Geet*. Delhi: Hind Pocket Books, ca. 1958.

Urdu Rubaiyat. Translated by Prakash Pandit. Delhi: Hind Pocket Books, n.d.

Vidyalankar, Satyakam. *Mukta*. Delhi: Hind Pocket Books, n.d.

OTHER BOOKS, ARTICLES, AND DISSERTATIONS

Abbas, K. A. *I Am Not an Island: An Experiment in Autobiography*. Delhi: Vikas Publishing, 1977.

AbuKhalil, As'ad. "*U.S. Intervention in Lebanon, 1958 and 1982: Presidential Decisionmaking*, by Agnes G. Korbani." *Middle East Journal*, no. 3 (1993): 530.

Adorno, Theodor. *The Philosophy of Modern Music*. Translated by Anne G. Mitchell and Wesley V. Blomster. 1949; London: Continuum International Publishing Group, 2003.

Adorno, Theodor W., and J. M. Bernstein. *The Culture Industry: Selected Essays on Mass Culture*. London: Routledge, 1991.

Ahluwalia, Sanjam. *Reproductive Restraints: Birth Control in India, 1877–1947*. Champaign: Illinois University Press, 2008.

Allen, James. *Atma Rahasya*. Translated by Dayachandra Goyalinka. Allahabad: Hindi Sahitya Bhandar, 1918.

Allen, Rob, and Thijs van den Berg, eds. *Serialization in Popular Culture*. London: Routledge, 2014.

Amarkant. "Hatyare." In *Pratinidhi Kahaniyaan*, 105–12. Delhi: Rajkamal, 1984.

Appiah, Kwame Anthony. *Cosmopolitanism: Ethics in a World of Strangers*. New York: W. W. Norton, 2006.

Ashk, Neelabh, ed. *Hindi sahitya ka maukhik Itihas*. Vol. 1. Wardha: Mahatma Gandhi Antarashtriya Hindi Vishwavidyalay, 2004.

———. *Hindi sahitya ka maukhik Itihas*. Vol. 3. Wardha: Mahatma Gandhi Antarrashtriya Hindi Vishwavidyalay, 2004.

Balasubramanian, Aditya. *Toward a Free Economy: Swatantra and Opposition Politics in Democratic India*. Princeton, NJ: Princeton University Press, 2023.

Bandivedekar, Chandrakant. "Patrakar Bharti." In *Dharmvir Bharti: Vyaktitva aur Krititva*. Delhi: Sahitya Akademi, 2001.

Baxendale, John. "Priestley and the Highbrows." In *Middlebrow Literary Cultures: The Battle of the Brows, 1920–1960*, edited by Erica Brown and Mary Grover. New York: Palgrave Macmillan, 2012.

Beetham, Margaret. *A Magazine of Her Own? Domesticity and Desire in the Woman's Magazine, 1800–1914*. London: Routledge, 1996.

Berry, Kim. "Lakshmi and the Scientific Housewife: A Transnational Account of Indian Women's Development and Production of an Indian Modernity." *Economic and Political Weekly* 38 (January 1, 2003): 1055–68.

Bhandari, Mannu. "Ek sahityik tukka." In *Dilli Ti Haus*, edited by Baldev Vanshi. Delhi: National, 2009.

Bharati, Dharamvir. "Falling Stars." In *Chander and Sudha*. Translated by Poonam Saxena. Delhi: Penguin, 2015.

Bharti, Dharmvir. *Deshantar* (1960). In *Dharmavir Bharti Granthavali*, edited by Chandrakant Bandiwadekar, vol. 8. Delhi: Vani Prakashan, 1998.

———. *Dharmvir Bharti se Sakshatkar*. Edited by Pushpa Bharti. Delhi: Bhartiya Gyanpith, 1998.

Bharti, Kanta. *Ret ki machli*. Delhi: Lokbharti Prakashan, 2008.

Bhattacharjee, Shobhana. "Indian Travel Writing." In *The Routledge Companion to Travel Writing*, edited by Carl Thompson, 125–38. Oxford: Routledge, 2016.

Bhaumik, Someshwar. *Cinema and Censorship: The Politics of Control in India*. New Delhi: Orient BlackSwan, 2009.

"Bhumika." In *Agyeya Rachna Sagar*, 13–52. Delhi: Prabhat Prakashan, 2011.

Bourdieu, Pierre. *Distinction: A Social Critique of the Judgment of Taste.* London: Routledge & Kegan Paul, 1984.

———. *The Rules of Art: Genesis and Structure of the Literary Field.* Cambridge: Polity, 1996.

Briggs, Asa. "Samuel Smiles: The Gospel of Self-Help." In Victorian Values: *Personalities and Perspectives in Nineteenth Century Society*, edited by Gordon Marsden. London: Routledge, 1998.

Brooks, Peter. *The Melodramatic Imagination: Balzac, Henry James, Melodrama, and the Mode of Excess*. New Haven, CT: Yale University Press, 1976.

Butalia, Urvashi. *The Other Side of Silence: Voices from the Partition of India.* Durham, NC: Duke University Press, 2000.

Certeau, Michel de. *The Practice of Everyday Life*. Berkeley: University of California Press, 1984.

Chartier, Roger. "Laborers and Voyagers: From the Text to the Reader." *Diacritics* 22, no. 2 (1992): 49–61.

Chakrabarty, Dipesh, Carol Breckenridge, Homi K. Bhabha, and Sheldon Pollock, "Cosmopolitanisms." In *Cosmopolitanism*, edited by Carol A. Breckenridge, Sheldon Pollock, Homi K. Bhabha, and Dipesh Chakrabarty, 1–15. Durham, NC: Duke University Press, 2002.

Chatterjee, Partha. "The Nationalist Resolution of the Women's Question." In *Recasting Women: Essays in Indian Colonial History*, edited by Kumukum Sangari and Sudesh Vaid, 233–53. New Brunswick, NJ: Rutgers University Press, 1990.

Chatterjee, Rimi B. *Empires of the Mind: A History of the Oxford University Press in India under the Raj*. New York: Oxford University Press, 2006.

———. Five Centuries of Print: The book in India, Old and New." Himal Magazine, 21 May 2011. https://www.himalmag.com/cover/five-centuries-of-print-2011.

Chibber, Vivek. *Locked in Place: State-Building and Capitalist Industrialization in India, 1940–1970*. Princeton, NJ: Princeton University Press, 2003.

Cohen, Benjamin. "Negotiating Differences: India's Language Policy." In *Social Difference and Constitutionalism in Pan-Asia*, edited by Susan H. Williams, 27–52. Cambridge: Cambridge University Press, 2014.

Dalmia, Vasudha. "Generic Questions: Bharatendu Harishchandra and Women's Issues." In *Hindu Pasts: Women, Religion, Histories*, 251–85. New York: SUNY Press, 2017.

———. *The Nationalization of Hindu Traditions: Bhāratendu Hariśchandra and Nineteenth-Century Benaras*. New York: Oxford University Press, 1997.

Dalmia, Vasudha, and Sanjeev Kumar, eds. *Balabodhini*. Delhi: Rajkamal, 2014.

Darnton, Robert. "What Is the History of Books?" *Daedalus* 111, no. 3 (1982): 65–83.

———. "'What Is the History of Books?' Revisited." *Modern Intellectual History* 4, no. 3 (November 2007): 495–508.

Das Gupta, Jyotirindra. *Language Conflict and National Development: Group Politics and National Language Policy in India*. Berkeley: University of California Press, 1970.

De, Rohit. "'Commodities must be controlled': Economic Crimes and Market Discipline in India (1939–55)." *International Journal of Law in Context* 10 (2014): 277–94.

———. *A People's Constitution: The Everyday Life of Law in the Indian Republic*. Princeton, NJ: Princeton University Press, 2018.

Derrida, Jacques, and Avital Ronell. "The Law of Genre." *Critical Inquiry* 7, no. 1 (1980): 55–81.

Desai, Santosh. *Mother Pious Lady: Making Sense of Everyday India*. New Delhi: HarperCollins, 2010.

Devitt, Amy J. "Generalizing about Genre: New Conceptions of an Old Concept." *College Composition and Communication* 44, no. 4 (December 1993): 573–86.

Dimitrova, Diana, ed. *The Other in South Asian Religion, Literature and Film: Perspectives on Otherism and Otherness*. New York: Routledge, 2014.

Diwan, Paras. *Modern Hindu Law: Codified and Uncodified*. Allahabad: Allahabad Law Agency, 2021.

Duggal, K. S. *Book Publishing in India*. New Delhi: Marwah, 1980.

Dwyer, Rachel. "Fire and Rain, The Tramp and The Trickster: Romance and the Family in the Early Films of Raj Kapoor." *South Asianist* 2 (1 January 2013): 9–32.

———. "Mumbai Middlebrow: Ways of Thinking about the Middle Ground in Hindi Cinema." In *Middlebrow Cinema*, edited by Sally Faulkner, 51–67. London: Routledge, 2016.

Dwyer, Rachel, and Divia Patel. *Cinema India: The Visual Culture of Hindi Film*. New Brunswick, NJ: Rutgers University Press, 2002.

Farr, Cecilia Konchar, and Tom Perrin. "Introduction: Inventing the Middlebrow." *Post45*, 1 July 2016. https://post45.org/2016/07/introduction-inventing-the-middlebrow/.

Fernandes, Leela. *India's New Middle Class: Democratic Politics in an Era of Economic Reform*. Minneapolis: University of Minnesota Press, 2006.

Freier, Monika. "Cultivating Emotions: The Gita Press and Its Agenda of Social and Spiritual Reform." *South Asian History and Culture* 3, no. 3 (1 July 2012): 397–413.

Gandhi, M. K. *Thoughts on National Language*. Ahmedabad: Navajivan, 1956.

Ghosh, Anindita. *Power in Print: Popular Publishing and the Politics of Language and Culture in a Colonial Society, 1778–1905*. New Delhi: Oxford University Press, 2006.

Gonzalez, J. A. "A Contemporary Look at Pierre Bourdieu's 'Photography: A Middle-Brow Art.'" *Visual Anthropology Review* 8, no. 1 (Spring 1992): 126–31.

Gould, William. *Bureaucracy, Community and Influence: Society and the State in India, 1930–1960s*. London: Routledge, 2011.

———. "From Subjects to Citizens? Rationing, Refugees and the Publicity of Corruption over Independence in UP." *Modern Asian Studies* 45, no. 1 (January 2011): 33–56.

Green, Nile. *Sufism: A Global History*. Oxford: Wiley-Blackwell, 2012.

Greenberg, Clement. *The Collected Essays and Criticism*. Edited by John O'Brian. Chicago: University of Chicago Press, 1986.

Gupta, Abhijit, and Swapan Chakravorty, eds. *Print Areas: Book History in India*. Delhi: Permanent Black, 2004.

———, eds. *Movable Type: Book History in India*. Delhi: Permanent Black, 2008.

———, eds. *New Word Order: Transnational Themes in Book History*. Calcutta: Worldview, 2011.

Gupta, Charu. *The Gender of Caste: Representing Dalits in Print*. Seattle: University of Washington Press, 2016.

———. *Sexuality, Obscenity, Community: Women, Muslims, and the Hindu Public in Colonial India*. New Delhi: Permanent Black, 2001.

Gupta, Dharmendra. *Laghu Patrikayein aur Sahityik Patrakarita*. Delhi: Takshila Prakashan, 2000.

Gupta, Manmath Nath. *Pragativad ki ruprekha: sahitya aur samaj ke vibhinn pakshon tatha rachnaon ka pragati-parak vishlesan*. Delhi: Atamaram and Sons, 1952.

Gyanranjan. "Vagabond Nights." Translated by Sara Rai. In *The Last Bungalow: Writings on Allahabad*, edited by Arvind Krishna Mehrotra, 305–15. Delhi: Penguin, 2007.

Hardgrove, Anne. *Community and Public Culture: The Marwaris in Calcutta*. New Delhi: Oxford University Press, 2004.

Harrison, K. C. "Highbrow, Lowbrow, No-Brow: Women's Reading Practices and the Vitality of New-Format Fiction." *Reconstruction: Studies in Contemporary Culture* 11, no. 3 (2011).

Haug, Wolfgang Fritz. *Critique of Commodity Aesthetics*. Minneapolis: University of Minneapolis Press, 1986.

Haynes, Douglas. *The Emergence of Brand-Name Capitalism in Late Colonial India Advertising and the Making of Modern Conjugality*. London: Bloomsbury, 2022.

Haynes, Douglas E., Abigail McGowan, Tirthankar Roy, and Haruka Yanagisawa, eds. *Towards a History of Consumption in South Asia*. New Delhi: Oxford University Press, 2010.

Hofmeyr, Isobel. *Gandhi's Printing Press: Experiments in Slow Reading*. Cambridge, MA: Harvard University Press, 2013.

Horta, Paulo Lemos, and Kwame Anthony Appiah. *Cosmopolitanisms*. Edited by Bruce Robbins. New York: New York University Press, 2017.

India Yearbook, 1954. Delhi: Publications Division, 1955.

Jain, Kajri. *Gods in the Bazaar: The Economies of Indian Calendar Art*. Durham, NC: Duke University Press, 2007.

Jalil, Rakshanda. *Liking Progress, Loving Change: A Literary History of the Progressive Writers' Movement in Urdu*. New Delhi: Oxford University Press, 2014.

Jameson, Fredric. *The Cultural Turn: Selected Writings on the Postmodern, 1983–1998*. London: Verso, 2009.

Jauss, Hans Robert. *Toward an Aesthetic of Reception*. Minneapolis: University of Minnesota Press, 1982.

Jia, Yan. "Trans-Asian Popular Aesthetics." *Journal of World Literature* 4, no. 4 (2019): 530–51.

Johri, Meera. "Vishwanath, Prakashan Rajpal and Sons ki Janm Shatabdi par poorna smaran." 1:09:17 hours, posted 27 July 2020. https://www.facebook.com/105694072811330/videos/936042983562848.

Joshi, Priya. "Reading in the Public Eye: The Circulation of British Fiction in Indian Libraries, c. 1835–1901." In *Literary History. Essays on the Nineteenth Century*, edited by Stuart Blackburn and Vasudha Dalmia, 280–326. Delhi: Permanent Black, 2013.

Joshi, Sanjay. "Contesting Histories and Nationalist Geographies: A Comparison of School Textbooks in India and Pakistan." *South Asian History and Culture* 1, no. 3 (2010): 357–77.

———. *Fractured Modernity: Making of a Middle Class in Colonial North India*. New Delhi: Oxford University Press, 2001.

Joshi, S. T. "Establishing the Canon of Weird Fiction." *Journal of the Fantastic in the Arts* 14, no. 3 (55) (Fall 2003): 333–41.

Joshi, Vijay. *India's Long Road: The Search for Prosperity*. New Delhi: Oxford University Press, 2017.

Kaliya, Ravindra. *Ghalib chuti sharab*. Delhi: Vani Prakashan, 2000.

———. "Ti haus hamara dusra ghar tha." In *Dilli Tī Haus*, edited by Baldev Vanshi, 333–43. Delhi: National, 2009.

Kamleshwar, "Ti Haus: Ab na rahe ve peene wale." In *Dilli Ti Haus*, edited by Baldev Vanshi. Delhi: National, 2009.

———. *Adharshilayein: Yadon ke chiragh*. Delhi: Rajpal & Sons, 1992.

Kanda, K. C. *Masterpieces of Urdu Ghazal from the 17th to the 20th Century*. Delhi: Sterling, 1992.

Kant, Immanuel. "Idea of a Universal History with a Cosmopolitan Purpose," in *Political Writings*. Edited by H. S. Reiss. Cambridge: Cambridge University Press, 1991.

Kapur, Geeta. "Mythic Material in Indian Cinema." *Journal of Arts and Ideas*, no. 14–15 (July–December 1987): 79–108.

Kaur, Ravinder. *Since 1947: Partition Narratives among Punjabi Migrants of Delhi*. Oxford: Oxford University Press, 2018.

Keating, Christine. *Decolonizing Democracy: Transforming the Social Contract in India*. University Park: Pennsylvania State University Press, 2011.

Kennedy, A. B. *The International Ambitions of Mao and Nehru: National Efficacy Beliefs and the Making of Foreign Policy*. Cambridge: Cambridge University Press, 2012.

Kesavan, B. S. *History of Printing and Publishing in India: A Story of Cultural Re-Awakening*. Vol. 3, *Origins of Printing and Publishing in the Hindi Heartland*. New Delhi: National Book Trust, India, 1997.

Khan, Yasmin. *The Great Partition: The Making of India and Pakistan*. New Haven, CT: Yale University Press, 2007.

Khilnani, Sunil. "Fifties: Looking Back, for Lessons." *India Today*, 2 July 2007.

Kohli, Kanta. *Ret ki machli*. Delhi: Lokbharti Prakashan, 2008.

Krynicki, Annie Krieger. *Captive Princess: Zebunissa, Daughter of Emperor Aurangzeb*. Karachi, Pakistan: Oxford University Press, 2005.

Kumar, Sukrita Paul. *Narrating Partition: Texts, Interpretations, Ideas*. New Delhi: Indialog, 2004.

Lathan, Sean, and Robert Scholes. "The Rise of Periodical Studies." *Publications of the Modern Language Association of America* 121, no. 2 (March 2006): 517.

Lelyveld, David. "The Fate of Hindustani: Colonial Knowledge and the Project of a National Language." In *Orientalism and the Postcolonial Predicament*, edited by Carol A. Breckenridge and Peter van der Veer, 189–214. Philadelphia: University of Pennsylvania Press, 1993.

———. "Words as Deeds: Gandhi and Language." In *Competing Nationalisms in South Asia*, edited by Paul R. Brass and Achin Vanaik, 172–86. New Delhi: Orient Longman, 2002.

Littlewood, Derek, and Peter Stockwell, eds. *Impossibility Fiction: Alternativity—Extrapolation-Speculation*. Atlanta, GA: Brill Rodopi, 1996.

Lunn, David. "Denying Difference: Poetic Tastes and Practices across the Divide." In "Looking for Common Ground: Aspects of Cultural Production in Hindi/Urdu, 1900–1947," 119–87. Unpublished diss., SOAS, University of London, 2012.

Lutgendorf, Philip. "Making Tea in India: Chai, Capitalism, Culture." *Thesis Eleven* 113, no. 1 (December 2012): 11–31.

Machve, Prabhakar Balvant. *From Self to Self: Reminiscences of a Writer*. New Delhi: Vikas,, 1977.

Majchrowicz, Daniel. *The World in Words: Travel Writing and the Global Imagination in Muslim South Asia*. Cambridge: Cambridge University Press, 2023.

Majeed, Javed. *Autobiography, Travel and Postnational Identity: Gandhi, Nehru and Iqbal*. New York: Palgrave Macmillan, 2007.

Malhan, Sangita P. Menon, *The TOI Story: How a Newspaper Changed the Rules of the Game*. Delhi: HarperCollins, 2013.

Malhotra, D. N. *Dare to Publish: Memoirs of a Publisher Who Pioneered the Paperback Revolution in India*. New Delhi: Clarion Books-Hind Pocket Books, 2004.

———. "Publishing of Paperbacks." In *50 years of Book Publishing in India since Independence*, edited by D. N. Malhotra, 219–23. New Delhi: Federation of Indian Publishers, 1998.

Malhotra, D. N., and Narendra Kumar, eds. *Indian Publishing since Independence*. Delhi: Bookman's Club, 1980.

Mandhwani, Aakriti. "Communism, Congress and the Early Cold War: A Perspective from Late 1940s Magazines." In *Handbook of Postcolonial Print Cultures*, edited by Neelam Srivastava, Rajeswari Sunder Rajan, and Jack Webb, 25–38. New York: Bloomsbury, 2023.

———. "From the Colloquial to the 'Literary': Hindi Pulp's Journey from the Streets to the Bookshelves." In *Indian Genre Fiction: Past and Future Histories*, 189-202, edited by Bodhisattva Chattopadhyay, Aakriti Mandhwani, and Anwesha Maity. Delhi: Routledge, 2018.

———. "The Hindi Library and the Making of an Archive: The Hindi Sahitya Sammelan from 1911 to 1973." *South Asia: Journal of South Asian Studies* 43, no. 3 (June 2020): 522–36.

———. "Review of *Gita Press and the Making of Hindu India*." *Indian Economic & Social History Review* 54, no. 2 (April 2017): 286.

Mani, Preetha. "Feminine Desire Is Human Desire: Women Writing Feminism in Postindependence India." *Comparative Studies of South Asia, Africa and the Middle East* 36 (1 January 2016): 21–41.

———. "Gender, Genre, and the Idea of Indian Literature: The Short Story in Hindi and Tamil, 1950–1970." PhD diss., University of California, Berkeley, 2012.

———. *The Idea of Indian Literature: Gender, Genre, and Comparative Method*. Evanston, IL: Northwestern University Press, 2022.

Maniquis, Robert M. "Review of *The Melodramatic Imagination: Balzac, Henry James, Melodrama, and the Mode of Excess*, by Peter Brooks." *Nineteenth-Century Fiction* 32, no. 4 (1978): 483–90.

Masood, Javed. "Catering to Indian and British Tastes: Gender in Early Indian Print Advertisements." *Tasveer Ghar: A Digital Archive of South Asian Popular Visual Culture*. Accessed 3 February 2017. http://www.tasveergharindia.net/essay/catering-indian-british-tastes.html.

Matthews, Jill Julius. "Review of *A Magazine of Her Own? Domesticity and Desire in the Woman's Magazine, 1800–1914; Inarticulate Longings: The 'Ladies' Home Journal,' Gender*, and The *Promises of Consumer Culture*, by Margaret Beetham and Jennifer Scanlon." *Signs* 24, no. 1 (Autumn 1998): 248–50.

McCleery, Alistair. "The Return of the Publisher to Book History: The Case of Allen Lane." *Book History* 5, no. 1 (12 December 2002): 161–85.

McGarr, Peter. "After Nehru, What? Britain, the United States, and the Other Transfer of Power in India, 1960–64." *International History Review* 33, no. 1 (May 2011): 115–42.

———. *The Cold War in South Asia: Britain, the United States and the Indian Subcontinent, 1945–1965*. Cambridge: Cambridge University Press, 2013.

McGowan, Abigail. "An All-Consuming Subject? Women and Consumption in Late-Nineteenth and Early-Twentieth-Century Western India." *Journal of Women's History* 18, no. 4 (2006): 31–54.

———. "Modernity at Home: Leisure, Autonomy and the New Woman in India." *Tasveer Ghar: A Digital Archive of South Asian Popular Visual Culture*. Accessed 1 February 2017. http://www.tasveergharindia.net/essay/modernity-leisure-autonomy-woman.html.

McGregor, R. S. *The Oxford Hindi-English Dictionary*. Oxford: Oxford University Press, 1993.

———. "The Rise of Standard Hindi and Early Hindi Prose Fiction." *Journal of the Royal Asiatic Society of Great Britain and Ireland*, no. 3/4 (1967): 114–32.

Mehrotra, Arvind Krishna, *The Last Bungalow: Writings on Allahabad*. New Delhi: Penguin Books, 2006.

Mehta, Rini Bhattacharya, and Debali Mookerjea-Leonard, eds. *The Indian Partition in Literature and Films: History, Politics and Aesthetics*. London: Routledge, 2015.

Menon, Nikhil. *Planning Democracy: Modern India's Quest for Development*. Cambridge: Cambridge University Press, 2022.

Menon, Ritu, and Kamla Bhasin, eds. *Borders and Boundaries: Women in India's Partition*. New Delhi: Kali for Women, 1998.

Mercer, Ben. "The Paperback Revolution: Mass-Circulation Books and the Cultural Origins of 1968 in Western Europe." *Journal of the History of Ideas* 72, no. 4 (21 October 2011): 613–36.

Mitchell, Sally. "Review of *A Magazine of Her Own? Domesticity and Desire in the Woman's Magazine, 1800–1914*, by Margaret Beetham." *Victorian Studies* 40, no. 2 (1997): 337–39.

Mody, Sujata. "Literary Self-Determination and the Disciplinary Boundaries of Hindi Literature in the Early Twentieth Century." *South Asia Research* 32, no. 3 (November 2012): 233.

———. *The Making of Modern Hindi: Literary Authority in Colonial North India*. New Delhi: Oxford University Press, 2018.

Moitra, Bishwadeep. "Triangle River Tango." *Outlook Magazine*, 5 February 2022. https://www.outlookindia.com/search?q=triangle%20river%20tango.

Mukerjee, Kaushik. "Coca-Cola's Branding Strategies in India." *ICFAI Journal of Brand Management* 5, no. 1 (2008): 34–48.

Mukhopadhyay, Priyasha. *Required Reading: Empire and Its Forms of Writing, 1857–1914*. Princeton, NJ: Princeton University Press, 2024.

Mukul, Akshaya. *Gita Press and the Making of Hindu India*. Delhi: HarperCollins, 2015.

Murphy, Sharon. "Imperial Reading? The East India Company's Lending Libraries for Soldiers, c. 1819–1834." *Book History* 12, no. 1 (2009): 74–99.

———. "Libraries, Schoolrooms, and Mud Godowns: Formal Scenes of Reading at East India Company Stations in India, c. 1819–1835." *Journal of the Royal Asiatic Society*, Series 3, 21, 4 (2011): 459–67.

Naipaul, V. S. "Women's Era." In *A Million Mutinies Now*. Delhi: Viking, 1991.

Nandan, Kanhaiyalal. *Guzrā Kahā̃- Kahā̃ Se: ātmakathatmak Saṃsmaraṇa*. Delhi: Rajpal & Sons, 2007.

———. *Kahna Zaroori Tha*. Delhi: Samyik Prakashan, 2009.

Neale, Steve. "Melodrama and Tears." *Screen* 27, no. 6 (11 December 1986): 6–23.

Nerlekar, Anjali. *Bombay Modern: Arun Kolatkar and Bilingual Literary Culture*. Evanston, IL: Northwestern University Press, 2016.

Newbigin, Eleanor. *The Hindu Family and the Emergence of Modern India: Law, Citizenship and Community*. Cambridge: Cambridge University Press, 2013.

———. "A Post-Colonial Patriarchy? Representing Family in the Indian Nation-State." *Modern Asian Studies* 44 (2010): 121–44.

Nijhawan, Shobna. *Women and Girls in the Hindi Public Sphere: Periodical Literature in Colonial North India*. New Delhi: Oxford University Press, 2012.

Nussbaum, Martha. "Kant and Cosmopolitanism." In *The Cosmopolitanism Reader*, edited by Garrett W. Brown and David Held, 27–44. Cambridge: Polity, 2010.

Orsini, Francesca. *Before the Divide: Hindi and Urdu Literary Culture*. New Delhi: Orient Blackswan, 2011.

———. "Booklets and Sants: Religious Publics and Literary History." *South Asia: Journal of South Asian Studies* 38, no. 3 (July 2015): 435–49.

———. *The Hindi Public Sphere, 1920–1940: Language and Literature in the Age of Nationalism*. New Delhi: Oxford University Press, 2002.

———. ed. *The History of the Book in South Asia*. Farnham, U.K.: Ashgate, 2013.

———. Introduction to *The Oxford India Premchand*, translated by David Rubin, Alok Rai, and Christopher King, vii–xxix. New Delhi: Oxford University Press, 2004.

———. "Literary Activism: Hindi Magazines, the Short Story and the World." In *The Form of Ideology and the Ideology of Form: Cold War, Decolonization and Third World Print Cultures*, edited by Francesca Orsini, Neelam Srivastava, and Laetitia Zecchini, 99–136. UK: OpenBook, 2022.

———. *Print and Pleasure: Popular Literature and Entertaining Fictions in Colonial North India*. Ranikhet, India: Permanent Black, 2009.

Pande, Ira. *Diddi: My Mother's Voice*. New Delhi: Penguin, 2005.

Pandey, Gyanendra. "The Prose of Otherness." In *Subaltern Studies: Writings on South Asian History and Society, vol. 8, Essays in Honour of Ranajit Guha*, edited by David Arnold and David Hardiman, 188–221. Delhi: Oxford University Press, 1994.

———. *Remembering Partition: Violence, Nationalism and History in India*. Delhi: Cambridge University Press, 2001.

Parsons, Rahul. "The Bazaar and the Bari: Calcutta, Marwaris, and the World of Hindi Letters." PhD diss., University of California, Berkeley, December 2012.

Pernau, Margrit, Helge Jordheim, Emmanuelle Saada, Christian Bailey, Einar Wigen, Orit Bashkin, Mana Kia et al. *Civilizing Emotions: Concepts in Nineteenth-Century Asia and Europe*. Oxford: Oxford University Press, 2015.

Pinney, Christopher. *Photos of the Gods: The Printed Image and Political Struggle in India*. London: Reaktion, 2004.

Pollentier, Caroline. "Configuring Middleness: Bourdieu, l'Art Moyen and the Broadbrow." In *Middlebrow Literary Cultures: The Battle of the Brows, 1920–1960*, edited by Erica Brown and Mary Grover, 37–51. New York: Palgrave Macmillan, 2012.

Prasad, Madhava. *Ideology of the Hindi Film: A Historical Construction*. Delhi: Oxford University Press, 2000.

Prasad, Ritika. "Railway Bookselling and the Politics of Print in India: The Case of A. H. Wheeler." *Book History* 24, no. 1 (Spring 2021): 115–45.

Pratik, Ashok K. Shah. *Upanyaskar Guru Dutt: Ek Anusheelan*. Mathura: Jawahar Pustakalaya, 1988.

Press and Advertisers YearBook. New Delhi: India News & Feature Alliance (INFA), 1964.

Price, Leah. *How to Do Things with Books in Victorian Britain*. Princeton, NJ: Princeton University Press, 2012.

Radway, Janice. "The Book-of-the-Month Club and the General Reader: On the Uses of 'Serious' Fiction." *Critical Inquiry* 14, no. 3 (1988): 516–38.

———. *A Feeling for Books: The Book- of-the-Month Club, Literary Taste, and Middle Class Desire*. Chapel Hill: University of North Carolina Press, 1997.

Rai, Alok. *Hindi Nationalism*. London: Sangam Books, 2001.

———. "Reading *Pratik* through Agyeya: Reading Agyeya through *Pratik*." In *Hindi Modernism: Rethinking Agyeya and His Times*, edited by Vasudha Dalmia, 17–30. Berkeley: Center for South Asia Studies, 2012.

Rai, Gopal. *Hindi Kahani ka Itihaas: 1900–1950*. Delhi: Rajkamal Prakashan, 2011.

———. *Hindi sahitya par pathakon ki ruchi ka prabhav*. Patna, India: Grantha Niketana, 1965.

Ramamurthy, Priti. "All-Consuming Nationalism: The Indian Modern Girl in the 1920s and 1930s." In *The Modern Girl around the World: Consumption, Modernity, and Globalization*, edited by Alys Eve Weinbaum, Lynn M. Thomas, Priti Ramamurthy, Uta G. Poiger, Madeleine Y. Dong and Tani E. Barlow, 147–73. Durham, NC: Duke University Press, 2009.

Raman, V. Venkat. "Press Gagging: Implementation of Press Ordinances in the Madras Presidency, 1930 and 1932." *Proceedings of the Indian History Congress* 63 (2002): 546–60.

Ranjan, Prabhat. *Kothagoi*. Delhi: Vani Prakashan, 2015.

———. "Lugdi Sahitya ke Andhere Ujale." In *Diwan-e-Sarai: Media Vimarsh/Hindi Janpad*, edited by Ravikant and Sanjay Sharma, 82–91. Delhi: Sarai Media Lab-Sarai, 2002.

Rapple, Brendan A. "Matthew Arnold's Views on Modernity and a State System of Middle-Class Education in England: Some Continental Views." *Journal of General Education* 39, no. 4 (1988): 206–21.

Roadarmel, Gordon Charles. "The Theme of Alienation in the Modern Hindi Short Story." PhD diss., University of Michigan, 1969.

Robbins, Bruce, and Paulo Lemos Horta, eds. *Cosmopolitanisms*. New York: New York University Press, 2017.

Rosenstein, Lucy, ed. *New Poetry in Hindi: Nayī Kavita; An Anthology*. Translated by Lucy Rosenstein. London: Anthem Press, 2003.

Roy, Srirupa. *Beyond Belief: India and the Politics of Postcolonial Nationalism*. Durham, NC: Duke University Press, 2007.

Rubin, Joan Shelley. *The Making of Middle/brow Culture*. Chapel Hill: University of North Carolina Press, 1992.

Sadana, Rashmi. *English Heart, Hindi Heartland: The Political Life of Literature in India*. Berkeley: University of California Press, 2012.

Saint, Tarun K. *Witnessing Partition: Memory, History, Fiction*. New Delhi: Routledge, 2010.

Saral, Manmohan. "*Dharmyug ka Samay: Patracarita se juri yad, kuchh karhvi, kuchh mithi*." Accessed May 6, 2017. http://www.hindisamay.com/contentDetail.aspx?id=5567&pageno=1.

Sarkar, Tanika. "Gandhi and Social Relations." In *The Cambridge Companion to Gandhi*, edited by Judith M. Brown and Anthony Parel, 173–96. Cambridge: Cambridge University Press, 2011.

Schomer, Karine. *Mahadevi Varma and the Chhayavad Age of Modern Hindi Poetry*. Berkeley: University of California Press, 1983.

Sharma, Chinmay. "Many Mahabharatas: Linking Mythic Re-tellings in Contemporary India." PhD diss., SOAS, University of London, 2017.

Sharma, Ravikant. "Architecture of Intellectual Sociality: Tea and Coffeehouses in Post-Colonial Delhi." *City, Culture and Society* 7, no. 4 (December 2016): 275–81.

———. "Words in Motion Pictures: A Social History of Language of 'Hindi Cinema' (c. 1931 till the Present)." PhD diss., University of Delhi, 2016.

Sharma "Ugra," Pandey Bechan. *Chocolate, and Other Writings on Male Homoeroticism*. Translated by Ruth Vanita. Durham, NC: Duke University Press, 2009.

Sharp, Joanne. *Condensing the Cold War: "Reader's Digest" and American Identity*. Minneapolis: University of Minnesota Press, 2000.

Sherman, Taylor C. "From 'Grow More Food' to 'Miss a Meal': Hunger, Development and the Limits of Post-Colonial Nationalism in India, 1947–1957." *South Asia: Journal of South Asian Studies* 36, no. 4 (1 December 2013): 571–88.

Shukla, Vinod Kumar. *Naukar ki kameez*. New Delhi: Rajkamal Prakashan, 1979.

———. *The Servant's Shirt*. Translated by Satti Khanna. Delhi: Penguin, 1999. 17.

Siegel, Benjamin. *Hungry Nation: Food, Famine, and the Making of Modern India*. Cambridge: Cambridge University Press, 2018.

———. "'Self-Help Which Ennobles a Nation': Development, Citizenship, and the Obligations of Eating in India's Austerity Years." *Modern Asian Studies* 50, no. 3 (May 2016): 975–1018.

Sil, Narasingha P. *The Life of Sharatchandra Chattopadhyay: Drifter and Dreamer*. Madison, NJ: Fairleigh Dickinson University Press, 2011.

Singh, Amrik. "School Level Text Books." In *50 Years of Book Publishing in India since Independence*, edited by D. N. Malhotra, 202–9. Delhi: FIPA, 1998.

Smiles, Samuel. *Thrift*. London: John Murray, 1892. https://www.gutenberg.org/cache/epub/14418/pg14418-images.html.

Sreenivas, Mytheli. *Reproductive Politics and the Making of Modern India*. Seattle: University of Washington Press, 2021.

Srivastava, Sanjay. *Passionate Modernity: Sexuality, Class and Consumption in India*. Delhi: Routledge, 2007.

Stark, Ulrike. *An Empire of Books: The Naval Kishore Press and the Diffusion of the Printed Word in Colonial India*. Ranikhet: Permanent Black, 2007.

Subramanian, Samanth. "Supreme Being: How Samir Jain Created the Modern Indian Newspaper Industry." 1 December 2012. https://caravanmagazine.in/reportage/supreme-being.

Swirski, Peter. *From Lowbrow to Nobrow*. Montreal: McGill-Queen's University Press, 2005.

Ts, Redactie. "Ten Questions to a Periodical Scholar." *Tijdschrift Voor Tijdschriftstudies*, 23 December 2013.

Uberoi, Patricia. "From Goddess to Pin-Up: Icons of Femininity in Indian Calendar Art, 1955–1995." In *Of Women: Icons / Stars / Feasts*, edited by Pooja Sood, 7–9. New Delhi: Eicher Gallery, 1996.

———. "Legislating the Family in Post-Independence India." In *Women of India: Colonial and Post-Colonial Periods*, edited by Bharati Ray, 26–52. Delhi: Sage, 2005.

———. "'Unity in Diversity?' Dilemmas of Nationhood in Indian Calendar Art." *Contributions to Indian Sociology* 36, no. 1–2 (1 February 2002): 191–232.

Usman, Yasser. *Rajesh Khanna: The Untold Story of India's First Superstar*. New Delhi: Penguin Books India, 2014.

van Rees, Kees, Jeroen Vermunt, and Marc Verboord. "Cultural Classifications under Discussion Latent Class Analysis of Highbrow and Lowbrow Reading." *Poetics* 26, no. 5–6 (1 August 1999): 349–65.

Vanshi, Baldev, ed. *Dilli Ti Haus*. Delhi: National, 2009.

Varma, Pavan K. *The Great Indian Middle Class*. Delhi: Penguin, 2007.

Varughese, Emma Dawson. *Genre Fiction of New India: Post-Millennial Receptions of "Weird" Narratives*. Routledge Studies in Contemporary Literature. New York: Routledge, 2017.

Vasudevan, Ravi. *The Melodramatic Public: Film Form and Spectatorship in Indian Cinema*. New York: Palgrave Macmillan, 2011.

———. "Shifting Codes, Dissolving Identities." *Third Text* 10, no. 34 (June 2008): 59–77.

Veer, Peter van der. *Imperial Encounters: Religion and Modernity in India and Britain*. Princeton, NJ: Princeton University Press, 2011.

Verma, Keshav Chandra. *Parimal: Smritiyaan aur Dastavez*. Allahabad: Pradeepan, 2003.

Verma, Nirmal. "Returning to One's Country." In *India and Europe: Selected Essays*, edited by Alok Bhalla, 63–68. Shimla: Indian Institute of Advanced Study, 2000.

Virdi, Jyotika. "Reverence, Rape—and Then Revenge: Popular Hindi Cinema's 'Women's Film.'" In *Killing Women: The Visual Culture of Gender and Violence*, edited by Annette Burfoot and Susan Lord, 251–72. Waterloo: Wilfrid Laurier University Press, 2006.

Viswanathan, Gauri. *Outside the Fold: Conversion, Modernity, and Belief*. Princeton, NJ: Princeton University Press, 1998.

Wood, Ruth Pirsig. *Lolita in Peyton Place: Highbrow, Middlebrow, and Lowbrow Novels of the 1950s*. London: Taylor & Francis, 1995.

Woolf, Virginia. *The Death of the Moth, and Other Essays*. London: Harcourt, Brace, 1942. https://gutenberg.net.au/ebooks12/1203811h.html.

Yadav, Rajendra. *Ek Duniya Samanantar*. Delhi: Radhakrishna Prakashan, 1996.

Yang, Anand. *Bazaar India: Markets, Society, and the Colonial State in Gangetic Bihar*. Berkeley: University of California Press, 1998.

Yashpal. *Jhootha Sach*. Delhi: Lokbharati Prakashan, 2010.

Zamindar, Vazira Fazila-Yacoobali. *The Long Partition and the Making of Modern South Asia: Refugees, Boundaries, Histories*. New York: Columbia University Press, 2007.

Zecchini, Laetitia. *Arun Kolatkar and Literary Modernism in India: Moving Lines*. London: Bloomsbury, 2014.

———. "The Meanings, Forms and Exercise of 'Freedom': The Indian PEN and the Indian Committee for Cultural Freedom (1930s–1960s)." In *The Form of Ideology and the Ideology of Form: Cold War, Decolonization and Third World Print Cultures*, edited by Francesca Orsini, Neelam Srivastava, and Laetitia Zecchini, 177–214. UK: OpenBook, 2022.

WEBSITES (ARTICLES AND ENTRIES)

Allen, James. "Eight Pillars of Prosperity." In *The James Allen Free Library*. Accessed 5 February 2018. http://james-allen.in1woord.nl/?text=eight-pillars-of-prosperity.

Cambridge Dictionary, s.v. "lowbrow." Accessed 23 March 2017. http://dictionary.cambridge.org/dictionary/english/lowbrow.

"Catering to Indian and British Tastes: Gender in Early Indian print Advertisements." Accessed 3 February 2018. http://www.tasveerghar.net/cmsdesk/essay/74/.

Chatterjee, Rimi B. "Five Centuries of Print." *Himal Magazine*, May 2011. http://www.himalmag.com/component/content/article/4408-five-centuries-of-print html (no longer available).

Comic World. "# Dharamyug." 30 April 2017. http://comic-guy.blogspot.com/2010/04/dharamyug.html.

"*Dharmyug ki yad mein anutha ayojan*." Accessed 10 April 2017. http://hindimedia.in/3/news/A-unique-event-in-memory-of-Dharmayug.

Hindi Media. "Dharmyug ki yaad mein ek anutha ayojan." Accessed 10 April 2017. http://hindimedia.in/3/news/A-unique-event-in-memory-of-Dharmayug.

Hindustani, Prakash. "Dr Dharmvir Bharti: Hindi patrakarita ke shikhar puruṣ." *Gadya Kosh*. Accessed 1 June 2020. https://tinyurl.com/9dfhbr4x.

———. "Mere sampadak Dr Dharmvir Bharti." Accessed 7 May 2017. http://www.prakashhindustani.com/index.php/mere-sampadak/61-drdharveerbharti.

"The Launch of Penguin Books and the Role of F. W. Woolworth." *The Woolworths Museum*. Accessed 31 January 2018. https://www.woolworthsmuseum.co.uk/stat-penguin.html#:~:text=Shortly%20after%20founding%20Penguin%20Books,to%20become%20its%20Managing%20Editor.

Mishra, Samiratmaj. "Indian Man Waits Six Decades for University Award." BBC News, 23 March 2012. http://www.bbc.co.uk/news/world-asia-india-17485479.

Monier-Williams Sanskrit-English Dictionary, 1899, s.v. "dharmyug." Accessed 25 April 2017. http://www.sanskrit-lexicon.uni-koeln.d/monier/.

Online Etymology Dictionary, s.v. "lowbrow." Accessed 27 March 2017. http://www.etymonline.com/index.php?term=lowbrow&allowed_in_frame=0.

"Penguin Random House Acquires Respected Hindi Publisher Hind Pocket Books." *Hindustan Times*, 29 June 2018. https://www. hindustantimes.

com/books/penguin-random-house-acquires-respected-hindi-publisher-hind-pocket-books/story-n5DXW4331PpsD5JTK4HAaN.html.

Saral, Manmohan. "Dharmyug ka Samay: Patrakarita se juri yaad, kuchh karvi, kuchh mithi." Accessed 6 May 2017. http://www.hindisamay.com/contentDetail.aspx?id=5567&pageno=1.

"Shanti Prasad Jain, Indian Industrialist and Philanthropist." *New York Times*, 28 October 1977. http://www.nytimes.com/ 1977/10/28/archives/obituary-6-no-title.html.

"A Story Book Book Story." *The Woolworths Museum*. Accessed 31 January 2018. https://www.woolworthsmuseum.co.uk/stat-penguin.html#:~:text=Shortly%20after%20founding%20Penguin%20Books,to%20become%20its%20Managing%20Editor.

VISUAL MEDIA/DOCUMENTARIES

Poonchi, Liaqat Jafri. "Guftugu with Salma Sidiqqui." YouTube video, 21:12 minutes. Posted 16 June 2014. https://www.youtube.com/watch?v=2ZdtGU1IeUQ.

Prakash, Uday. "Dharmvir Bharati." YouTube video, 46:59 minutes. Posted 2 August 2014. https://www.youtube.com/watch?v=vcrTFaUpIL4&t=1990s.

Rajya Sabha TV. "*Guftugu* with D N Malhotra." YouTube video, 28:39 minutes. Posted 30 March 2012. https://www.youtube.com/watch?v=Bh7lKGMxDAk.

Rekhta. "Krishan Chander Documentary Based on His Life and Work by Rekhta.org." YouTube video, 27 minutes. Posted 22 November 2014. https://www.youtube.com/watch?v=s_RyFSsND6M.

Sahapedia. "Pushpa Bharati in Conversation." YouTube video, 45:42 minutes. Posted 14 July 2016. https://www.youtube.com/watch?v=nWSBQgxadKk.

INDEX